C-835 CAREER EXAMINATION SERIES

This is your
PASSBOOK for...

General Mechanic (USPS)

Test Preparation Study Guide
Questions & Answers

COPYRIGHT NOTICE

This book is SOLELY intended for, is sold ONLY to, and its use is RESTRICTED to individual, bona fide applicants or candidates who qualify by virtue of having seriously filed applications for appropriate license, certificate, professional and/or promotional advancement, higher school matriculation, scholarship, or other legitimate requirements of education and/or governmental authorities.

This book is NOT intended for use, class instruction, tutoring, training, duplication, copying, reprinting, excerption, or adaptation, etc., by:

1) Other publishers
2) Proprietors and/or Instructors of "Coaching" and/or Preparatory Courses
3) Personnel and/or Training Divisions of commercial, industrial, and governmental organizations
4) Schools, colleges, or universities and/or their departments and staffs, including teachers and other personnel
5) Testing Agencies or Bureaus
6) Study groups which seek by the purchase of a single volume to copy and/or duplicate and/or adapt this material for use by the group as a whole without having purchased individual volumes for each of the members of the group
7) Et al.

Such persons would be in violation of appropriate Federal and State statutes.

PROVISION OF LICENSING AGREEMENTS – Recognized educational, commercial, industrial, and governmental institutions and organizations, and others legitimately engaged in educational pursuits, including training, testing, and measurement activities, may address request for a licensing agreement to the copyright owners, who will determine whether, and under what conditions, including fees and charges, the materials in this book may be used them. In other words, a licensing facility exists for the legitimate use of the material in this book on other than an individual basis. However, it is asseverated and affirmed here that the material in this book CANNOT be used without the receipt of the express permission of such a licensing agreement from the Publishers. Inquiries re licensing should be addressed to the company, attention rights and permissions department.

All rights reserved, including the right of reproduction in whole or in part, in any form or by any means, electronic or mechanical, including photocopying, recording, or by any information storage and retrieval system, without permission in writing from the Publisher.

Copyright © 2024 by
National Learning Corporation

212 Michael Drive, Syosset, NY 11791
(516) 921-8888 • www.passbooks.com
E-mail: info@passbooks.com

PUBLISHED IN THE UNITED STATES OF AMERICA

PASSBOOK® SERIES

THE *PASSBOOK® SERIES* has been created to prepare applicants and candidates for the ultimate academic battlefield – the examination room.

At some time in our lives, each and every one of us may be required to take an examination – for validation, matriculation, admission, qualification, registration, certification, or licensure.

Based on the assumption that every applicant or candidate has met the basic formal educational standards, has taken the required number of courses, and read the necessary texts, the *PASSBOOK® SERIES* furnishes the one special preparation which may assure passing with confidence, instead of failing with insecurity. Examination questions – together with answers – are furnished as the basic vehicle for study so that the mysteries of the examination and its compounding difficulties may be eliminated or diminished by a sure method.

This book is meant to help you pass your examination provided that you qualify and are serious in your objective.

The entire field is reviewed through the huge store of content information which is succinctly presented through a provocative and challenging approach – the question-and-answer method.

A climate of success is established by furnishing the correct answers at the end of each test.

You soon learn to recognize types of questions, forms of questions, and patterns of questioning. You may even begin to anticipate expected outcomes.

You perceive that many questions are repeated or adapted so that you can gain acute insights, which may enable you to score many sure points.

You learn how to confront new questions, or types of questions, and to attack them confidently and work out the correct answers.

You note objectives and emphases, and recognize pitfalls and dangers, so that you may make positive educational adjustments.

Moreover, you are kept fully informed in relation to new concepts, methods, practices, and directions in the field.

You discover that you are actually taking the examination all the time: you are preparing for the examination by "taking" an examination, not by reading extraneous and/or supererogatory textbooks.

In short, this PASSBOOK®, used directedly, should be an important factor in helping you to pass your test.

GENERAL MECHANIC (U.S.P.S.)

DUTIES:

General Mechanics perform semiskilled preventive, corrective, and predictive maintenance tasks associated with the upkeep and operation of various types of mail processing equipment, buildings, building equipment, customer service equipment, and delivery equipment. Maintenance positions require extensive technical skills.

United States Postal Service Test M/N 931

EXHIBIT A

Test M/N 931 covers the following Knowledge, Skills, and Abilities:

(1) **Knowledge of basic mechanics** refers to the theory of operation, terminology, usage, and characteristics of basic mechanical principles as they apply to such things as gears, pulleys, cams, pawls, power transmissions, linkages, fasteners, chains, sprockets, and belts; and including hoisting, rigging, roping, pneumatics, and hydraulic devices.

(2) **Knowledge of basic electricity** refers to the theory, terminology, usage, and characteristics of basic electrical principles such as Ohm's Law, Kirchoff's Law, and magnetism, as they apply to such things as AC-DC circuitry and hardware, relays, switches, and circuit breakers.

(3) **Knowledge of basic electronics** refers to the theory, terminology, usage, and characteristics of basic electronic principles concerning such things as solid state devices, vacuum tubes, coils, capacitors, resistors, and basic logic circuitry.

(5) **Knowledge of safety procedures and equipment** refers to the knowledge of industrial hazards (e.g., mechanical, chemical, electrical, electronic) and procedures and techniques established to avoid injuries to self and others such as lock-out devices, protective clothing, and waste disposal techniques.

(12) **Knowledge of refrigeration** refers to the theory, terminology, usage, and characteristics of refrigeration principles as they apply to such things as the refrigeration cycle, compressors, condensers, receivers, evaporators, metering devices, and refrigerant oils.

(13) **Knowledge of heating, ventilation, and air conditioning (HVAC) equipment operation** refers to the knowledge of equipment operation such as safety considerations, start-up, shut-down, and mechanical/electrical operating characteristics of HVAC equipment (e.g., chillers, direct expansion units, window units, heating equipment). This does not include the knowledge of refrigeration.

(19) **Ability to perform basic mathematical computations** refers to the ability to perform basic calculations such as addition, subtraction, multiplication and division with whole numbers, fractions and decimals.

(20) **Ability to perform more complex mathematics** refers to the ability to perform calculations such as basic algebra, geometry, scientific notation, and number conversions, as applied to mechanical, electrical and electronic applications.

(21) **Ability to apply theoretical knowledge to practical applications** refers to mechanical, electrical and electronic maintenance applications such as inspection, troubleshooting equipment repair and modification, preventive maintenance, and installation of electrical equipment.

(22) **Ability to detect patterns** refers to the ability to observe and analyze qualitative factors such as number progressions, spatial relationships, and auditory and visual patterns. This includes combining information and determining how a given set of numbers, objects, or sounds are related to each other.

(23) **Ability to use written reference materials** refers to the ability to locate, read, and comprehend text material such as handbooks, manuals, bulletins, directives, checklists and route sheets.

(26) **Ability to follow instructions** refers to the ability to comprehend and execute written and oral instructions such as work orders, checklists, route sheets, and verbal directions and instructions.

(31) **Ability to use hand tools** refers to knowledge of, and proficiency with, various hand tools. This ability involves the safe and efficient use and maintenance of such tools as screwdrivers, wrenches, hammers, pliers, chisels, punches, taps, dies, rules, gauges, and alignment tools.

(35) **Ability to use technical drawings** refers to the ability to read and comprehend technical materials such as diagrams, schematics, flow charts, and blueprints.

(36) **Ability to use test equipment** refers to the knowledge of, and proficiency with, various types of mechanical, electrical and electronic test equipment such as VOMS, oscilloscopes, circuit tracers, amprobes, and tachometers.

(37) **Ability to solder** refers to the knowledge of, and the ability to safely and effectively apply, the appropriate soldering techniques.

EXHIBIT B

The following positions use Test M/N 931:

Position Title	Register Number
Area Maintenance Specialist	M11
Area Maintenance Technician	M12
Assistant Engineman	M01
Blacksmith-Welder	M36
Building Maintenance Custodian	M13
Building Equipment Mechanic	M02
Carpenter	M14
Elevator Mechanic	M37
Engineman	M04
Fireman	M05
Fireman-Laborer	M06
General Mechanic	M39
Industrial Equipment Mechanic	M40
Letter Box Mechanic (Shop)	M41
Machinist	M42
Maintenance Electrician	M16
Mason	M21
Mechanic Helper	M44
Oiler, MPE	M45
Painter	M22
Painter/Finisher	M23
Plumber	M24
Postal Machines Mechanic	M46
Postal Maintenance Trainee A&B	M47
Scale Mechanic	M48
Stationary Engineer	M09

UNITED STATES POSTAL SERVICE

SAMPLE QUESTIONS - TEST M/N 931

The purpose of this booklet is to illustrate the types of questions that will be used in Test M/M 931. The samples will also show how the questions in the test are to be answered.

Test M/N 931 measures 16 Knowledge, Skills, and Abilities (KSAs) used by a variety of maintenance positions. Exhibit A lists the actual KSAs that are measured, and Exhibit B lists the positions that use this examination. However, not all KSAs that are measured in this test are scored for every position listed. The qualification standard for each position lists the KSAs required for the position. Only those questions that measure KSAs required for the position(s) for which you are applying will be scored for the position(s).

The suggested answers to each question are lettered A, B, C, etc. Select the BEST answer and make a heavy pencil mark in the corresponding space on the Sample Answer Sheet. Each mark must be dense black. Each mark must cover more than half the space and must not extend into neighboring spaces. If the answer to Sample 1 is B, you would mark the Sample Answer Sheet like this:

After recording your answers, compare them with those in the Correct Answers to Sample Questions. If they do not agree, carefully re-read the questions that were missed to get a clear understanding of what each question is asking.

During the test, directions for answering questions in Part I will be given orally, either by a cassette tape or by the examiner. You are to listen closely to the directions and follow them. To practice for this part of the test you might have a friend read the direction to you while you mark your answers on the Sample Answer Sheet. Directions for answering questions in Part II will be completely described in the test booklet.

STUDY CAREFULLY BEFORE YOU GO TO THE EXAMINATION ROOM

PART I

In Part I of the test, you will be told to follow directions by writing in a test booklet and then on an answer sheet. The test booklet will have lines of material like the following five samples:

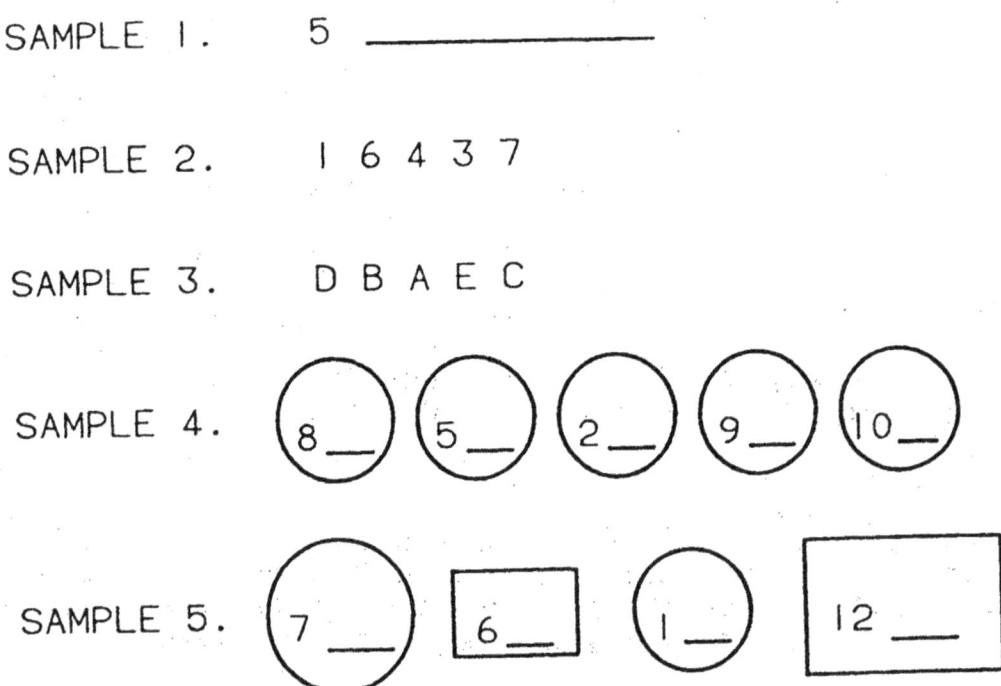

To practice this test, have someone read the instructions on the next page to you and you follow the instructions. When they tell you to darken the space on the Sample Answer Sheet, use the one on this page.

```
              SAMPLE ANSWER SHEET
  1 Ⓐ Ⓑ Ⓒ Ⓓ Ⓔ     5 Ⓐ Ⓑ Ⓒ Ⓓ Ⓔ     9 Ⓐ Ⓑ Ⓒ Ⓓ Ⓔ
  2 Ⓐ Ⓑ Ⓒ Ⓓ Ⓔ     6 Ⓐ Ⓑ Ⓒ Ⓓ Ⓔ    10 Ⓐ Ⓑ Ⓒ Ⓓ Ⓔ
  3 Ⓐ Ⓑ Ⓒ Ⓓ Ⓔ     7 Ⓐ Ⓑ Ⓒ Ⓓ Ⓔ    11 Ⓐ Ⓑ Ⓒ Ⓓ Ⓔ
  4 Ⓐ Ⓑ Ⓒ Ⓓ Ⓔ     8 Ⓐ Ⓑ Ⓒ Ⓓ Ⓔ    12 Ⓐ Ⓑ Ⓒ Ⓓ Ⓔ
```

Instructions to be read (the words in parentheses should not be read aloud).

You are to follow the instructions that I shall read to you. I cannot repeat them.

Look at the samples. Sample 1 has a number and a line beside it. On the line write an A. (Pause 2 seconds.) Now on the Sample Answer Sheet, find number 5 (pause 2 seconds) and darken the space for the letter you just wrote on the line. (Pause 2 seconds.)

Look at Sample 2. (Pause slightly.) Draw a line under the third number. (Pause 2 seconds.) Now look on the Sample Answer Sheet, find the number under which you just drew a line and darken space B as in baker for that number. (Pause 5 seconds.)

Look at Sample 3. (Pause slightly.) Draw a line under the third letter in the line. (Pause 2 seconds.) Now on your Sample Answer Sheet, find number 9 (pause 2 seconds) and darken the space for the letter under which you drew a line. (Pause 5 seconds.)

Look at the five circles in Sample 4. (Pause slightly.) Each circle has a number and a line in it. Write D as in dog on the blank in the last circle. (Pause 2 seconds.) Now on the Sample Answer Sheet, darken the space for the number-letter combination that is in the circle you just wrote in. (Pause 5 seconds.)

Look at Sample 5. (Pause slightly.) There are two circles and two boxes of different sizes with numbers in them. (Pause slightly.) If 4 is more than 2 and if 5 is less than 3, write A in the smaller circle. (Pause slightly.) Otherwise write C in the larger box. (Pause 2 seconds.) Now on the Sample Answer Sheet, darken the space for the number-letter combination in the circle or box in which you just wrote. (Pause 5 seconds.)

Now look at the Sample Answer Sheet. (Pause slightly.) You should have darkened spaces 4B, 5A, 9A, 10D, and 12C on the Sample Answer Sheet. (If the person preparing to take the examination made any mistakes, try to help him or her understand why the mistakes are wrong.)

HOW TO TAKE A TEST

I. YOU MUST PASS AN EXAMINATION

A. *WHAT EVERY CANDIDATE SHOULD KNOW*

Examination applicants often ask us for help in preparing for the written test. What can I study in advance? What kinds of questions will be asked? How will the test be given? How will the papers be graded?

As an applicant for a civil service examination, you may be wondering about some of these things. Our purpose here is to suggest effective methods of advance study and to describe civil service examinations.

Your chances for success on this examination can be increased if you know how to prepare. Those "pre-examination jitters" can be reduced if you know what to expect. You can even experience an adventure in good citizenship if you know why civil service exams are given.

B. *WHY ARE CIVIL SERVICE EXAMINATIONS GIVEN?*

Civil service examinations are important to you in two ways. As a citizen, you want public jobs filled by employees who know how to do their work. As a job seeker, you want a fair chance to compete for that job on an equal footing with other candidates. The best-known means of accomplishing this two-fold goal is the competitive examination.

Exams are widely publicized throughout the nation. They may be administered for jobs in federal, state, city, municipal, town or village governments or agencies.

Any citizen may apply, with some limitations, such as the age or residence of applicants. Your experience and education may be reviewed to see whether you meet the requirements for the particular examination. When these requirements exist, they are reasonable and applied consistently to all applicants. Thus, a competitive examination may cause you some uneasiness now, but it is your privilege and safeguard.

C. *HOW ARE CIVIL SERVICE EXAMS DEVELOPED?*

Examinations are carefully written by trained technicians who are specialists in the field known as "psychological measurement," in consultation with recognized authorities in the field of work that the test will cover. These experts recommend the subject matter areas or skills to be tested; only those knowledges or skills important to your success on the job are included. The most reliable books and source materials available are used as references. Together, the experts and technicians judge the difficulty level of the questions.

Test technicians know how to phrase questions so that the problem is clearly stated. Their ethics do not permit "trick" or "catch" questions. Questions may have been tried out on sample groups, or subjected to statistical analysis, to determine their usefulness.

Written tests are often used in combination with performance tests, ratings of training and experience, and oral interviews. All of these measures combine to form the best-known means of finding the right person for the right job.

II. HOW TO PASS THE WRITTEN TEST

A. NATURE OF THE EXAMINATION

To prepare intelligently for civil service examinations, you should know how they differ from school examinations you have taken. In school you were assigned certain definite pages to read or subjects to cover. The examination questions were quite detailed and usually emphasized memory. Civil service exams, on the other hand, try to discover your present ability to perform the duties of a position, plus your potentiality to learn these duties. In other words, a civil service exam attempts to predict how successful you will be. Questions cover such a broad area that they cannot be as minute and detailed as school exam questions.

In the public service similar kinds of work, or positions, are grouped together in one "class." This process is known as *position-classification*. All the positions in a class are paid according to the salary range for that class. One class title covers all of these positions, and they are all tested by the same examination.

B. FOUR BASIC STEPS

1) Study the announcement

How, then, can you know what subjects to study? Our best answer is: "Learn as much as possible about the class of positions for which you've applied." The exam will test the knowledge, skills and abilities needed to do the work.

Your most valuable source of information about the position you want is the official exam announcement. This announcement lists the training and experience qualifications. Check these standards and apply only if you come reasonably close to meeting them.

The brief description of the position in the examination announcement offers some clues to the subjects which will be tested. Think about the job itself. Review the duties in your mind. Can you perform them, or are there some in which you are rusty? Fill in the blank spots in your preparation.

Many jurisdictions preview the written test in the exam announcement by including a section called "Knowledge and Abilities Required," "Scope of the Examination," or some similar heading. Here you will find out specifically what fields will be tested.

2) Review your own background

Once you learn in general what the position is all about, and what you need to know to do the work, ask yourself which subjects you already know fairly well and which need improvement. You may wonder whether to concentrate on improving your strong areas or on building some background in your fields of weakness. When the announcement has specified "some knowledge" or "considerable knowledge," or has used adjectives like "beginning principles of…" or "advanced … methods," you can get a clue as to the number and difficulty of questions to be asked in any given field. More questions, and hence broader coverage, would be included for those subjects which are more important in the work. Now weigh your strengths and weaknesses against the job requirements and prepare accordingly.

3) Determine the level of the position

Another way to tell how intensively you should prepare is to understand the level of the job for which you are applying. Is it the entering level? In other words, is this the position in which beginners in a field of work are hired? Or is it an intermediate or advanced level? Sometimes this is indicated by such words as "Junior" or "Senior" in the class title. Other jurisdictions use Roman numerals to designate the level – Clerk I, Clerk II, for example. The word "Supervisor" sometimes appears in the title. If the level is not indicated by the title, check the description of duties. Will you be working under very close supervision, or will you have responsibility for independent decisions in this work?

4) Choose appropriate study materials

Now that you know the subjects to be examined and the relative amount of each subject to be covered, you can choose suitable study materials. For beginning level jobs, or even advanced ones, if you have a pronounced weakness in some aspect of your training, read a modern, standard textbook in that field. Be sure it is up to date and has general coverage. Such books are normally available at your library, and the librarian will be glad to help you locate one. For entry-level positions, questions of appropriate difficulty are chosen – neither highly advanced questions, nor those too simple. Such questions require careful thought but not advanced training.

If the position for which you are applying is technical or advanced, you will read more advanced, specialized material. If you are already familiar with the basic principles of your field, elementary textbooks would waste your time. Concentrate on advanced textbooks and technical periodicals. Think through the concepts and review difficult problems in your field.

These are all general sources. You can get more ideas on your own initiative, following these leads. For example, training manuals and publications of the government agency which employs workers in your field can be useful, particularly for technical and professional positions. A letter or visit to the government department involved may result in more specific study suggestions, and certainly will provide you with a more definite idea of the exact nature of the position you are seeking.

III. KINDS OF TESTS

Tests are used for purposes other than measuring knowledge and ability to perform specified duties. For some positions, it is equally important to test ability to make adjustments to new situations or to profit from training. In others, basic mental abilities not dependent on information are essential. Questions which test these things may not appear as pertinent to the duties of the position as those which test for knowledge and information. Yet they are often highly important parts of a fair examination. For very general questions, it is almost impossible to help you direct your study efforts. What we can do is to point out some of the more common of these general abilities needed in public service positions and describe some typical questions.

1) General information

Broad, general information has been found useful for predicting job success in some kinds of work. This is tested in a variety of ways, from vocabulary lists to questions about current events. Basic background in some field of work, such as sociology or economics, may be sampled in a group of questions. Often these are principles which have become familiar to most persons through exposure rather than through formal training. It is difficult to advise you how to study for these questions; being alert to the world around you is our best suggestion.

2) Verbal ability

An example of an ability needed in many positions is verbal or language ability. Verbal ability is, in brief, the ability to use and understand words. Vocabulary and grammar tests are typical measures of this ability. Reading comprehension or paragraph interpretation questions are common in many kinds of civil service tests. You are given a paragraph of written material and asked to find its central meaning.

3) Numerical ability

Number skills can be tested by the familiar arithmetic problem, by checking paired lists of numbers to see which are alike and which are different, or by interpreting charts and graphs. In the latter test, a graph may be printed in the test booklet which you are asked to use as the basis for answering questions.

4) Observation

A popular test for law-enforcement positions is the observation test. A picture is shown to you for several minutes, then taken away. Questions about the picture test your ability to observe both details and larger elements.

5) Following directions

In many positions in the public service, the employee must be able to carry out written instructions dependably and accurately. You may be given a chart with several columns, each column listing a variety of information. The questions require you to carry out directions involving the information given in the chart.

6) Skills and aptitudes

Performance tests effectively measure some manual skills and aptitudes. When the skill is one in which you are trained, such as typing or shorthand, you can practice. These tests are often very much like those given in business school or high school courses. For many of the other skills and aptitudes, however, no short-time preparation can be made. Skills and abilities natural to you or that you have developed throughout your lifetime are being tested.

Many of the general questions just described provide all the data needed to answer the questions and ask you to use your reasoning ability to find the answers. Your best preparation for these tests, as well as for tests of facts and ideas, is to be at your physical and mental best. You, no doubt, have your own methods of getting into an exam-taking mood and keeping "in shape." The next section lists some ideas on this subject.

IV. KINDS OF QUESTIONS

Only rarely is the "essay" question, which you answer in narrative form, used in civil service tests. Civil service tests are usually of the short-answer type. Full instructions for answering these questions will be given to you at the examination. But in case this is your first experience with short-answer questions and separate answer sheets, here is what you need to know:

1) Multiple-choice Questions

Most popular of the short-answer questions is the "multiple choice" or "best answer" question. It can be used, for example, to test for factual knowledge, ability to solve problems or judgment in meeting situations found at work.

A multiple-choice question is normally one of three types—
- It can begin with an incomplete statement followed by several possible endings. You are to find the one ending which *best* completes the statement, although some of the others may not be entirely wrong.
- It can also be a complete statement in the form of a question which is answered by choosing one of the statements listed.

- It can be in the form of a problem – again you select the best answer.

Here is an example of a multiple-choice question with a discussion which should give you some clues as to the method for choosing the right answer:

When an employee has a complaint about his assignment, the action which will *best* help him overcome his difficulty is to
    A. discuss his difficulty with his coworkers
    B. take the problem to the head of the organization
    C. take the problem to the person who gave him the assignment
    D. say nothing to anyone about his complaint

In answering this question, you should study each of the choices to find which is best. Consider choice "A" – Certainly an employee may discuss his complaint with fellow employees, but no change or improvement can result, and the complaint remains unresolved. Choice "B" is a poor choice since the head of the organization probably does not know what assignment you have been given, and taking your problem to him is known as "going over the head" of the supervisor. The supervisor, or person who made the assignment, is the person who can clarify it or correct any injustice. Choice "C" is, therefore, correct. To say nothing, as in choice "D," is unwise. Supervisors have and interest in knowing the problems employees are facing, and the employee is seeking a solution to his problem.

2) True/False Questions

The "true/false" or "right/wrong" form of question is sometimes used. Here a complete statement is given. Your job is to decide whether the statement is right or wrong.

SAMPLE: A roaming cell-phone call to a nearby city costs less than a non-roaming call to a distant city.

This statement is wrong, or false, since roaming calls are more expensive.
This is not a complete list of all possible question forms, although most of the others are variations of these common types. You will always get complete directions for answering questions. Be sure you understand *how* to mark your answers – ask questions until you do.

V. RECORDING YOUR ANSWERS

Computer terminals are used more and more today for many different kinds of exams.
For an examination with very few applicants, you may be told to record your answers in the test booklet itself. Separate answer sheets are much more common. If this separate answer sheet is to be scored by machine – and this is often the case – it is highly important that you mark your answers correctly in order to get credit.
An electronic scoring machine is often used in civil service offices because of the speed with which papers can be scored. Machine-scored answer sheets must be marked with a pencil, which will be given to you. This pencil has a high graphite content which responds to the electronic scoring machine. As a matter of fact, stray dots may register as answers, so do not let your pencil rest on the answer sheet while you are pondering the correct answer. Also, if your pencil lead breaks or is otherwise defective, ask for another.

Since the answer sheet will be dropped in a slot in the scoring machine, be careful not to bend the corners or get the paper crumpled.

The answer sheet normally has five vertical columns of numbers, with 30 numbers to a column. These numbers correspond to the question numbers in your test booklet. After each number, going across the page are four or five pairs of dotted lines. These short dotted lines have small letters or numbers above them. The first two pairs may also have a "T" or "F" above the letters. This indicates that the first two pairs only are to be used if the questions are of the true-false type. If the questions are multiple choice, disregard the "T" and "F" and pay attention only to the small letters or numbers.

Answer your questions in the manner of the sample that follows:

32. The largest city in the United States is
    A. Washington, D.C.
    B. New York City
    C. Chicago
    D. Detroit
    E. San Francisco

1) Choose the answer you think is best. (New York City is the largest, so "B" is correct.)
2) Find the row of dotted lines numbered the same as the question you are answering. (Find row number 32)
3) Find the pair of dotted lines corresponding to the answer. (Find the pair of lines under the mark "B.")
4) Make a solid black mark between the dotted lines.

VI. BEFORE THE TEST

Common sense will help you find procedures to follow to get ready for an examination. Too many of us, however, overlook these sensible measures. Indeed, nervousness and fatigue have been found to be the most serious reasons why applicants fail to do their best on civil service tests. Here is a list of reminders:

- Begin your preparation early – Don't wait until the last minute to go scurrying around for books and materials or to find out what the position is all about.
- Prepare continuously – An hour a night for a week is better than an all-night cram session. This has been definitely established. What is more, a night a week for a month will return better dividends than crowding your study into a shorter period of time.
- Locate the place of the exam – You have been sent a notice telling you when and where to report for the examination. If the location is in a different town or otherwise unfamiliar to you, it would be well to inquire the best route and learn something about the building.
- Relax the night before the test – Allow your mind to rest. Do not study at all that night. Plan some mild recreation or diversion; then go to bed early and get a good night's sleep.
- Get up early enough to make a leisurely trip to the place for the test – This way unforeseen events, traffic snarls, unfamiliar buildings, etc. will not upset you.
- Dress comfortably – A written test is not a fashion show. You will be known by number and not by name, so wear something comfortable.

- Leave excess paraphernalia at home – Shopping bags and odd bundles will get in your way. You need bring only the items mentioned in the official notice you received; usually everything you need is provided. Do not bring reference books to the exam. They will only confuse those last minutes and be taken away from you when in the test room.
- Arrive somewhat ahead of time – If because of transportation schedules you must get there very early, bring a newspaper or magazine to take your mind off yourself while waiting.
- Locate the examination room – When you have found the proper room, you will be directed to the seat or part of the room where you will sit. Sometimes you are given a sheet of instructions to read while you are waiting. Do not fill out any forms until you are told to do so; just read them and be prepared.
- Relax and prepare to listen to the instructions
- If you have any physical problem that may keep you from doing your best, be sure to tell the test administrator. If you are sick or in poor health, you really cannot do your best on the exam. You can come back and take the test some other time.

VII. AT THE TEST

The day of the test is here and you have the test booklet in your hand. The temptation to get going is very strong. Caution! There is more to success than knowing the right answers. You must know how to identify your papers and understand variations in the type of short-answer question used in this particular examination. Follow these suggestions for maximum results from your efforts:

1) Cooperate with the monitor

The test administrator has a duty to create a situation in which you can be as much at ease as possible. He will give instructions, tell you when to begin, check to see that you are marking your answer sheet correctly, and so on. He is not there to guard you, although he will see that your competitors do not take unfair advantage. He wants to help you do your best.

2) Listen to all instructions

Don't jump the gun! Wait until you understand all directions. In most civil service tests you get more time than you need to answer the questions. So don't be in a hurry. Read each word of instructions until you clearly understand the meaning. Study the examples, listen to all announcements and follow directions. Ask questions if you do not understand what to do.

3) Identify your papers

Civil service exams are usually identified by number only. You will be assigned a number; you must not put your name on your test papers. Be sure to copy your number correctly. Since more than one exam may be given, copy your exact examination title.

4) Plan your time

Unless you are told that a test is a "speed" or "rate of work" test, speed itself is usually not important. Time enough to answer all the questions will be provided, but this does not mean that you have all day. An overall time limit has been set. Divide the total time (in minutes) by the number of questions to determine the approximate time you have for each question.

5) Do not linger over difficult questions

If you come across a difficult question, mark it with a paper clip (useful to have along) and come back to it when you have been through the booklet. One caution if you do this – be sure to skip a number on your answer sheet as well. Check often to be sure that you have not lost your place and that you are marking in the row numbered the same as the question you are answering.

6) Read the questions

Be sure you know what the question asks! Many capable people are unsuccessful because they failed to *read* the questions correctly.

7) Answer all questions

Unless you have been instructed that a penalty will be deducted for incorrect answers, it is better to guess than to omit a question.

8) Speed tests

It is often better NOT to guess on speed tests. It has been found that on timed tests people are tempted to spend the last few seconds before time is called in marking answers at random – without even reading them – in the hope of picking up a few extra points. To discourage this practice, the instructions may warn you that your score will be "corrected" for guessing. That is, a penalty will be applied. The incorrect answers will be deducted from the correct ones, or some other penalty formula will be used.

9) Review your answers

If you finish before time is called, go back to the questions you guessed or omitted to give them further thought. Review other answers if you have time.

10) Return your test materials

If you are ready to leave before others have finished or time is called, take ALL your materials to the monitor and leave quietly. Never take any test material with you. The monitor can discover whose papers are not complete, and taking a test booklet may be grounds for disqualification.

VIII. EXAMINATION TECHNIQUES

1) Read the general instructions carefully. These are usually printed on the first page of the exam booklet. As a rule, these instructions refer to the timing of the examination; the fact that you should not start work until the signal and must stop work at a signal, etc. If there are any *special* instructions, such as a choice of questions to be answered, make sure that you note this instruction carefully.

2) When you are ready to start work on the examination, that is as soon as the signal has been given, read the instructions to each question booklet, underline any key words or phrases, such as *least, best, outline, describe* and the like. In this way you will tend to answer as requested rather than discover on reviewing your paper that you *listed without describing*, that you selected the *worst* choice rather than the *best* choice, etc.

3) If the examination is of the objective or multiple-choice type – that is, each question will also give a series of possible answers: A, B, C or D, and you are called upon to select the best answer and write the letter next to that answer on your answer paper – it is advisable to start answering each question in turn. There may be anywhere from 50 to 100 such questions in the three or four hours allotted and you can see how much time would be taken if you read through all the questions before beginning to answer any. Furthermore, if you come across a question or group of questions which you know would be difficult to answer, it would undoubtedly affect your handling of all the other questions.

4) If the examination is of the essay type and contains but a few questions, it is a moot point as to whether you should read all the questions before starting to answer any one. Of course, if you are given a choice – say five out of seven and the like – then it is essential to read all the questions so you can eliminate the two that are most difficult. If, however, you are asked to answer all the questions, there may be danger in trying to answer the easiest one first because you may find that you will spend too much time on it. The best technique is to answer the first question, then proceed to the second, etc.

5) Time your answers. Before the exam begins, write down the time it started, then add the time allowed for the examination and write down the time it must be completed, then divide the time available somewhat as follows:
   - If 3-1/2 hours are allowed, that would be 210 minutes. If you have 80 objective-type questions, that would be an average of 2-1/2 minutes per question. Allow yourself no more than 2 minutes per question, or a total of 160 minutes, which will permit about 50 minutes to review.
   - If for the time allotment of 210 minutes there are 7 essay questions to answer, that would average about 30 minutes a question. Give yourself only 25 minutes per question so that you have about 35 minutes to review.

6) The most important instruction is to *read each question* and make sure you know what is wanted. The second most important instruction is to *time yourself properly* so that you answer every question. The third most important instruction is to *answer every question*. Guess if you have to but include something for each question. Remember that you will receive no credit for a blank and will probably receive some credit if you write something in answer to an essay question. If you guess a letter – say "B" for a multiple-choice question – you may have guessed right. If you leave a blank as an answer to a multiple-choice question, the examiners may respect your feelings but it will not add a point to your score. Some exams may penalize you for wrong answers, so in such cases *only*, you may not want to guess unless you have some basis for your answer.

7) Suggestions
   a. Objective-type questions
      1. Examine the question booklet for proper sequence of pages and questions
      2. Read all instructions carefully
      3. Skip any question which seems too difficult; return to it after all other questions have been answered
      4. Apportion your time properly; do not spend too much time on any single question or group of questions

5. Note and underline key words – *all, most, fewest, least, best, worst, same, opposite*, etc.
6. Pay particular attention to negatives
7. Note unusual option, e.g., unduly long, short, complex, different or similar in content to the body of the question
8. Observe the use of "hedging" words – *probably, may, most likely*, etc.
9. Make sure that your answer is put next to the same number as the question
10. Do not second-guess unless you have good reason to believe the second answer is definitely more correct
11. Cross out original answer if you decide another answer is more accurate; do not erase until you are ready to hand your paper in
12. Answer all questions; guess unless instructed otherwise
13. Leave time for review

b. Essay questions
1. Read each question carefully
2. Determine exactly what is wanted. Underline key words or phrases.
3. Decide on outline or paragraph answer
4. Include many different points and elements unless asked to develop any one or two points or elements
5. Show impartiality by giving pros and cons unless directed to select one side only
6. Make and write down any assumptions you find necessary to answer the questions
7. Watch your English, grammar, punctuation and choice of words
8. Time your answers; don't crowd material

8) Answering the essay question

Most essay questions can be answered by framing the specific response around several key words or ideas. Here are a few such key words or ideas:

M's: manpower, materials, methods, money, management
P's: purpose, program, policy, plan, procedure, practice, problems, pitfalls, personnel, public relations

a. Six basic steps in handling problems:
1. Preliminary plan and background development
2. Collect information, data and facts
3. Analyze and interpret information, data and facts
4. Analyze and develop solutions as well as make recommendations
5. Prepare report and sell recommendations
6. Install recommendations and follow up effectiveness

b. Pitfalls to avoid
1. *Taking things for granted* – A statement of the situation does not necessarily imply that each of the elements is necessarily true; for example, a complaint may be invalid and biased so that all that can be taken for granted is that a complaint has been registered

2. *Considering only one side of a situation* – Wherever possible, indicate several alternatives and then point out the reasons you selected the best one
3. *Failing to indicate follow up* – Whenever your answer indicates action on your part, make certain that you will take proper follow-up action to see how successful your recommendations, procedures or actions turn out to be
4. *Taking too long in answering any single question* – Remember to time your answers properly

IX. AFTER THE TEST

Scoring procedures differ in detail among civil service jurisdictions although the general principles are the same. Whether the papers are hand-scored or graded by machine we have described, they are nearly always graded by number. That is, the person who marks the paper knows only the number – never the name – of the applicant. Not until all the papers have been graded will they be matched with names. If other tests, such as training and experience or oral interview ratings have been given, scores will be combined. Different parts of the examination usually have different weights. For example, the written test might count 60 percent of the final grade, and a rating of training and experience 40 percent. In many jurisdictions, veterans will have a certain number of points added to their grades.

After the final grade has been determined, the names are placed in grade order and an eligible list is established. There are various methods for resolving ties between those who get the same final grade – probably the most common is to place first the name of the person whose application was received first. Job offers are made from the eligible list in the order the names appear on it. You will be notified of your grade and your rank as soon as all these computations have been made. This will be done as rapidly as possible.

People who are found to meet the requirements in the announcement are called "eligibles." Their names are put on a list of eligible candidates. An eligible's chances of getting a job depend on how high he stands on this list and how fast agencies are filling jobs from the list.

When a job is to be filled from a list of eligibles, the agency asks for the names of people on the list of eligibles for that job. When the civil service commission receives this request, it sends to the agency the names of the three people highest on this list. Or, if the job to be filled has specialized requirements, the office sends the agency the names of the top three persons who meet these requirements from the general list.

The appointing officer makes a choice from among the three people whose names were sent to him. If the selected person accepts the appointment, the names of the others are put back on the list to be considered for future openings.

That is the rule in hiring from all kinds of eligible lists, whether they are for typist, carpenter, chemist, or something else. For every vacancy, the appointing officer has his choice of any one of the top three eligibles on the list. This explains why the person whose name is on top of the list sometimes does not get an appointment when some of the persons lower on the list do. If the appointing officer chooses the second or third eligible, the No. 1 eligible does not get a job at once, but stays on the list until he is appointed or the list is terminated.

X. HOW TO PASS THE INTERVIEW TEST

The examination for which you applied requires an oral interview test. You have already taken the written test and you are now being called for the interview test – the final part of the formal examination.

You may think that it is not possible to prepare for an interview test and that there are no procedures to follow during an interview. Our purpose is to point out some things you can do in advance that will help you and some good rules to follow and pitfalls to avoid while you are being interviewed.

What is an interview supposed to test?

The written examination is designed to test the technical knowledge and competence of the candidate; the oral is designed to evaluate intangible qualities, not readily measured otherwise, and to establish a list showing the relative fitness of each candidate – as measured against his competitors – for the position sought. Scoring is not on the basis of "right" and "wrong," but on a sliding scale of values ranging from "not passable" to "outstanding." As a matter of fact, it is possible to achieve a relatively low score without a single "incorrect" answer because of evident weakness in the qualities being measured.

Occasionally, an examination may consist entirely of an oral test – either an individual or a group oral. In such cases, information is sought concerning the technical knowledges and abilities of the candidate, since there has been no written examination for this purpose. More commonly, however, an oral test is used to supplement a written examination.

Who conducts interviews?

The composition of oral boards varies among different jurisdictions. In nearly all, a representative of the personnel department serves as chairman. One of the members of the board may be a representative of the department in which the candidate would work. In some cases, "outside experts" are used, and, frequently, a businessman or some other representative of the general public is asked to serve. Labor and management or other special groups may be represented. The aim is to secure the services of experts in the appropriate field.

However the board is composed, it is a good idea (and not at all improper or unethical) to ascertain in advance of the interview who the members are and what groups they represent. When you are introduced to them, you will have some idea of their backgrounds and interests, and at least you will not stutter and stammer over their names.

What should be done before the interview?

While knowledge about the board members is useful and takes some of the surprise element out of the interview, there is other preparation which is more substantive. It *is* possible to prepare for an oral interview – in several ways:

1) Keep a copy of your application and review it carefully before the interview

This may be the only document before the oral board, and the starting point of the interview. Know what education and experience you have listed there, and the sequence and dates of all of it. Sometimes the board will ask you to review the highlights of your experience for them; you should not have to hem and haw doing it.

2) Study the class specification and the examination announcement

Usually, the oral board has one or both of these to guide them. The qualities, characteristics or knowledges required by the position sought are stated in these documents. They offer valuable clues as to the nature of the oral interview. For example, if the job involves supervisory responsibilities, the announcement will usually indicate that knowledge of modern supervisory methods and the qualifications of the candidate as a supervisor will be tested. If so, you can expect such questions, frequently in the form of a hypothetical situation which you are expected to solve. NEVER go into an oral without knowledge of the duties and responsibilities of the job you seek.

3) Think through each qualification required

Try to visualize the kind of questions you would ask if you were a board member. How well could you answer them? Try especially to appraise your own knowledge and background in each area, *measured against the job sought*, and identify any areas in which you are weak. Be critical and realistic – do not flatter yourself.

4) Do some general reading in areas in which you feel you may be weak

For example, if the job involves supervision and your past experience has NOT, some general reading in supervisory methods and practices, particularly in the field of human relations, might be useful. Do NOT study agency procedures or detailed manuals. The oral board will be testing your understanding and capacity, not your memory.

5) Get a good night's sleep and watch your general health and mental attitude

You will want a clear head at the interview. Take care of a cold or any other minor ailment, and of course, no hangovers.

What should be done on the day of the interview?

Now comes the day of the interview itself. Give yourself plenty of time to get there. Plan to arrive somewhat ahead of the scheduled time, particularly if your appointment is in the fore part of the day. If a previous candidate fails to appear, the board might be ready for you a bit early. By early afternoon an oral board is almost invariably behind schedule if there are many candidates, and you may have to wait. Take along a book or magazine to read, or your application to review, but leave any extraneous material in the waiting room when you go in for your interview. In any event, relax and compose yourself.

The matter of dress is important. The board is forming impressions about you – from your experience, your manners, your attitude, and your appearance. Give your personal appearance careful attention. Dress your best, but not your flashiest. Choose conservative, appropriate clothing, and be sure it is immaculate. This is a business interview, and your appearance should indicate that you regard it as such. Besides, being well groomed and properly dressed will help boost your confidence.

Sooner or later, someone will call your name and escort you into the interview room. *This is it.* From here on you are on your own. It is too late for any more preparation. But remember, you asked for this opportunity to prove your fitness, and you are here because your request was granted.

What happens when you go in?

The usual sequence of events will be as follows: The clerk (who is often the board stenographer) will introduce you to the chairman of the oral board, who will introduce you to the other members of the board. Acknowledge the introductions before you sit down. Do not be surprised if you find a microphone facing you or a stenotypist sitting by. Oral interviews are usually recorded in the event of an appeal or other review.

Usually the chairman of the board will open the interview by reviewing the highlights of your education and work experience from your application – primarily for the benefit of the other members of the board, as well as to get the material into the record. Do not interrupt or comment unless there is an error or significant misinterpretation; if that is the case, do not hesitate. But do not quibble about insignificant matters. Also, he will usually ask you some question about your education, experience or your present job – partly to get you to start talking and to establish the interviewing "rapport." He may start the actual questioning, or turn it over to one of the other members. Frequently, each member undertakes the questioning on a particular area, one in which he is perhaps most competent, so you can expect each member to participate in the examination. Because time is limited, you may also expect some rather abrupt switches in the direction the questioning takes, so do not be upset by it. Normally, a board member will not pursue a single line of questioning unless he discovers a particular strength or weakness.

After each member has participated, the chairman will usually ask whether any member has any further questions, then will ask you if you have anything you wish to add. Unless you are expecting this question, it may floor you. Worse, it may start you off on an extended, extemporaneous speech. The board is not usually seeking more information. The question is principally to offer you a last opportunity to present further qualifications or to indicate that you have nothing to add. So, if you feel that a significant qualification or characteristic has been overlooked, it is proper to point it out in a sentence or so. Do not compliment the board on the thoroughness of their examination – they have been sketchy, and you know it. If you wish, merely say, "No thank you, I have nothing further to add." This is a point where you can "talk yourself out" of a good impression or fail to present an important bit of information. Remember, *you close the interview yourself.*

The chairman will then say, "That is all, Mr. _____, thank you." Do not be startled; the interview is over, and quicker than you think. Thank him, gather your belongings and take your leave. Save your sigh of relief for the other side of the door.

How to put your best foot forward

Throughout this entire process, you may feel that the board individually and collectively is trying to pierce your defenses, seek out your hidden weaknesses and embarrass and confuse you. Actually, this is not true. They are obliged to make an appraisal of your qualifications for the job you are seeking, and they want to see you in your best light. Remember, they must interview all candidates and a non-cooperative candidate may become a failure in spite of their best efforts to bring out his qualifications. Here are 15 suggestions that will help you:

1) Be natural – Keep your attitude confident, not cocky

If you are not confident that you can do the job, do not expect the board to be. Do not apologize for your weaknesses, try to bring out your strong points. The board is interested in a positive, not negative, presentation. Cockiness will antagonize any board member and make him wonder if you are covering up a weakness by a false show of strength.

2) Get comfortable, but don't lounge or sprawl

Sit erectly but not stiffly. A careless posture may lead the board to conclude that you are careless in other things, or at least that you are not impressed by the importance of the occasion. Either conclusion is natural, even if incorrect. Do not fuss with your clothing, a pencil or an ashtray. Your hands may occasionally be useful to emphasize a point; do not let them become a point of distraction.

3) Do not wisecrack or make small talk

This is a serious situation, and your attitude should show that you consider it as such. Further, the time of the board is limited – they do not want to waste it, and neither should you.

4) Do not exaggerate your experience or abilities

In the first place, from information in the application or other interviews and sources, the board may know more about you than you think. Secondly, you probably will not get away with it. An experienced board is rather adept at spotting such a situation, so do not take the chance.

5) If you know a board member, do not make a point of it, yet do not hide it

Certainly you are not fooling him, and probably not the other members of the board. Do not try to take advantage of your acquaintanceship – it will probably do you little good.

6) Do not dominate the interview

Let the board do that. They will give you the clues – do not assume that you have to do all the talking. Realize that the board has a number of questions to ask you, and do not try to take up all the interview time by showing off your extensive knowledge of the answer to the first one.

7) Be attentive

You only have 20 minutes or so, and you should keep your attention at its sharpest throughout. When a member is addressing a problem or question to you, give him your undivided attention. Address your reply principally to him, but do not exclude the other board members.

8) Do not interrupt

A board member may be stating a problem for you to analyze. He will ask you a question when the time comes. Let him state the problem, and wait for the question.

9) Make sure you understand the question

Do not try to answer until you are sure what the question is. If it is not clear, restate it in your own words or ask the board member to clarify it for you. However, do not haggle about minor elements.

10) Reply promptly but not hastily

A common entry on oral board rating sheets is "candidate responded readily," or "candidate hesitated in replies." Respond as promptly and quickly as you can, but do not jump to a hasty, ill-considered answer.

11) Do not be peremptory in your answers

A brief answer is proper – but do not fire your answer back. That is a losing game from your point of view. The board member can probably ask questions much faster than you can answer them.

12) Do not try to create the answer you think the board member wants

He is interested in what kind of mind you have and how it works – not in playing games. Furthermore, he can usually spot this practice and will actually grade you down on it.

13) Do not switch sides in your reply merely to agree with a board member

Frequently, a member will take a contrary position merely to draw you out and to see if you are willing and able to defend your point of view. Do not start a debate, yet do not surrender a good position. If a position is worth taking, it is worth defending.

14) Do not be afraid to admit an error in judgment if you are shown to be wrong
The board knows that you are forced to reply without any opportunity for careful consideration. Your answer may be demonstrably wrong. If so, admit it and get on with the interview.

15) Do not dwell at length on your present job
The opening question may relate to your present assignment. Answer the question but do not go into an extended discussion. You are being examined for a *new* job, not your present one. As a matter of fact, try to phrase ALL your answers in terms of the job for which you are being examined.

Basis of Rating
Probably you will forget most of these "do's" and "don'ts" when you walk into the oral interview room. Even remembering them all will not ensure you a passing grade. Perhaps you did not have the qualifications in the first place. But remembering them will help you to put your best foot forward, without treading on the toes of the board members.

Rumor and popular opinion to the contrary notwithstanding, an oral board wants you to make the best appearance possible. They know you are under pressure – but they also want to see how you respond to it as a guide to what your reaction would be under the pressures of the job you seek. They will be influenced by the degree of poise you display, the personal traits you show and the manner in which you respond.

ABOUT THIS BOOK

This book contains tests divided into Examination Sections. Go through each test, answering every question in the margin. We have also attached a sample answer sheet at the back of the book that can be removed and used. At the end of each test look at the answer key and check your answers. On the ones you got wrong, look at the right answer choice and learn. Do not fill in the answers first. Do not memorize the questions and answers, but understand the answer and principles involved. On your test, the questions will likely be different from the samples. Questions are changed and new ones added. If you understand these past questions you should have success with any changes that arise. Tests may consist of several types of questions. We have additional books on each subject should more study be advisable or necessary for you. Finally, the more you study, the better prepared you will be. This book is intended to be the last thing you study before you walk into the examination room. Prior study of relevant texts is also recommended. NLC publishes some of these in our Fundamental Series. Knowledge and good sense are important factors in passing your exam. Good luck also helps. So now study this Passbook, absorb the material contained within and take that knowledge into the examination. Then do your best to pass that exam.

EXAMINATION SECTION

EXAMINATION SECTION
TEST 1

DIRECTIONS: Each question or incomplete statement is followed by several suggested answers or completions. Select the one that BEST answers the question or completes the statement. *PRINT THE LETTER OF THE CORRECT ANSWER IN THE SPACE AT THE RIGHT.*

Questions 1-3.

DIRECTIONS: Questions 1 through 3, inclusive, are to be answered in accordance with the American Standard Graphical Symbols for Pipe Fittings, Valves, and Piping and American Standard Graphical Symbols for Heating, Ventilating and Air Conditioning.

1. The symbol ⊙⊢ shown on a piping drawing represents a _____ elbow.

   A. turned down
   B. reducing
   C. long radius
   D. turned up

2. The symbol ⊢▭⊣ shown on a heating drawing represents a(n)

   A. expansion joint
   B. hanger or support
   C. heat exchanger
   D. air eliminator

3. The symbol ⊢⋈⊣ shown on a piping drawing represents a _____ gate valve.

   A. welded
   B. flanged
   C. screwed
   D. bell and spigot

4. The MAIN purpose for the inspection of plant equipment, buildings, and facilities is to

   A. determine the quality of maintenance work of all the trades
   B. prevent the overstocking of equipment and materials used in maintenance work
   C. forecast normal maintenance jobs for existing equipment, buildings, and facilities
   D. prevent unscheduled interruptions of operating equipment and excessive deterioration of buildings and facilities

5. Of the following devices, the one that is used to determine the rating, in cubic feet per minute, of a unit ventilator is a(n)

   A. psychrometer
   B. pyrometer
   C. anemometer
   D. manometer

6. A number of 4' x 6' skids loaded with material are to be stored. Assume that the total weight of each loaded skid is 1200 pounds and that the maximum allowable floor load is 280 lbs. per sq. ft.
   The MAXIMUM number of skids that can be stacked vertically without exceeding the MAXIMUM allowable floor load is

   A. 4
   B. 5
   C. 6
   D. 7

7. Specifications which contain the term *slump test* would MOST likely refer to

   A. lumber   B. paint   C. concrete   D. water

8. Of the following sizes of copper conductors, the one which has the LEAST current-carrying capacity is _____ AWG.

   A. 000   B. 0   C. 8   D. 12

9. The size of a steel beam is shown on a steel drawing as W 8 x 15.
   In accordance with the latest edition of the Steel Construction Manual of the American Institute of Steel Construction, the number 8 in W 8 x 15 represents the beam's *approximate*

   A. depth   B. flange thickness
   C. width   D. web thickness

10. For expediting control functions such as work methods, planning, scheduling, and work measurement, EQUIPMENT RECORDS must contain specific data.
    Of the following, the data which is NOT usually indicated on an EQUIPMENT RECORD card is

    A. machinery and parts specifications numbers
    B. a breakdown history
    C. a preventive maintenance history
    D. salvage value on the open market

11. Refrigeration piping, valves, fittings, and related parts used in the construction and installation of refrigeration systems shall conform to the

    A. American Society of Mechanical Engineers Boiler and Pressure Vessel Code
    B. American Standards Association Code for Pressure Piping
    C. Pipe Fabrication Institute Standards
    D. Underwriters Laboratory Standards

12. The maintenance term *downtime* means MOST NEARLY the

    A. period of time in which a machine is out of service
    B. routine replacement of parts or materials to a piece of equipment
    C. labor required for clean-up of equipment to insure its proper operation
    D. maintenance work which is confined to checking, adjusting, and lubrication of equipment

13. A supplier quotes a list price of $172.00 less 15 and 10 percent for twelve tools.
    The ACTUAL cost for these twelve tools is MOST NEARLY

    A. $146   B. $132   C. $129   D. $112

14. Of the following colors of electrical conductor coverings, the one which indicates a conductor used SOLELY for grounding portable or fixed electrical equipment is

    A. blue   B. green   C. red   D. black

15. A *medium duty* type of scaffold is one on which the working load on the platform surface must NOT exceed _____ pounds per square foot.

    A. 50   B. 70   C. 90   D. 110

16. Assume that a mechanic is using a powder-actuated tool and the cartridge misfires. According to recommended safe practices regarding a misfired cartridge, the FIRST course of action the mechanic should take is to

    A. place the misfired cartridge carefully into a metal container filled with water
    B. carefully reload the tool with the misfired cartridge and try it again
    C. immediately bury the misfired cartridge at least two feet in the ground
    D. remove the wadding from the misfired cartridge and empty the powder into a pail of sand

16._____

17. The ratings used in classifying fire resistant building construction materials are MOST frequently expressed in

    A. Btu's   B. hours   C. temperatures   D. pounds

17._____

18. The only legible portion of the nameplate on a piece of equipment reads: *208 volts, 3 phase, 10 H.P.*
    This data would MOST NEARLY indicate that the piece of equipment is a(n)

    A. amplifier   B. fixture ballast
    C. motor   D. rectifier

18._____

19. Of the following items relating to the maintenance of roofs, the one which is of the LEAST value in a preventive maintenance program for roofs is knowledge of the

    A. roofing specifications   B. application procedures
    C. process of deterioration   D. frequency of rainstorms

19._____

20. In an oxyacetylene cutting outfit, the color of the hose that is connected to the oxygen cylinder is USUALLY

    A. white   B. yellow   C. red   D. green

20._____

21. Assume that a welding generator is to be used to weld partitions made of 18 gauge steel. Of the following settings, the BEST one to use would be a _____ setting of voltage and a _____ setting of amperage.

    A. high; high   B. high; low   C. low; high   D. low; low

21._____

22. According to the administrative code, when color marking is used, potable water lines shall be painted

    A. yellow   B. blue   C. red   D. green

22._____

23. A set of mechanical plan drawings is drawn to a scale of 1/8" = 1 foot.
    If a length of pipe measures 15 7/16" on the drawing, the ACTUAL length of the pipe is _____ feet.

    A. 121.5   B. 122.5   C. 123.5   D. 124.5

23._____

24. A portion of a specification states: *Concrete, other than that placed under water, should be compacted and worked into place by spading or puddling.*
    The MAIN reason why *spading and puddling* is required is to

    A. insure that all water in the concrete mix is brought to the surface
    B. eliminate stone pockets and large bubbles of air

24._____

3

C. provide a means to obtain a spade full of concrete for test purposes
D. make allowances for *bleeding and segregation* of the concrete

25. Assume that the following statement appears in a construction contract: *Payment will be made for the number of pounds of bar reinforcement incorporated in the work as shown on the plans.*
    This type of contract is MOST likely

    A. cost plus   B. lump sum   C. subcontract   D. unit price

26. Partial payments to outside contractors are USUALLY based on the

    A. breakdown estimate submitted after the contract was signed
    B. actual cost of labor and material plus overhead and profit
    C. estimate of work completed which is generally submitted periodically
    D. estimate of material delivered to the job

27. Building contracts usually require that estimates for changes made in the field be submitted for approval before the work can start.
    The MAIN reason for this requirement is to

    A. make sure that the contractor understands the change
    B. discourage such changes
    C. keep the contractor honest
    D. enable the department to control its expenses

28. An *addendum* to contract specifications means MOST NEARLY

    A. a substantial completion payment to the contractor for work almost completed
    B. final acceptance of the work by authorities of all contract work still to be done
    C. additional contract provisions issued in writing by authorities prior to receipt of bids
    D. work other than that required by the contract at the time of its execution

29. Of the following terms, the one which is usually NOT used to describe the types of payments to outside contractors for work done is the _____ payment.

    A. partial payment   B. substantial completion
    C. final   D. surety

30. Of the following metals, the one which is a ferrous metal is

    A. cast iron   B. brass   C. bronze   D. babbit

31. Assume that you have assigned six mechanics to do a job that must be finished in four days. At the end of three days, your men have completed only two-thirds of the job. In order to complete the job on time and because the job is such that it cannot be speeded up, you should assign a MINIMUM of _____ extra men.

    A. 3   B. 4   C. 5   D. 6

32. Of the following traps, the one which is NORMALLY used to retain steam in a heating unit or piping is the _____ trap.

    A. P   B. running   C. float   D. bell

33. Of the following materials, the one which is a convenient and powerful adhesive for cementing tears in canvas jackets that are wrapped around warm pipe insulation is   33.____

    A. cylinder oil
    B. wheat paste
    C. water glass
    D. latex paint

34. Pipe chases should be provided with an access door PRIMARILY to provide means to   34.____

    A. replace piping lines
    B. either inspect or manipulate valves
    C. prevent condensate from forming on the pipes
    D. check the chase for possible structural defects

35. Electric power is measured in   35.____

    A. volts   B. amperes   C. watts   D. ohms

KEY (CORRECT ANSWERS)

1.	D	16.	A
2.	A	17.	B
3.	B	18.	C
4.	D	19.	D
5.	C	20.	D
6.	B	21.	B
7.	C	22.	D
8.	D	23.	C
9.	A	24.	B
10.	D	25.	D
11.	B	26.	C
12.	A	27.	D
13.	B	28.	C
14.	B	29.	D
15.	A	30.	A

31. A
32. C
33. C
34. B
35. C

TEST 2

DIRECTIONS: Each question or incomplete statement is followed by several suggested answers or completions. Select the one that BEST answers the question or completes the statement. *PRINT THE LETTER OF THE CORRECT ANSWER IN THE SPACE AT THE RIGHT.*

1. The HIGHEST quality tools should

   A. always be bought
   B. never be bought
   C. be bought when they offer an overall advantage
   D. be bought only for foreman

2. Master keys should have no markings that will identify them as such.
   This statement is

   A. *false;* it would be impossible to keep records about them without such markings
   B. *true;* markings are subject to alteration and vandalization
   C. *false;* without such markings, they would be too lightly regarded by those to whom issued
   D. *true;* markings would only highlight their value to a potential wrongdoer

3. For a foreman to usually delay for a few weeks handling grievances his men make is a

   A. *poor* practice; it can affect the morale of the men
   B. *good* practice; it will discourage grievances
   C. *poor* practice; the causes of grievances usually disappear if action is delayed
   D. *good* practice; most employee grievances are not justified

4. Whenever an important change in procedure is contemplated, some foremen make a point of discussing the matter with their subordinates in order to get their viewpoint on the proposed change.
   In general, this practice is advisable MAINLY for the reason that

   A. subordinates can often see the effects of procedural changes more clearly than foremen
   B. the foreman has an opportunity to explain the advantages of the new procedure
   C. future changes will be welcomed if subordinates are kept informed
   D. participation in work planning helps to build a spirit of cooperation among employees

5. An estimate of employee morale could LEAST effectively be appraised by

   A. checking accident and absenteeism records
   B. determining the attitudes of employees toward their job
   C. examining the number of requests for emergency leaves of absence
   D. reviewing the number and nature of employee suggestions

6. Assume that you are a foreman and that a visitor at the job site asks you what your crew is doing.
   You should

A. respectfully decline to answer since all questions must be answered by the proper authority
B. answer as concisely as possible but discourage undue conversation
C. refer the man to your superiors
D. give the person complete details of the job

7. Cooperation can BEST be obtained from the general public by

   A. siding with them whenever they have a complaint
   B. sticking carefully to your work and ignoring everything else
   C. explaining the department's objectives and why the public must occasionally be temporarily inconvenienced
   D. listening politely to their complaints and telling them that the complaints will be forwarded to the main office

8. While you are working for the city, a man says to you that one of the rules of your job doesn't make sense and he gets mad.
   You should say to him

   A. Leave me alone so I can get my work done
   B. Everyone must follow the rules
   C. Let me tell you the reason for the rule
   D. I'm only doing my job so don't get mad at me

9. One approach to preparing written reports to superiors is to present first the conclusions and recommendations and then the data on which the conclusions and recommendations are based.
   The use of this approach is BEST justified when the

   A. data completely support the conclusions and recommendations
   B. superiors lack the specific training and experience required to understand and interpret the data
   C. data contain more information than is required for making the conclusions and recommendations
   D. superiors are more interested in the conclusions and recommendations than in the data

10. The MOST important reason why separate paragraphs might be used in writing a report is that this

    A. makes it easier to understand the report
    B. permits the report to be condensed
    C. gives a better appearance to the report
    D. prevents accidental elimination of important facts

11. On a drawing, the following standard cross-section represents MOST NEARLY

    A. sand   B. concrete   C. earth   D. rock

12. On a drawing, the following standard cross-section represents MOST NEARLY

    A. malleable iron B. steel
    C. bronze D. lead

13. On a piping plan drawing, the symbol represents a 90° _____ elbow.

    A. flanged B. screwed
    C. bell and spigot D. welded

14. On a drawing, the symbol ⋘⋘ represents

    A. stone B. steel C. glass D. wood

15. On a heating piping drawing, the symbol ―/―/―/― represents piping.

    A. high-pressure steam B. medium-pressure steam
    C. low-pressure D. hot water supply

16. Of the following devices, the one that is LEAST frequently used to attach a piece of equipment to concrete or masonry walls is a(n)

    A. carriage bolt B. through bolt
    C. lag screw D. expansion bolt

17. A vapor barrier is usually installed in conjunction with

    A. drainage piping B. roof flashing
    C. building insulation D. wood sheathing

Questions 18-20.

DIRECTIONS: Questions 18 through 20 are to be answered in accordance with the following table

	Man Days Borough 1 Oct. Nov.	Man Days Borough 2 Oct. Nov.	Man Days Borough 3 Oct. Nov.	Man Days Borough 4 Oct. Nov.
Carpenter	70 100	35 180	145 205	120 85
Plumber	95 135	195 100	70 130	135 80
House Painter	90 90	120 80	85 85	95 195
Electrician	120 110	135 155	120 95	70 205
Blacksmith	125 145	60 180	205 145	80 125

18. In accordance with the above table, if the average daily pay of the five trades listed above is $47.50, the approximate labor cost of work done by the five trades during the month of October for Borough 1 is MOST NEARLY

    A. $22,800 B. $23,450 C. $23,750 D. $26,125

19. In accordance with the above table, the Borough which MOST NEARLY made up 22.4% of the total plumbing work force for the month of November is Borough

    A. 1   B. 2   C. 3   D. 4

20. In accordance with the above table, the average man days per month per Borough spent on electrical work for all Boroughs combined is MOST NEARLY

    A. 120   B. 126   C. 130   D. 136

21. Of the following percentages of carbon, the one that would indicate a medium carbon steel is

    A. 0.2%   B. 0.4%   C. 0.8%   D. 1.2%

22. A *screw pitch gage* measures only the

    A. looseness of threads
    B. tightness of threads
    C. number of threads per inch
    D. gage number

23. Assume that you are to make an inspection of a building to determine the need for painting.
    Of the following tools, the one which is LEAST needed to aid you in your inspection is a

    A. sharp penknife   B. putty knife
    C. lightweight tack hammer D. six-foot rule

24. A *slump test* for concrete is used MAINLY to measure the concrete's

    A. strength   B. consistency   C. flexibility   D. porosity

25. Specifications which contain the term *kiln dried* would MOST likely refer to

    A. asphalt shingles   B. brick veneer
    C. paint lacquer   D. lumber

26. In accordance with established jurisdictional work procedures among the trades, the person you would assign to replace a malfunctioning fire sprinkler head would be a

    A. plumber   B. laborer   C. housesmith   D. steamfitter

27. Of the following types of union shops, the one which is illegal under the Taft-Hartley Law is the _____ shop.

    A. closed   B. open
    C. union   D. union representative

28. Of the following types of contracts, the one that in city work would MOST likely be limited to emergency work *only* is

    A. lump-sum
    B. unit-price
    C. cost-plus
    D. partial cost-plus and lump-sum

29. Of the following qualifications of outside work contractors, the one which is the LEAST important requirement for determining eligible contractors is

    A. availability
    B. size of work force
    C. experience
    D. location of business

30. Of the following piping materials, the one that combines the physical strength of mild steel with the corrosion resistance of gray iron is

    A. grade A steel
    B. grey cast iron
    C. welded wrought iron
    D. ductile iron

31. Assume that a can of red lead paint needs to be thinned slightly.
    Of the following, the one that should be used is

    A. turpentine
    B. lacquer thinner
    C. water
    D. alcohol

32. Assume that a trench is 42" wide, 5' deep, and 100' long. If the unit price of excavating the trench is $35 per cubic yard, the cost of excavating the trench is MOST NEARLY

    A. $2,275 B. $5,110 C. $7,000 D. $21,000

33. Of the following uses, the one for which a bituminous compound would usually be used is to

    A. prevent corrosion of buried steel tanks
    B. increase the strength of concrete
    C. caulk water pipes
    D. paint inside wood columns

34. An electrical drawing is drawn to a scale of 1/4" = 1'.
    If a length of conduit on the drawing measures 7 3/8", the actual length of the conduit, in feet, is MOST NEARLY

    A. 7.5' B. 15.5' C. 22.5' D. 29.5'

35. Of the following steam heating systems, the one that operates under both vacuum and low pressure conditions, without using a vacuum pump, is generally known as a _____ system.

    A. one pipe low pressure
    B. vacuum
    C. vapor
    D. high pressure

36. Of the following valve trim symbols, the one which designates a valve trim made of monel material is

    A. 8-18 B. NI-CU C. SM D. MI

37. A replacement part for a piece of equipment is to be made of S.A.E. 4047 steel.
    This material is MOST likely a _____ steel.

    A. wrought
    B. nickel
    C. chrome-vanadium
    D. molybdenum

38. A metallic underground water piping system is to be used as a means of grounding. Of the following statements concerning use of this system, the one that is MOST NEARLY CORRECT is that this use is

    A. not permitted
    B. permitted where available
    C. absolutely required
    D. permitted only in certain cases

39. For pipe sizes up to 8", schedule 40 pipe is identical to _____ pipe.

    A. standard
    B. extra strong
    C. double extra strong
    D. type M copper

40. Assume that a shop is undergoing a general housecleaning, and all excess unused materials have been removed. *Clean-up work,* as pertains to painting in this case, means MOST NEARLY

    A. a thorough two-coat paint job
    B. only that surface which was marred to be painted
    C. a one-coat job to *freshen things up*
    D. only that iron work is to be painted

41. The *United States Standard Gage* is used to measure sheet metal thicknesses of

    A. iron and steel
    B. aluminum
    C. copper
    D. tin

42. Headers and stretchers are used in the construction of

    A. floors
    B. walls
    C. ceilings
    D. roofs

Questions 43-44.

DIRECTIONS: Questions 43 and 44, inclusive, are to be answered in accordance with the following paragraph.

For cast iron pipe lines, the middle ring or sleeve shall have beveled ends and shall be high quality cast iron. The middle ring shall have a minimum wall thickness of 3/8" for pipe up to 8", 7/16" for pipe 10" to 30", and 1/2" for pipe over 30", nominal diameter. Minimum length of middle ring shall be 5" for pipe up to 10", 6" for pipe 10" to 30", and 10" for pipe 30" nominal diameter and larger. The middle ring shall not have a center pipe stop, unless otherwise specified.

43. As used in the above paragraph, the word *beveled* means MOST NEARLY

    A. straight
    B. slanted
    C. curved
    D. rounded

44. In accordance with the above paragraph, the middle ring of a 24" nominal diameter pipe would have a minimum wall thickness and length of _____ thick and _____ long.

    A. 3/8"; 5"
    B. 3/8"; 6"
    C. 7/16"; 6"
    D. 1/2"; 6"

45. A work order is NOT usually issued for which one of the following jobs:

    A. Repairing wood door frames
    B. Taking daily inventory
    C. Installing electric switches in maintenance shop
    D. Repairing a number of valves in boiler room

46. Of the following statements, the one which usually does NOT pertain to preventative maintenance programs is

    A. periodic inspection of facilities
    B. lubrication of equipment
    C. minor repair of equipment
    D. complete replacement of deteriorated equipment

Questions 47-50.

DIRECTIONS: Questions 47 through 50, inclusive, are based on the sketch of metal sheet shown below. (Sketch not to scale.)

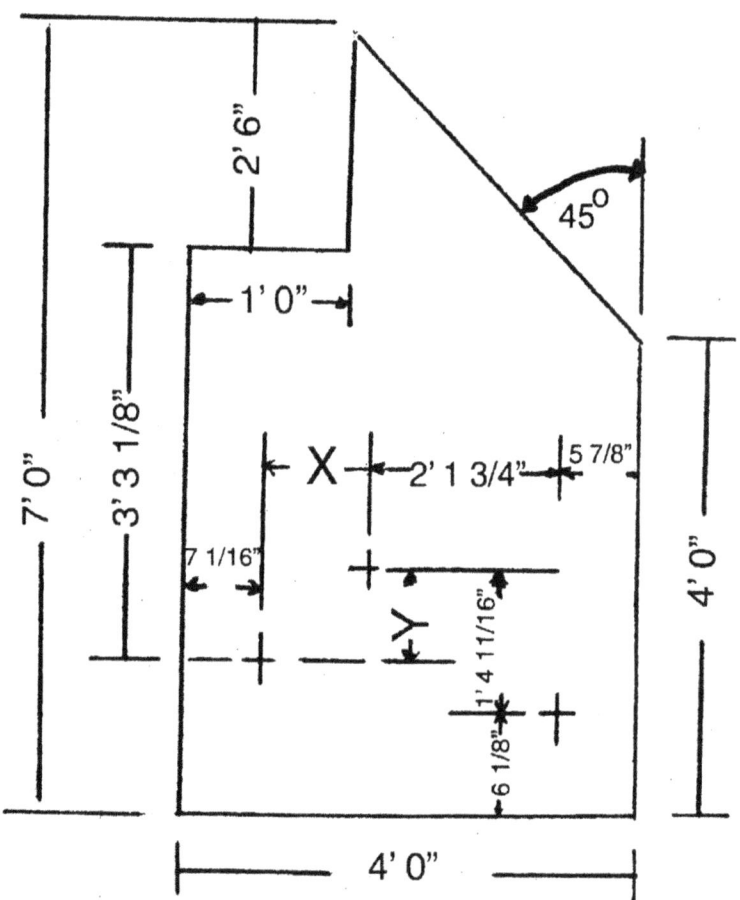

47. From the above sketch, the distance marked X is MOST NEARLY

    A. 5 1/4"   B. 6 5/16"   C. 7 1/8"   D. 9 5/16"

48. From the above sketch, the distance marked Y is MOST NEARLY   48._____

   A. 5 11/16"   B. 6 3/16"   C. 7 5/16"   D. 8 11/16"

49. In reference to the above sketch, if each piece is made from a rectangular piece of metal   49._____
    measuring 4' x 7', the percent of waste material is MOST NEARLY

   A. 10%   B. 15%   C. 25%   D. 30%

50. In reference to the above sketch, if the metal is 1/4" thick and weighs 144 pounds per   50._____
    cubic foot, the net weight of one piece would be MOST NEARLY _____ pounds.

   A. 51   B. 63   C. 75   D. 749

KEY (CORRECT ANSWERS)

1. C	11. A	21. B	31. A	41. A
2. D	12. C	22. C	32. A	42. B
3. A	13. A	23. D	33. A	43. B
4. D	14. D	24. B	34. D	44. C
5. C	15. B	25. D	35. C	45. B
6. B	16. A	26. D	36. B	46. D
7. C	17. C	27. A	37. D	47. D
8. C	18. C	28. C	38. B	48. D
9. D	19. B	29. D	39. A	49. C
10. A	20. B	30. D	40. C	50. B

EXAMINATION SECTION
TEST 1

DIRECTIONS: Each question or incomplete statement is followed by several suggested answers or completions. Select the one that BEST answers the question or completes the statement. *PRINT THE LETTER OF THE CORRECT ANSWER IN THE SPACE AT THE RIGHT.*

1. The composition of plumber's solder for wiping is APPROXIMATELY (ratio of tin to lead)   1.____

   A. 40-60   B. 50-50   C. 60-40   D. 70-30

2. A device used to lift sewage to the level of a sewer from a floor below the sewer grade is known as a(n)   2.____

   A. elevator   B. ejector   C. sump   D. conveyer

3. A check valve in a piping system will   3.____

   A. permit excessive pressures in a boiler
   B. eliminate water hammer
   C. permit water to flow in only one direction
   D. control the rate of flow of water

4. The chemical MOST frequently used to clean drains clogged with grease is   4.____

   A. muriatic acid   B. soda ash
   C. ammonia   D. caustic soda

5. To test for leaks in a newly installed C.I. waste stack,   5.____

   A. oil of peppermint is poured into the top of the stack
   B. smoke under pressure is pumped into the stack
   C. a water meter is used to measure the water flow
   D. dye is placed in the system at the top of the stack

6. When installing a catch basin, the outlet should be located   6.____

   A. at the same level as the inlet
   B. above the inlet
   C. below the inlet
   D. at the invert

7. The copper float in a low down water tank is perforated so that water enters the ball. As a result, the tank will   7.____

   A. flush once, and then will not operate again
   B. not flush at all
   C. not flush completely
   D. continue to flush, but water will be wasted

8. If water leaks from the stem of a faucet when the faucet is opened, the _____ should be   8.____

   A. faucet; replaced   B. cap nut; rethreaded
   C. seat; reground   D. packing; replaced

15

9. In a hot water heating system, it may be necessary to *bleed* radiators to

   A. relieve high steam pressure
   B. permit entrapped, air to escape
   C. allow condensate to return to the boiler
   D. drain off waste water

10. When painting raw wood, puttying of nail holes should be done

    A. 24 hours before the prime coat
    B. immediately before the prime coat
    C. after the prime coat and before the second coat
    D. after the second coat and before the finish

11. In general, the one of the following that will dry *tack free* in the SHORTEST time is

    A. lacquer   B. varnish   C. enamel   D. oil paint

12. The *vehicle* MOST frequently used in paints for exterior wood surfaces is

    A. white lead   B. linseed oil
    C. japan   D. varnish

13. Painting of an interior plastered wall is usually delayed until the plaster is dry. If this practice is NOT followed, the paint might

    A. chalk   B. fade   C. run   D. blister

14. A *sealer* applied over knots and pitch streaks to prevent *bleeding* through paint is

    A. shellac   B. lacquer
    C. coal tar   D. carnauba wax

15. Painting of outside steel in near freezing (32° F) weather is poor practice MAINLY because

    A. the paint will not dry properly
    B. ice will form in the thinner
    C. more paint is required
    D. paint fumes are dangerous

16. When repainting exterior woodwork that has a glossy finish, good adhesion of paint is BEST obtained by first

    A. *washing* the work with diluted lye
    B. *dulling* the work with sandpaper
    C. *warming* the work with an electric heater
    D. *roughening* the work with a rasp

17. The one of the following methods of cleaning steelwork prior to painting that is NOT commonly used on exterior work, such as bridges, is

    A. sandblasting   B. flame cleaning
    C. wire brushing   D. pickling

18. When spraying oil paints, the type of gun and nozzle preferred is a _____ feed gun, _____ mix nozzle.

    A. pressure; internal
    B. pressure, external
    C. syphon; internal
    D. syphon; external

19. When opening a bag of cement, you find that the cement is lumpy.
    The cement should be

    A. discarded and not used at all
    B. crushed before placing in the mixer
    C. used as is since the mixer will grind it
    D. well mixed with water and stored overnight before using

20. A 1:2:4 concrete mix by volume is specified.
    If 6 cubic feet of cement is to be used in the mix, the volume of sand to use is, in cubic feet,

    A. 3   B. 6   C. 12   D. 24

21. Honeycombing in concrete is BEST prevented by

    A. increasing water-cement ratio
    B. heating concrete in cold weather
    C. using mechanical vibrators
    D. adding calcium chloride

22. When a lightweight concrete is required, the one of the following that is COMMONLY used as an aggregate is

    A. gravel   B. brick chips   C. stone   D. cinders

23. A rubbed finish on concrete is USUALLY obtained by use of a

    A. carborundum brick
    B. garnet sanding belt
    C. fibre brush and wax
    D. pad of steel wool

24. A copper strip is frequently embedded in the concrete across a construction joint in a concrete wall.
    The purpose of this is to

    A. make a watertight joint
    B. bond the two parts of the wall together
    C. prevent unequal settlement
    D. retard temperature cracking

25. In brickwork laid in common bond, a header course USUALLY occurs in every _____ course.

    A. 2nd   B. 4th   C. 6th   D. 8th

26. Pointing of brickwork refers to

    A. cutting brick to fit
    B. patching mortar joints
    C. attaching brick veneer
    D. arranging brick in an arch

27. Furring is applied to brick walls to

    A. strengthen the wall
    B. waterproof the wall
    C. provide ventilation to prevent condensation
    D. provide a base for lathing

28. The FIRST coat in plaster work is *scratched* in order to

    A. remove excess plaster
    B. smooth the base for the second coat
    C. provide a bond for the second coat
    D. strengthen the base coat

29. An alloy used where resistance to corrosion is important is

    A. tungsten   B. mild steel   C. monel   D. tin

30. The size of iron pipe is given in terms of its nominal

    A. weight   B. inside diameter
    C. outside diameter   D. wall thickness

31. When preparing surfaces to be soldered, the FIRST step is

    A. tinning   B. sweating   C. heating   D. cleaning

32. To test for leaks in an acetylene torch, it is BEST that one use

    A. soapy water   B. a match
    C. a gas with a strong odor D. a pressure gauge

33. One advantage of using a Pittsburgh lock seam when joining two pieces of sheet metal is that, once formed in the shop, it may be assembled anywhere with a

    A. hickey   B. swage   C. template   D. mallet

34. White cast iron is

    A. hard and brittle   B. hard and ductile
    C. ductile and malleable   D. brittle and malleable

35. The gage used for measuring copper wire is

    A. U.S. Standard   B. Stubbs
    C. Washburn and Moen   D. Brown and Sharpe

36. The BEST flux to use when soldering copper wires in an electric circuit is

    A. sal ammoniac   B. zinc chloride
    C. rosin   D. borax

37. The spark test, to determine the approximate composition of an unknown metal, is made by

    A. holding the metal against a grinding wheel
    B. striking flint on the unknown metal
    C. connecting wires from a source of electric power to the metal and striking an arc with a bare wire
    D. heating with an oxyacetylene torch

38. The one of the following metals that is MOST commonly used for bearings is   38.____

    A. duraluminum   B. brass   C. babbit   D. lead

39. A *tailstock* is found on a   39.____

    A. drill press   B. shaper   C. planer   D. lathe

40. The BEST lubricant to use when cutting screw threads in steel is   40.____

    A. naphtha   B. 3-in-1 oil
    C. lard oil   D. linseed oil

41. When a high speed cutting tool is required, the tip is frequently made of   41.____

    A. carborundum   B. tungsten carbide
    C. bronze   D. vanadium

42. A nut is turned on a 3/4"-10 bolt.   42.____
    When the nut is turned five complete turns on this bolt, the distance it moves along the bolt

    A. depends on the type of thread   B. is 0.2 inches
    C. is 0.375 inches   D. is 0.5 inches

43. Of the following, the STRONGEST screw thread form is the   43.____

    A. Whitworth   B. Acme
    C. National Standard   D. V

44. *Knurling* refers to   44.____

    A. rolling depressions in a fixed pattern on a cylindrical surface
    B. turning between centers on a lathe
    C. making deep cuts in a flat plate with a milling machine
    D. drilling matching holes in bolt and nut for a cotter pin

45. A special device used to guide the drill as well as to hold the work when drilling is known   45.____
    as a

    A. dolly   B. jig   C. chuck   D. collet

46. Tools that have a *Morse taper* would be used on a   46.____

    A. milling machine   B. shaper
    C. planer   D. drill press

47. When tapping a blind hole in a plate, the FIRST tap to use is a   47.____

    A. plug   B. bottoming   C. lead   D. taper

48. An important safety practice to remember when cutting a rivet with a chisel is to wear   48.____

    A. leather gloves   B. steel toe shoes
    C. cup goggles   D. a hard hat

49. Electricians working around *live wires* should wear gloves made of 49.____

    A. asbestos   B. metal mesh   C. leather   D. rubber

50. Storage of oily rags presents a safety hazard because of possible 50.____

    A. fire   B. poisonous flames
    C. attraction of rats   D. leakage of oil

KEY (CORRECT ANSWERS)

1. A	11. A	21. C	31. D	41. B
2. B	12. B	22. D	32. A	42. D
3. C	13. D	23. A	33. D	43. B
4. D	14. A	24. A	34. A	44. A
5. B	15. A	25. C	35. B	45. B
6. C	16. B	26. B	36. C	46. D
7. D	17. D	27. D	37. A	47. D
8. D	18. A	28. C	38. C	48. C
9. B	19. A	29. C	39. D	49. D
10. C	20. C	30. B	40. C	50. A

TEST 2

DIRECTIONS: Each question or incomplete statement is followed by several suggested answers or completions. Select the one that BEST answers the question or completes the statement. *PRINT THE LETTER OF THE CORRECT ANSWER IN THE SPACE AT THE RIGHT.*

1. *Shimmying* of the front wheels of a truck is MOST frequently caused by 1.____

   A. worn front brake drums
   B. a worn differential gear
   C. a loose steering gear
   D. a dead shock absorber

2. The MOST important reason for maintaining correct air pressure in all tires of a truck is to 2.____

   A. prevent the truck from swerving when brakes are applied
   B. permit the truck to stop quicker in an emergency
   C. provide a smoother ride
   D. prevent excessive wear on the tires

3. The oil gage on the dashboard of a truck indicates 3.____

   A. the amount of oil in the pan
   B. the pressure at which the oil is being pumped
   C. if the oil filter is working
   D. the temperature of the oil in the motor

4. An unbalanced wheel on a truck is corrected by 4.____

   A. bending the rim slightly
   B. adjusting the king pin
   C. changing the ratio of caster to camber
   D. adding small weights to the rim

5. A cold motor on a truck should be warmed up in wintertime by 5.____

   A. turning on the heater and pouring warm water into the radiator
   B. allowing the motor to idle for a few minutes
   C. racing the motor
   D. alternately pressing the gas pedal to the floor and releasing it

6. The brake pedal on a truck goes to the floorboard when pushed. The one of the following that would cause this condition is 6.____

   A. air in the hydraulic system
   B. wet brakes
   C. excessive fluid in the cylinders
   D. a loose backing plate

7. The ammeter of a truck indicates no charge during operation even though the battery is run down. To find the fault, the generator field terminal is grounded. The ammeter now shows a charge. The part that is defective is the 7.____

   A. generator field coil
   B. armature
   C. brushes
   D. voltage regulator

8. The part used to control the ratio of air and gasoline in a truck engine is the

   A. bogie   B. filter   C. carburetor   D. pump

9. The MAIN purpose of a vacuum booster on a truck engine is to

   A. increase the manifold vacuum
   B. assist windshield wiper operation
   C. provide a steadier fuel flow
   D. govern engine speed

10. The purpose of grounding the frame of an electric motor is to

    A. prevent excessive vibration
    B. eliminate shock hazards
    C. reduce power requirements
    D. prevent overheating

11. The one of the following that is NOT part of an electric motor is a

    A. brush   B. rheostat   C. pole   D. commutator

12. An electrical transformer would be used to

    A. change current from AC to DC
    B. raise or lower the power
    C. raise or lower the voltage
    D. change the frequency

13. The piece of equipment that would be rated in ampere hours is a

    A. storage battery
    B. bus bar
    C. rectifier
    D. capacitor

14. A ballast is a necessity in a(n)

    A. motor generator set
    B. fluorescent lighting system
    C. oil circuit breaker
    D. synchronous converter

15. The power factor in an AC circuit is on when

    A. no current is flowing
    B. the voltage at the source is a minimum
    C. the voltage and current are in phase
    D. there is no load

16.

    1 OHM

    6V

    1 OHM

    Neglecting the internal resistance in the battery, the current flowing through the battery shown in the sketch above is _____ amp.

    A. 3   B. 6   C. 9   D. 12

17. When excess current flows, a circuit breaker is opened directly by the action of a   17._____

    A. condenser   B. transistor   C. relay   D. solenoid

18. The MAIN purpose of bridging in building floor construction is to   18._____

    A. spread floor loads evenly to joists
    B. reduce the number of joists required
    C. permit use of thinner subflooring
    D. reduce noise passage through floors

19. Of the following, the material MOST commonly used for subflooring is   19._____

    A. rock lath   B. insulation board
    C. plywood   D. transite

20. In connection with stair construction, the one of the following that is LEAST related to the others is   20._____

    A. tread   B. cap   C. nosing   D. riser

21. The type of nail MOST commonly used in flooring is   21._____

    A. common   B. cut   C. brad   D. casing

22. The edge joint of flooring boards is COMMONLY   22._____

    A. mortise and tenon   B. shiplap
    C. half lap   D. tongue and groove

23. The purpose of a ridge board in building construction is to   23._____

    A. locate corners of a building
    B. keep plaster work smooth
    C. support the ends of roof rafters
    D. conceal openings at the eaves

24. To prevent splintering of wood when using an auger bit,   24._____

    A. the bit should be hollow ground
    B. hold the piece of wood in a vise
    C. clamp a piece of scrap wood to the back of the piece being drilled
    D. use a slow speed on the drill press

25. End grain of a post can be MOST easily planed by use of a _____ plane.   25._____

    A. rafter   B. jack   C. fore   D. block

26. A butt gauge is used when   26._____

    A. hanging doors   B. laying out stairs
    C. making rafter cuts   D. framing studs

27. The one of the following grades of sandpaper with the FINEST grit is   27._____

    A. 0   B. 2/0   C. 1/2   D. 1

28. The sum of the following numbers, 3 7/8, 14 1/4, 6 7/16, 22 3/16, 8 1/2 is

    A. 55 1/16   B. 55 1/8   C. 55 3/16   D. 55 1/4

29. The area of the rectangular field shown in the diagram at the right is, in square feet,
    A. 29,456
    B. 29,626
    C. 29,716
    D. 29,836

    437 FT.

    68 ft

30. The cost of material is approximately 3/8ths of the total cost of a certain job. If the total cost of the job is $127.56, then the cost of material is MOST NEARLY

    A. $47.83   B. $48.24   C. $48.65   D. $49.06

31. A blueprint is drawn to a scale of 1/4" = 1'0". A line on the blueprint that is not dimensioned is measured with a ruler and found to be 3 3/8" long.
    The length represented by this line is

    A. 13'2"   B. 13'4"   C. 13'6"   D. 13'8"

32. A maintainer, in repairing a brick wall, spends one-half hour getting materials, forty-three minutes chipping and cleaning the wall, fifteen minutes mixing the mortar, and one hour and twenty-seven minutes in applying the brick and finishing.
    The total time spent on this repair job is _____ hours _____ minute(s).

    A. 2; 45   B. 2; 50   C. 2; 55   D. 3; 0

33. *Employees are responsible for the good care, proper maintenance, and <u>serviceable condition</u> of property issued or assigned to their use.*
    As used above, *serviceable condition* means MOST NEARLY

    A. capable of being repaired   B. fit for use
    C. ease of handling   D. minimum cost

34. *An employee shall be on the alert constantly for potential accident hazards.*
    As used above, *potential* means MOST NEARLY

    A. dangerous   B. careless   C. possible   D. frequent

Questions 35-37.

DIRECTIONS: Questions 35 to 37, inclusive, are to be answered in accordance with the following paragraph.

All cement work contracts, more or less, in setting. The contraction in concrete walls and other structures causes fine cracks to develop at regular intervals. The tendency to contract increases in direct proportion to the quantity of cement in the concrete. A rich mixture will contract more than a lean mixture. A concrete wall, which has been made of a very lean mixture and which has been built by filling only about one foot in depth of concrete in the form each day will frequently require close inspection to reveal the cracks.

35. According to the above paragraph,

   A. shrinkage seldom occurs in concrete
   B. shrinkage occurs only in certain types of concrete
   C. by placing concrete at regular intervals, shrinkage may be avoided
   D. it is impossible to prevent shrinkage

36. According to the above paragraph, the one of the factors which reduces shrinkage in concrete is the

   A. volume of concrete in wall
   B. height of each day's pour
   C. length of wall
   D. length and height of wall

37. According to the above paragraph, a rich mixture

   A. pours the easiest
   B. shows the largest amount of cracks
   C. is low in cement content
   D. need not be inspected since cracks are few

Questions 38-39.

   DIRECTIONS: Questions 38 and 39 are to be answered in accordance with the following paragraph.

Painting is done to preserve surfaces, and unless the surface is properly prepared, good preservation will not be possible. Apply paint only to clean dry surfaces. After a surface has been scaled, which means that all loose paint and rust are removed by chipping, scraping, and wire brushing, be sure all dust and dirt are completely removed.

38. According to the above paragraph, the MAIN purpose of painting a wall is to _____ the wall.

   A. clean
   B. waterproof
   C. protect
   D. remove dust from

39. According to the above paragraph,

   A. chipping, scraping, and wire brushing are the only methods permitted for cleaning surfaces
   B. painting is effective only when the surface is clean
   C. scaling refers only to the removal of rust
   D. paint may be applied on wet surfaces

40. The order in which the dimensions of stock are listed on a bill of materials is

   A. thickness, length, and width
   B. thickness, width, and length
   C. width, length, and thickness
   D. length, thickness, and width

41. The glue that will BEST withstand extreme exposure to moisture and water is _____ glue.

    A. polyvinyl
    B. resorcinol
    C. powdered resin
    D. protein

42. Four board feet of lumber, listed at $350.00 per M, will cost

    A. $3.50   B. $1.40   C. $1.30   D. $4.00

43. The cap iron or chip breaker stiffens the plane iron and

    A. protects the cutting edge
    B. curls the shaving
    C. regulates the thickness of the shaving
    D. reduces mouth gap

44. Coping-saw blades have teeth shaped like those on a _____ saw.

    A. dovetail   B. crosscut   C. back   D. rip

45. Of the following, the claw hammer that is BEST suited for general use in a woodworking shop is the _____ claw.

    A. straight
    B. bell-faced curved
    C. plain-faced curved
    D. adze eye curved

46. The natural binder which cements wood fibers together and makes wood solid is

    A. cellulose
    B. lignin
    C. alpha-cellulose
    D. trichocarpa

47. The plane that is BEST suited for trimming the bottom of a dado or lap joint is the _____ plane.

    A. block   B. router   C. rabbet   D. core-box

48. Brads are fasteners that are similar to _____ nails.

    A. escutcheon
    B. box
    C. finishing
    D. duplex head

49. The plane in which the plane iron is inserted with its bevel in the up position is the _____ plane.

    A. fore   B. rabbet   C. block   D. circular

50. Coating materials used to protect wood against fire USUALLY contain a water soluble fire-retardant such as

    A. ammonium chloride
    B. sodium perborate
    C. sodium silicate
    D. sal soda

KEY (CORRECT ANSWERS)

1. C	11. B	21. B	31. C	41. B
2. D	12. C	22. D	32. C	42. B
3. B	13. A	23. C	33. B	43. B
4. D	14. B	24. C	34. C	44. D
5. B	15. C	25. D	35. D	45. B
6. A	16. A	26. A	36. B	46. B
7. D	17. D	27. B	37. B	47. B
8. C	18. A	28. D	38. C	48. C
9. B	19. C	29. C	39. B	49. C
10. B	20. B	30. A	40. B	50. C

EXAMINATION SECTION

TEST 1

DIRECTIONS: Each question or incomplete statement is followed by several suggested answers or completions. Select the one that BEST answers the question or completes the statement. *PRINT THE LETTER OF THE CORRECT ANSWER IN THE SPACE AT THE RIGHT.*

Questions 1-17:
Use the following diagrams of tools to answer questions 1 through 17. (Tools are NOT drawn to scale.)

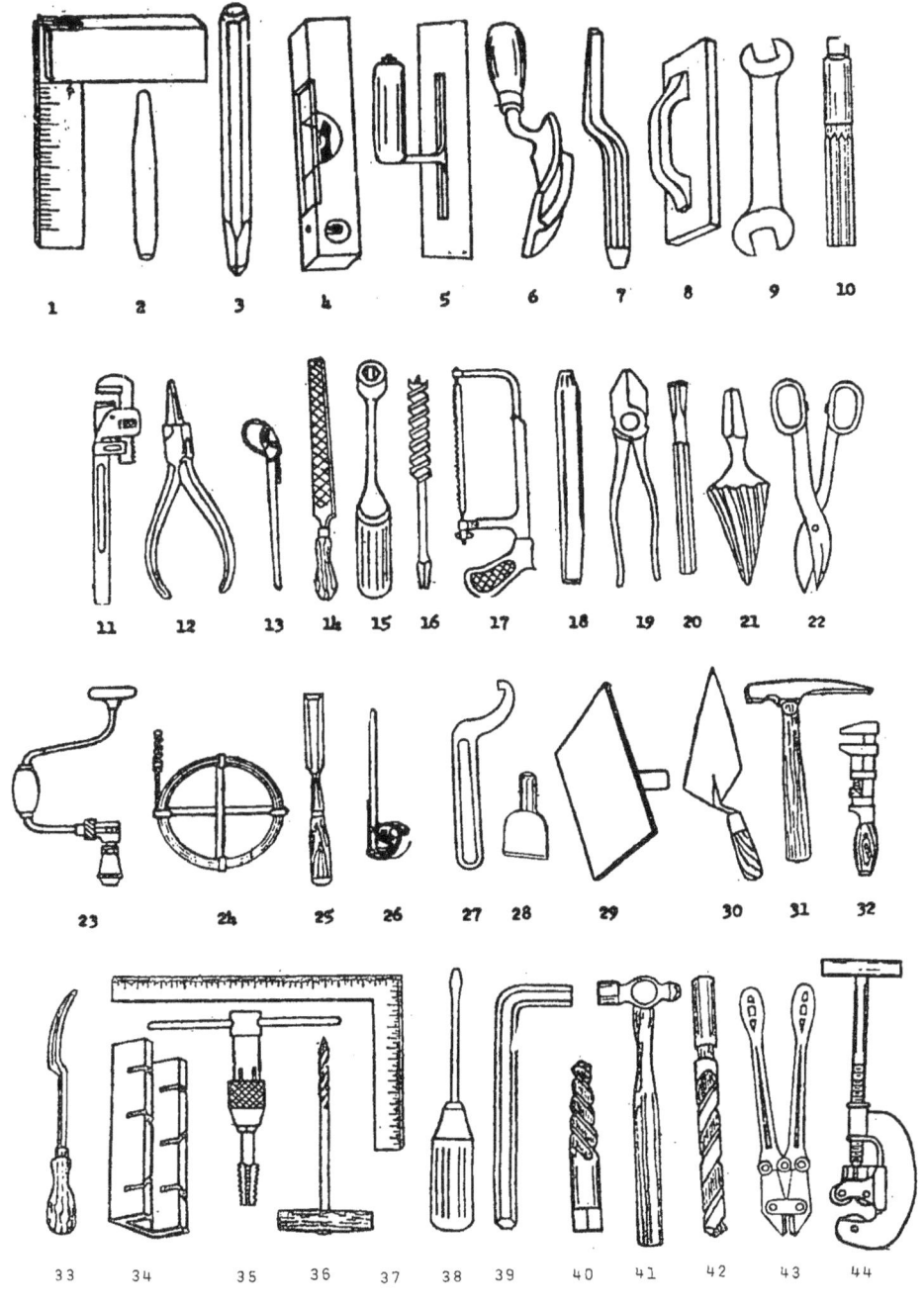

1. To tighten an elbow on a threaded pipe, a mechanic should use tool   1._____
   number
       A. 9   B. 11   C. 26   D. 32

2. To cut grooves in a newly poured cement floor, a mechanic should use   2._____
   tool number
       A. 5   B. 6   C. 28   D. 29

3. To "caulk" a lead joint, a mechanic should use tool number   3._____
       A. 7   B. 10   C. 25   D. 33

4. The term "snips" should be applied by a mechanic to tool number   4._____
       A. 12   B. 22   C. 36   D. 43

5. To slightly enlarge an existing 17/32" diameter hole in a metal plate, a   5._____
   mechanic should use tool number
       A. 3   B. 10   C. 14   D. 35

6. The term "snake" should be applied by a mechanic to tool number   6._____
       A. 21   B. 23   C. 24   D. 40

7. If the threaded portion of a 1/2" brass pipe breaks off inside a gate valve,   7._____
   the piece should be removed with tool number
       A. 15   B. 35   C. 39   D. 40

8. To cut a face brick into a bat, a mechanic should use tool number   8._____
       A. 3   B. 18   C. 25   D. 28

9. A mechanic should cut a 3" x 2" x 3/16" angle iron with tool number   9._____
       A. 3   B. 17   C. 22   D. 43

10. A mechanic should tighten a chrome-plated water supply pipe by using 10._____
    tool number
       A. 11   B. 19   C. 26   D. 32

11. The term "hawk" should be applied by a mechanic to tool number   11._____
       A. 28   B. 29   C. 30   D. 33

12. If your coworker asks you to pass him the "star" drill, you should hand him   12._____
    tool number
       A. 16   B. 20   C. 40   D. 42

13. After threading a 1" diameter piece of pipe, a mechanic should debur the   13._____
    inside by using tool number
       A. 14   B. 21   C. 36   D. 40

3 (#1)

14. A mechanic should apply the term "float" to tool number 14._____
    A. 4 B. 6 C. 8 D. 28

15. If a mechanic has to cut a dozen 15-inch lengths of 3/4" steel pipe for 15._____
    spacers, he should use tool number
    A. 18 B. 26 C. 43 D. 44

16. If a mechanic is erecting two structural steel plates and needs to line up 16._____
    the bolt holes, he should use tool number
    A. 2 B. 3 C. 33 D. 42

17. To cut reinforcing wire mesh to be used in a concrete floor, you should 17._____
    use tool number
    A. 7 B. 17 C. 18 D. 43

18. The MAIN reason for overhauling a power tool on a regular basis is to 18._____
    A. make the men more familiar with the tool
    B. keep the men busy during slack times
    C. insure that the tool is used occasionally
    D. minimize breakdowns

19. A mechanic should NOT press too heavily on a hacksaw while using it to 19._____
    cut through a steel rod because this may
    A. create flying steel particles
    B. bend the frame
    C. break the blade
    D. overheat the rod

20. Creosote is COMMONLY used with wood to 20._____
    A. speed up the seasoning   B. make the wood fireproof
    C. make painting easier   D. preserve the wood

21. A mitre box should be used to 21._____
    A. hold a saw while sharpening it
    B. store expensive tools
    C. hold a saw at a fixed angle
    D. encase steel beams for protection

22. Wood scaffold planks should be inspected 22._____
    A. at regular intervals   B. once a week
    C. before they are stored away D. each time before use

23. Continuous sheeting should be used when excavating deep trenches in 23._____
    A. rock   B. stiff clay
    C. firm earth   D. unstable soil

24. The MAIN reason for requiring that certain special tools be returned to the tool room after a job has been completed is that
    A. missing tools can be replaced
    B. the men will not need to care for the tools
    C. more tools will be available for use
    D. this permits easier inspection and maintenance of tools

24._____

25. The BEST material to use to extinguish an oil fire is
    A. sand   B. water   C. sawdust   D. gravel

25._____

26. A "Lally" column is
    A. fabricated from angles and plates
    B. fabricated by tying two channels together with lattice bars
    C. a steel member that has unequal sections
    D. a pipe fitted with a base plate at each end

26._____

27. The BEST action for you to take if you discover a small puddle of oil on the shop floor is to first
    A. have it cleaned up
    B. find out who spilled it
    C. discover the source of the leak
    D. cover it with newspaper

27._____

28. You should listen to your foreman even when he insists on explaining the procedure for a job you have done many times before because
    A. you can do the job the way you want when he leaves
    B. he may make an error and you can show that you know your job
    C. it is wise to humor him even if he is wrong
    D. you are required to do the job the way the foreman wants it

28._____

Questions 29-34:
Answer questions 29 through 34 by referring to the sketches that follow.

29. The indicated pressure is, MOST NEARLY, _____ psi.　　　　　　　　　29._____
    A. 132　　　　　B. 137　　　　　C. 143　　　　　D. 148

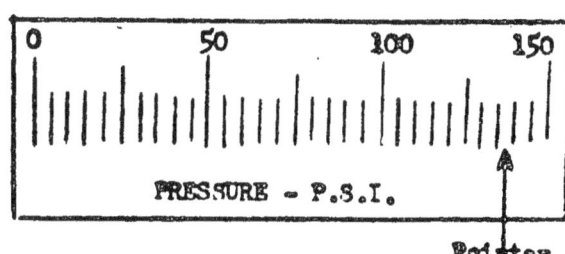

30. The LEAST number of shims, of any combination of thickness, required to　　30._____
    exactly fill the 1/4" gap shown is
    A. 7　　　　　B. 8　　　　　C. 9　　　　　D. 10

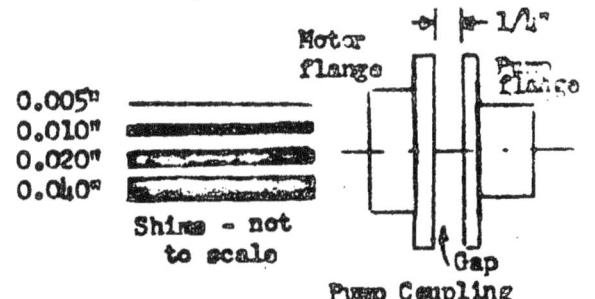

31. The dimension "X" on the keyway shown is　　　　　　　　　　　　31._____
    A. 3-3/8"　　　B. 3-9/16"　　　C. 3-3/4"　　　D. 4"

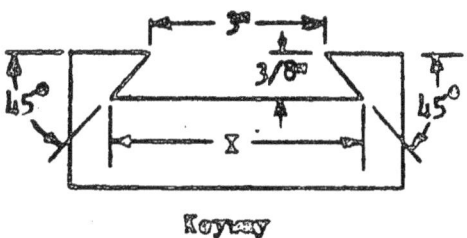

32. If the tank gauge reads 120 psi, then the pipe gauge should read ___ psi.　　32._____
    A. 80　　　　　B. 120　　　　　C. 180　　　　　D. 240

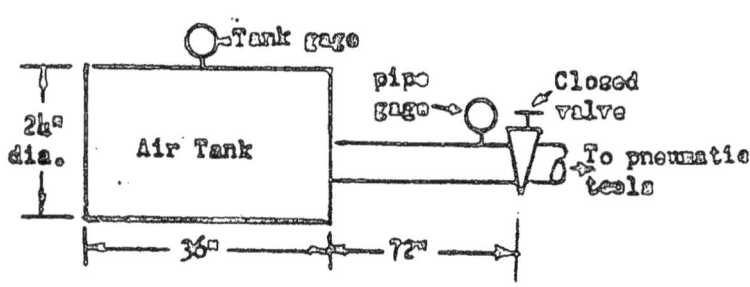

33. The MINIMUM number of feet of chainlink fence needed to completely enclose the storage yard shown is

    A. 278   B. 286   C. 295   D. 304   33._____

34. The distance "X" between the holes is

    A. 1-7/8"   B. 2-1/16" C. 2-3/8"   D. 2-9/16"   34._____

35. A rule requires all employees to report defective equipment to their superiors, even when the maintenance of the particular pieces of equipment is handled by someone else. The MAIN purpose of this rule is to   35._____

    A. determine who is doing the job improperly
    B. have repairs made before trouble occurs
    C. encourage all employees to be alert at all times
    D. reduce the cost of equipment

36. Some equipment is fitted with wing nuts. Such nuts are ESPECIALLY useful when   36._____

    A. the nut is to be wired closed
    B. space is limited
    C. the equipment is subject to vibration
    D. the nuts must be removed frequently

37. It is considered BAD practice to use water to put out electrical fires MAINLY because the water may   37._____

    A. rust the equipment
    B. short circuit the lines
    C. cause a serious shock
    D. damage the electrical insulation

38. The BEST instrument to use to make certain that two points, separated by a vertical distance of nine feet, are in perfect vertical alignment is a   38._____

    A. square   B. level   C. plumb bob   D. protractor

39. While you are being trained, you will be assigned to work with an experienced mechanic. It would be BEST for you to
    A. remind the mechanic that he is responsible for your training
    B. tell him frequently how much you know about the work
    C. let him do all the work while you observe closely
    D. be as cooperative and helpful a you can

40. If a measurement scaled from a drawing is one inch, and the scale of the drawing is 1/8 inch to the foot, then the one-inch measurement would represent an ACTUAL length of
    A. 8 feet   B. 2 feet   C. 1/8 of a foot   D. 8 inches

KEY (CORRECT ANSWERS)

1. B	11. B	21. C	31. C
2. B	12. B	22. D	32. B
3. A	13. B	23. D	33. D
4. B	14. C	24. D	34. A
5. B	15. D	25. A	35. B
6. C	16. A	26. D	36. D
7. D	17. D	27. A	37. C
8. D	18. D	28. D	38. C
9. B	19. C	29. B	39. D
10. C	20. D	30. A	40. A

TEST 2

DIRECTIONS: Each question or incomplete statement is followed by several suggested answers or completions. Select the one that BEST answers the question or completes the statement. *PRINT THE LETTER OF THE CORRECT ANSWER IN THE SPACE AT THE RIGHT.*

1. Cloth tapes should NOT be used when accurate measurements must be obtained because
    A. the numbers soon become worn and thus difficult to read
    B. there are not enough subdivisions of each inch on the tape
    C. the ink runs when wet, thus making the tape difficult to read
    D. small changes in the pull on the tape will make considerable differences in tape readings

1._____

2. It is considered GOOD practice to release the pressure from an air hose before uncoupling the hose connection because this avoids
    A. wasting air
    B. possible personal injury
    C. damage to the air tool
    D. damage to the air compressor

2._____

3. In brick construction, a structural steel member is used to support the wall above door and window openings. This member is called a
    A. purlin   B. sill   C. truss   D. lintel

3._____

4. The BEST procedure to use to properly ignite an oxyacetylene cutting torch is to
    A. crack the acetylene valve, apply the spark, and open the oxygen valve
    B. crack the acetylene valve, then the oxygen valve, and apply the spark
    C. crack the oxygen valve, then the acetylene valve, and apply the spark
    D. crack the oxygen valve, apply the spark, open the acetylene valve

4._____

5. The information in an accident report which may be MOST useful in helping to prevent similar-type accidents from happening is the
    A. cause of the accident   B. time of day it happened
    C. type of injuries suffered   D. number of people injured

5._____

6. The MAIN reason why each coat of paint should be of a different color when two coats of paint are specified is that
    A. cheaper paint can be used as the undercoat
    B. less care need be taken in applying the coats
    C. any missed areas will be easier to spot
    D. the colors do not have to be exact

6._____

7. To prevent manila hoisting ropes from raveling, the ends are
   A. moused   B. whipped   C. spliced   D. eyed

8. The MAIN advantage of aluminum ladders over wooden ladders is that they are
   A. much stronger   B. lighter
   C. cheaper   D. more stable

9. The splices in columns in steel construction are USUALLY made
   A. two feet above floor level   B. two feet below floor level
   C. at floor level   D. midway between floors

10. Open-end wrenches with small openings are generally made shorter in overall length than open-end wrenches with larger openings. The MOST important reason for this is to
    A. save material
    B. provide compactness
    C. prevent overstressing the wrench
    D. provide correct leverage

11. Galvanized steel wire is wire that has been coated with
    A. zinc   B. copper   C. tin   D. lead

12. "Camber" in a steel roof truss refers to the
    A. grade of steel used
    B. stress in the steel
    C. finish applied to the steel
    D. upward curve of the lower chord

13. A structural member is marked 8 WF 18. The 18 in this designation is the
    A. depth of the web
    B. width of the flange
    C. length of the member
    D. weight per foot

14. A strictly enforced safety rule in a rigging gang is that only one man gives the signals to the crane operator. However the ONE signal that anyone in the gang is allowed to give is the
    A. hoist-up signal   B. boom-down signal
    C. swing signal   D. stop signal

15. "Turnbuckles" are GENERALLY used to
    A. raise heavy loads   B. splice two cables
    C. tie a cable to a column   D. tighten a cable

16. If a mechanic opens the strands of a piece of manila rope and finds sawdust-like material inside the rope, it means the rope

  A. has dried out and must be re-oiled before use
  B. is relatively new
  C. has been damaged and should be discarded
  D. is to be used only for light loads until the sawdust has been cleaned out

16._____

Questions 17-21:
Refer to the passage below to answer questions 17 through 21.

REGULATIONS FOR SMALL GROUPS WHO MOVE FROM POINT TO POINT ON THE TRACKS

Employees who perform duties on the tracks in small groups and who move from point to point along the trainway, must be on the alert at all times and prepared to clear the track when a train approaches without unnecessarily slowing it down. Underground at all times, and out-of-doors between sunset and sunrise, such employees must not enter upon the tracks unless each of them is equipped with an approved light. Flashlights must not be used for protection by such groups. Upon clearing the track to permit a train to pass, each member of the group must give a proceed signal, by hand or light, to the motorman of the train. Whenever such small groups are working in an area protected by caution lights or flags, but are not members of the gang for whom the flagging protection was established, they must not give proceed signals to motormen. The purpose of this rule is to avoid a motorman's confusing such signal with that of the flagman who is protecting a gang. Whenever a small group is engaged in work of an engrossing nature or at any time when the view of approaching trains is limited by reason of curves or otherwise, one man of the group, equipped with a whistle, must be assigned properly to warn and protect the man or men at work and must not perform any other duties while so assigned.

17. If a small group of men are traveling along the tracks toward their work location and a train approaches, they should

  A. stop the train
  B. signal the motorman to go slowly
  C. clear the track
  D. stop immediately

17._____

18. Small groups may enter upon the tracks

  A. only between sunset and sunrise
  B. provided each has an approved light
  C. provided their foreman has a good flashlight
  D. provided each man has an approved flashlight

18._____

4 (#2)

19. After a small group has cleared the tracks in an area unprotected by caution lights or flags,
    A. each member must give the proceed signal to the motorman
    B. the foreman signals the motorman to proceed
    C. the motorman can proceed provided he goes slowly
    D. the last member off the tracks gives the signal to the motorman

19._____

20. If a small group is working in an area protected by the signals of a track gang, the members of the small group
    A. need not be concerned with train movement
    B. must give the proceed signal together with the track gang
    C. can delegate one of their members to give the proceed signal
    D. must not give the proceed signal

20._____

21. If the view of approaching trains is blocked, the small group should
    A. move to where they can see the trains
    B. delegate one of the group to warn and protect them
    C. keep their ears alert for approaching trains
    D. refuse to work at such locations

21._____

Questions 22-28:
Refer to the sketched below to answer questions 22 through 28.

22. The distance "Y" is
    A. 5/8"   B. 7/8"   C. 1-1/8"   D. 1-3/8"

22._____

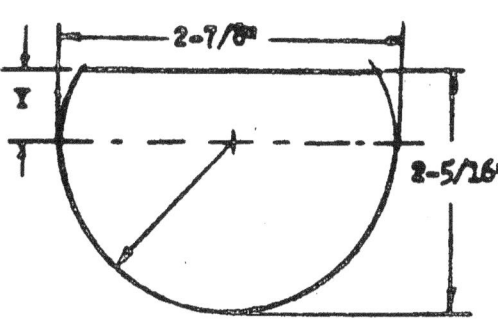

23. The sketch shows the float-operated trippers for operating a sump pump. If you want the pump to start sooner, you should
    A. lower the upper tripper   B. lower the lower tripper
    C. raise the upper tripper   D. raise the lower tripper

23._____

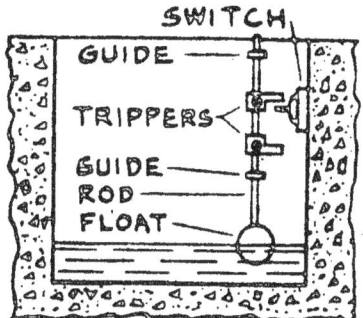

24. The width of the wood stud shown is 24._____
    A. 1-1/8"   B. 1-5/16"   C. 1-5/8"   D. 3-5/8"

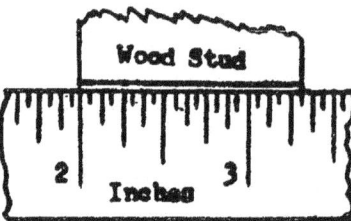

25. The right angle shown has been divided into four unequal parts. The 25._____
    number of degrees in angle "X" is
    A. 31°   B. 33°   C. 38°   D. 45°

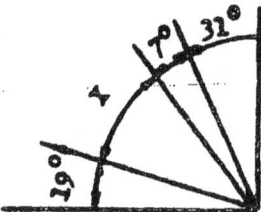

26. The reading on the meter shown is MOST NEARLY 26._____
    A. 0465   B. 0475   C. 0566   D. 1566

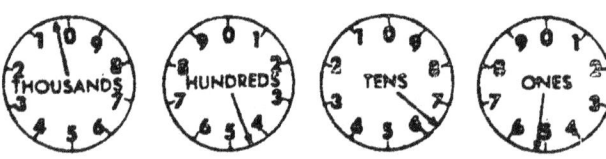

27. The length "X" of the slot shown is 27._____
    A. 2-3/8"   B. 2-7/16"   C. 2-1/2"   D. 2-9/16"

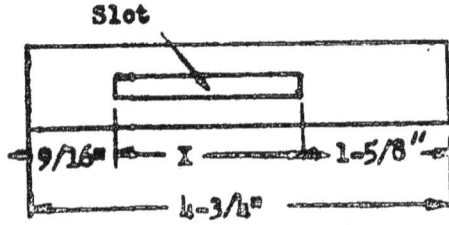

28. The volume of the bar shown is _____ cubic inches. 28._____
    A. 132   B. 356   C. 420   D. 516

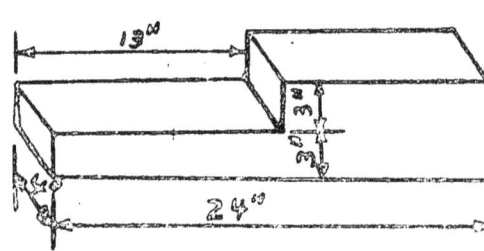

Questions 29-34:
Use the sketch below to answer questions 29 through 34.

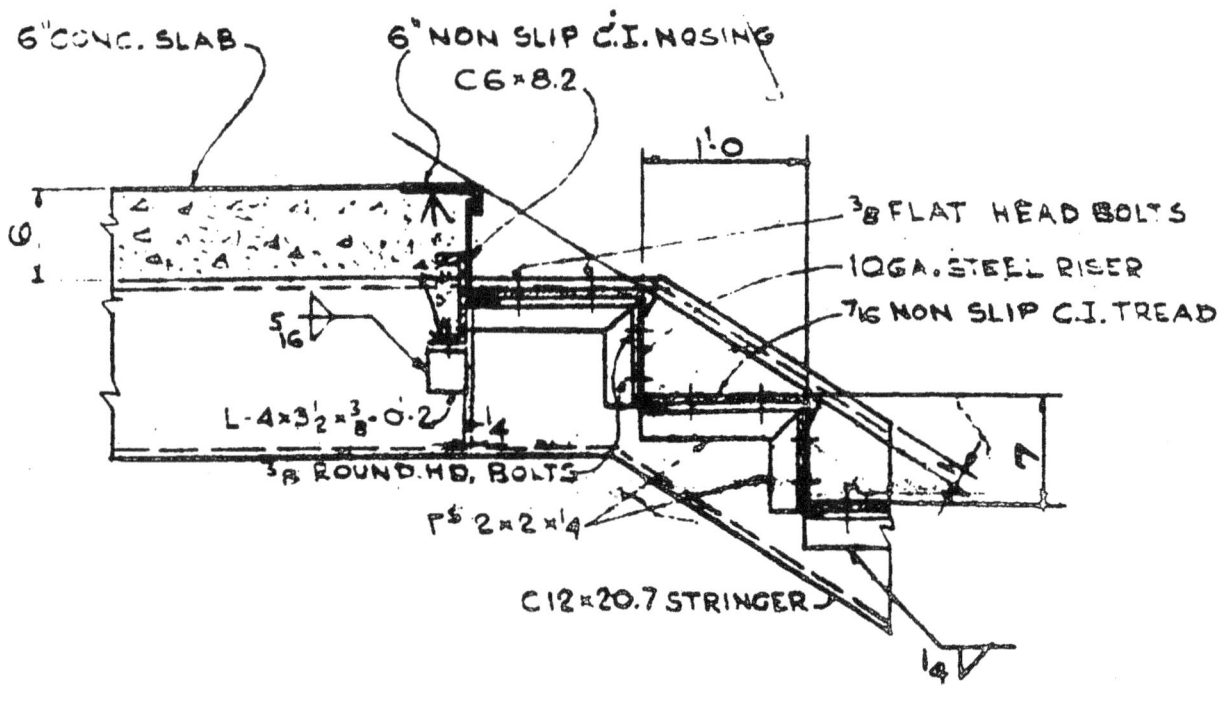

29. The stringer for this stair is a(n)
    A. I-beam   B. angle   C. H-beam   D. channel

30. The riser is made of
    A. concrete
    B. sheet metal
    C. cast iron
    D. wood

31. The 2 x 2 x 1/4 angles are secured to the stringer by
    A. 5/16" welds
    B. 1/4" welds
    C. 3/8" flat head bolts
    D. 3/8" round head bolts

32. The treads are made of
    A. concrete
    B. sheet metal
    C. cast iron
    D. wood

33. The height of the riser is
    A. 6"   B. 7"   C. 8"   D. 12"

34. The width of the tread is
    A. 6"   B. 7"   C. 8"   D. 12"

Questions 35-40:

DIRECTIONS: Questions 35 through 40 show the top view of an object in the first column, the front view of the same object in the second column, and four drawings in the third column, one of which correctly represents the RIGHT side view of the object. Select the CORRECT right side view. As a guide, the first one is an illustrative example, the correct answer of which is C.

35. _____
36. _____
37. _____
38. _____
39. _____
40. _____

KEY (CORRECT ANSWERS)

1. D	11. A	21. B	31. B
2. B	12. D	22. B	32. C
3. D	13. D	23. D	33. B
4. A	14. D	24. B	34. D
5. A	15. D	25. B	35. C
6. C	16. C	26. A	36. A
7. B	17. C	27. D	37. C
8. B	18. B	28. C	38. B
9. A	19. A	29. D	39. B
10. D	20. D	30. B	40. C

EXAMINATION SECTION
TEST 1

DIRECTIONS: Each question or incomplete statement is followed by several suggested answers or completions. Select the one that BEST answers the question or completes the statement. *PRINT THE LETTER OF THE CORRECT ANSWER IN THE SPACE AT THE RIGHT.*

1. The combustion efficiency of a boiler can be determined with a CO_2 indicator and the   1.____

    A. under fire draft
    B. boiler room humidity
    C. flue gas temperature
    D. outside air temperature

2. A quick, practical method of determining if the cast-iron waste pipe delivered to a job has been damaged in transit is to   2.____

    A. hydraulically test it
    B. "ring" each length with a hammer
    C. drop each length to see whether it breaks
    D. visually examine the pipe for cracks

3. An electrostatic precipitator is used to   3.____

    A. filter the air supply
    B. remove sludge from the fuel oil
    C. remove particles from the fuel gas
    D. supply samples for an Orsat analysis

4. The PRIMARY cause of cracking and spalling of refractory lining in the furnace of a steam generator is *most likely* due to   4.____

    A. continuous over-firing of boiler
    B. slag accumulation on furnace walls
    C. change in fuel from solid to liquid
    D. uneven heating and cooling within the refractory brick

5. The term "effective temperature" in air conditioning means   5.____

    A. the dry bulb temperature
    B. the average of the wet and dry bulb temperatures
    C. the square root of the product of wet and dry bulb temperatures
    D. an arbitrary index combining the effects of temperature, humidity, and movement

6. The piping in all buildings having dual water distribution systems should be identified by a color coding of _____ for potable water lines and _____ for non-potable water lines.   6.____

    A. green; red
    B. green; yellow
    C. yellow; green
    D. yellow; red

7. The breaking of a component of a machine subjected to excessive vibration is called   7.____

    A. tensile failure
    B. fatigue failure
    C. caustic embrittlement
    D. amplitude failure

45

8. The TWO MOST important factors to be considered in selecting fans for ventilating systems are

   A. noise and efficiency
   B. space available and weight
   C. first cost and dimensional bulk
   D. construction and arrangement of drive

9. In the modern power plant deaerator, air is removed from water to

   A. reduce heat losses in the heaters
   B. reduce corrosion of boiler steel due to the air
   C. reduce the load of the main condenser air pumps
   D. prevent pumps from becoming vapor bound

10. The abbreviations BOD, COD, and DO are associated with

    A. flue gas analysis
    B. air pollution control
    C. boiler water treatment
    D. water pollution control

11. The piping of a newly installed drainage system should be tested upon completion of the rough plumbing with a head of water of NOT LESS THAN _____ feet.

    A. 10   B. 15   C. 20   D. 25

12. Of the following statements concerning aquastats, the one which is CORRECT is:

    A. Aquastats may be obtained with either a narrow or wide range of settings
    B. Aquastats have a mercury tube switch which is controlled by the stack switch
    C. An aquastat is a device used to shut down the burner in the event of low water in the boiler
    D. An aquastat should be located about 4 inches above the normal water line of the boiler

13. The SAFEST way to protect the domestic water supply from contamination by sewage or non-potable water is to insert

    A. air gaps
    B. swing connections
    C. double check valves
    D. tanks with overhead discharge

14. The MAIN function of a back-pressure valve which is sometimes found in the connection between a water drain pipe and the sewer system is to

    A. equalize the pressure between the drain pipe and the sewer
    B. prevent sewer water from flowing into the drain pipe
    C. provide pressure to enable waste to reach the sewer
    D. make sure that there is not too much water pressure in the sewer line

15. Boiler water is neutral if its pH value is

    A. 0   B. 1   C. 7   D. 14

16. A domestic hot water mixing or tempering valve should be preceded in the hot water line by a   16.____

    A. strainer   B. foot valve
    C. check valve   D. steam trap

17. Between a steam boiler and its safety valve there should be   17.____

    A. no valve of any type
    B. a gate valve of the same size as the safety valve
    C. a swing check valve of at least the same size as the safety valve
    D. a cock having a clear opening equal in area to the pipe connecting the boiler and safety valve

18. A diagram of horizontal plumbing drainage lines should have cleanouts shown   18.____

    A. at least every 25 feet
    B. at least every 100 feet
    C. wherever a basin is located
    D. wherever a change in direction occurs

19. When a Bourdon gauge is used to measure steam pressures, some form of siphon or water seal must be maintained.   19.____
The reason for this is to

    A. obtain "absolute" pressure readings
    B. prevent steam from entering the gage
    C. prevent condensate from entering the gage
    D. obtain readings below atmospheric pressure

20. In a closed heat exchanger, oil is cooled by condensate which is to be returned to a boiler. In order to avoid the possibility of contaminating the condensate with oil should a tube fail in the oil cooler, it would be good practice to   20.____

    A. cool the oil by air instead of water
    B. treat the condensate with an oil solvent
    C. keep the oil pressure in the exchanger higher than the water pressure
    D. keep the water pressure in the exchanger higher than the oil pressure

21. A radiator thermostatic trap is used on a vacuum return type of heating system to   21.____

    A. release the pocketed air only
    B. reduce the amount of condensate
    C. maintain a predetermined radiator water level
    D. prevent the return of live steam to the return line

22. According to the color coding of piping, fire protection piping should be painted   22.____

    A. green   B. yellow   C. purple   D. red

23. The MAIN purpose of a standpipe system is to   23.____

    A. supply the roof water tank
    B. provide water for firefighting

C. circulate water for the heating system
D. provide adequate pressure for the water supply

24. The name "Saybolt" is associated with the measurement of   24.____

    A. viscosity   B. Btu content
    C. octane rating   D. temperature

25. Recirculation of conditioned air in an air-conditioned building is done MAINLY to   25.____

    A. reduce refrigeration tonnage required
    B. increase room entrophy
    C. increase air specific humidity
    D. reduce room temperature below the dewpoint

26. In a plumbing installation, vent pipes are GENERALLY used to   26.____

    A. prevent the loss of water seal from traps by evaporation
    B. prevent the loss of water seal due to several causes other than evaporation
    C. act as an additional path for liquids to flow through during normal use of a plumbing fixture
    D. prevent the backflow of water in a cross-connection between a drinking water line and a sewage line

27. The designation "150 W" cast on the bonnet of a gate valve is an indication of the   27.____

    A. water working temperature
    B. water working pressure
    C. area of the opening in square inches
    D. weight of the valve in pounds

28. In the city, the size soil pipe necessary in a sewage drainage system is determined by the   28.____

    A. legal occupancy of the building
    B. vertical height of the soil line
    C. number of restrooms connected to the soil line
    D. number of "fixture units" connected to the soil line

29. Fins or other extended surfaces are used on heat exchanger tubes when   29.____

    A. the exchanger is a water-to-water exchanger
    B. water is on one side of the tube and condensing steam on the other side
    C. the surface coefficient of heat transfer on both sides of the tube is high
    D. the surface coefficient of heat transfer on one side of the tube is low compared to the coefficient on the other side of the tube

30. A fusible plug may be put in a fire tube boiler as an emergency device to indicate low water level. The fusible plug is installed so that under normal operating conditions,   30.____

    A. both sides are exposed to steam
    B. one side is exposed to water and the other side to steam
    C. one side is exposed to steam and the other side to hot gases
    D. one side is exposed to the water and the other side to hot gases

31. Extra strong wrought-iron pipe, as compared to standard wrought-iron pipe of the same nominal size, has   31._____

    A. the same outside diameter but a smaller inside diameter
    B. the same inside diameter but a larger outside diameter
    C. a larger outside diameter and a smaller inside diameter
    D. larger inside and outside diameters

32. Fans may be rated on a dynamic or a static efficiency basis. The dynamic efficiency would *probably* be   32._____

    A. lower in value because of the energy absorbed by the air velocity
    B. the same as the static in the case of centrifugal blowers running at various speeds
    C. the same as the static in the case of axial flow blowers running at various speeds
    D. higher in value than the static

33. The function of the stack relay in an oil burner installation is to   33._____

    A. regulate the draft over the fire
    B. regulate the flow of fuel oil to the burner
    C. stop the motor if the oil has not ignited
    D. stop the motor if the water or steam pressure is too high

34. The type of centrifugal pump which is inherently balanced for hydraulic thrust is the   34._____

    A. double suction impeller type
    B. single suction impeller type
    C. single stage type
    D. multistage type

35. The specifications for a job using sheet lead calls for "4-lb. sheet lead." This means that each sheet should weigh   35._____

    A. 4 lbs.
    B. 4 lbs. per square
    C. 4 lbs. per square foot
    D. 4 lbs. per cubic inch

36. The total cooling load design conditions for a building are divided for convenience into two components.   36._____
    These are:

    A. infiltration and radiation
    B. sensible heat and latent heat
    C. wet and dry bulb temperatures
    D. solar heat gain and moisture transfer

37. The function of a Hartford loop used on some steam boilers is to   37._____

    A. limit boiler steam pressure
    B. limit temperature of the steam
    C. prevent high water levels in the boiler
    D. prevent back flow of water from the boiler into the return main

38. Vibration from a ventilating blower can be prevented from being transmitted to the duct work by

    A. installing straighteners in the duct
    B. throttling the air supply to the blower
    C. bolting the blower tightly to the duct
    D. installing a canvas sleeve at the blower outlet

39. A specification states that access panels to suspended ceiling will be of metal. The MAIN reason for providing access panels is to

    A. improve the insulation of the ceiling
    B. improve the appearance of the ceiling
    C. make it easier to construct the building
    D. make it easier to maintain the building

40. A plumber on a job reports that the steamfitter has installed a 3" steam line in a location at which the plans show the house trap. On inspecting the job, you should

    A. tell the steamfitter to remove the steam line
    B. study the condition to see if the house trap can be relocated
    C. tell the plumber and steamfitter to work it out between themselves and then report to you
    D. tell the plumber to find another location for the trap because the steamfitter has already completed his work

41. In the installation of any heating system, the MOST important consideration is that

    A. all elements be made of a good grade of cast iron
    B. all radiators and connectors be mounted horizontally
    C. the smallest velocity of flow of heating medium be used
    D. there be proper clearance between hot surfaces and surrounding combustible material

42. Which one of the following is the PRIMARY object in drawing up a set of specifications for materials to be purchased?

    A. Control of quality
    B. Outline of intended use
    C. Establishment of standard sizes
    D. Location and method of inspection.

43. The drawing which should be used as a LEGAL reference when checking completed construction work is the _____ drawing.

    A. contract   B. assembly
    C. working or shop   D. preliminary

Questions 44-50.

DIRECTIONS: Questions 44 through 50 refer to the plumbing drawing shown below.

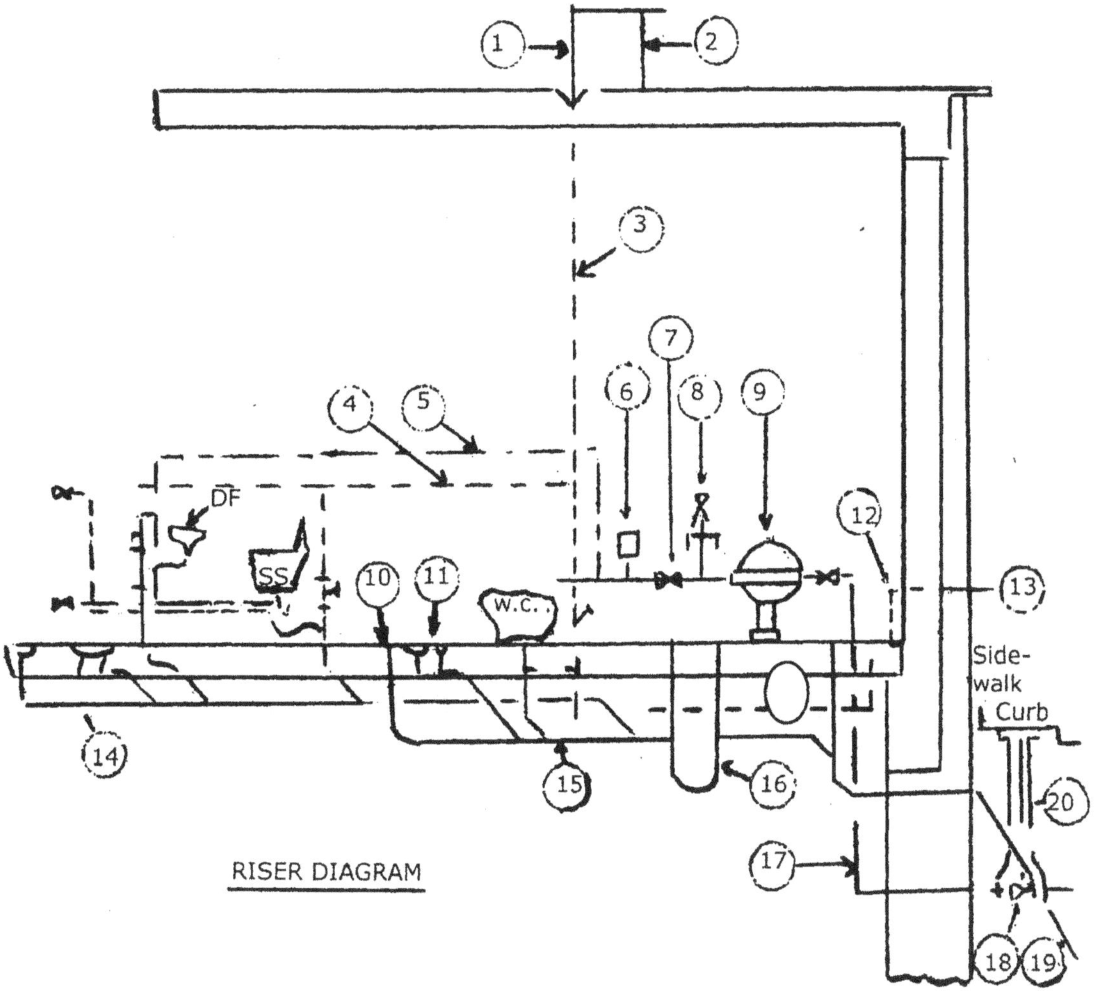

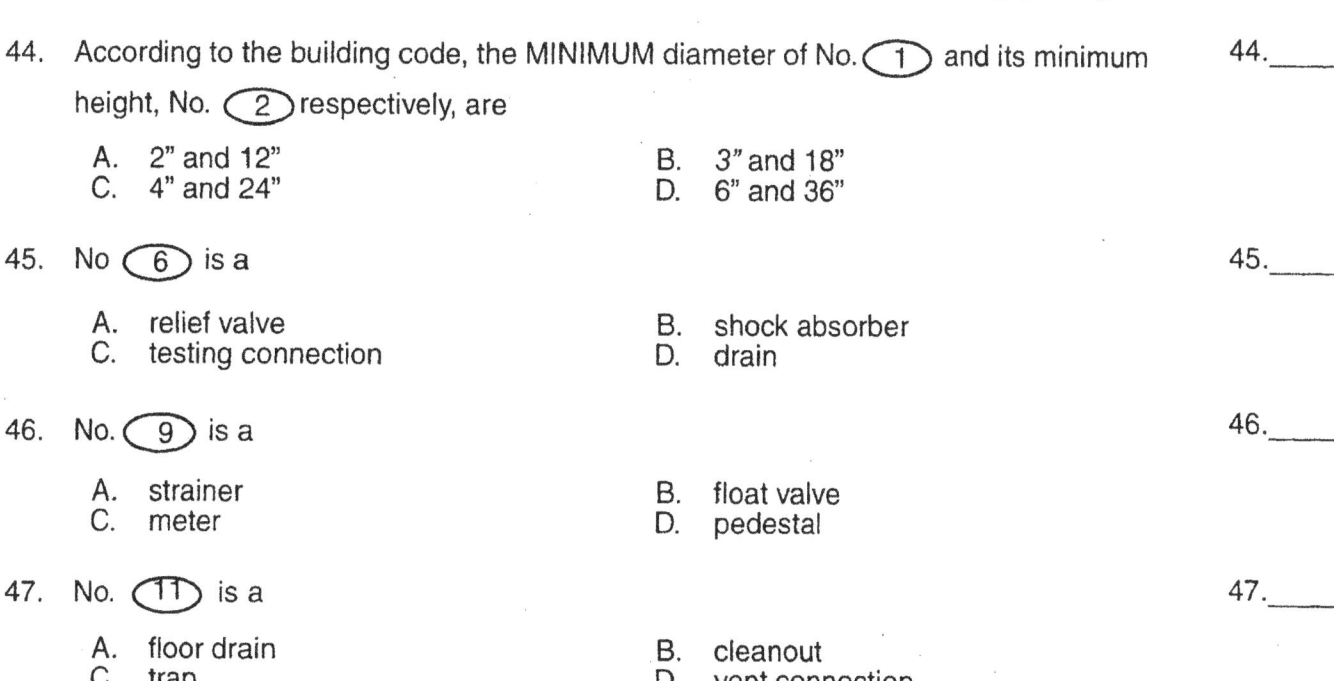

RISER DIAGRAM

44. According to the building code, the MINIMUM diameter of No. ① and its minimum height, No. ② respectively, are

    A. 2" and 12"
    B. 3" and 18"
    C. 4" and 24"
    D. 6" and 36"

44._____

45. No. ⑥ is a

    A. relief valve
    B. shock absorber
    C. testing connection
    D. drain

45._____

46. No. ⑨ is a

    A. strainer
    B. float valve
    C. meter
    D. pedestal

46._____

47. No. ⑪ is a

    A. floor drain
    B. cleanout
    C. trap
    D. vent connection

47._____

48. No. ⑬ is a

   A. standpipe
   C. sprinkler head
   B. air inlet
   D. cleanout

49. The size of No. ⑯ is

   A. 2" x 2"
   C. 3" x 3"
   B. 2" x 3"
   D. 4" x 4"

50. No. ⑱ is a

   A. pressure reducing valve
   B. butterfly valve
   C. curb cock
   D. sprinkler head

KEY (CORRECT ANSWERS)

1. C	11. A	21. D	31. A	41. D
2. B	12. C	22. D	32. D	42. A
3. C	13. A	23. B	33. C	43. A
4. D	14. B	24. A	34. A	44. C
5. D	15. C	25. A	35. C	45. B
6. B	16. A	26. B	36. B	46. C
7. B	17. A	27. B	37. D	47. A
8. A	18. D	28. D	38. D	48. B
9. B	19. B	29. D	39. D	49. D
10. D	20. D	30. D	40. B	50. C

EXAMINATION SECTION
TEST 1

DIRECTIONS: Each question or incomplete statement is followed by several suggested answers or completions. Select the one that BEST answers the question or completes the statement. *PRINT THE LETTER OF THE CORRECT ANSWER IN THE SPACE AT THE RIGHT.*

1. In refrigerating work, the term *automatic* expansion valve refers to a

   A. thermostatic expansion valve
   B. high side float valve
   C. capillary tube used to produce a pressure drop
   D. constant pressure expansion valve

   1.____

2. In a given refrigerating system, the ratio of the heat absorbed in the evaporator to the heat equivalent of the energy supplied by the compressor is 4.5.
The theoretical horsepower per ton of refrigeration is MOST NEARLY

   A. 0.69   B. 0.87   C. 1.04   D. 1.73

   2.____

3. In an air-water vapor mixture, the temperature which is the measure of the total heat of the mixture is the

   A. dewpoint
   B. dry bulb
   C. sum of dry bulb and wet bulb
   D. wet bulb

   3.____

4. In a refrigerating system, the

   A. refrigerating capacity of the machine is equal to the ice-making capacity of the plant
   B. standard ton is the abstraction of 12,000 Btu per hour
   C. rectifier of the absorption system is on the low pressure side
   D. cooling water temperature for a CO_2 system should be as high as possible

   4.____

5. In a two-stage double-acting air compressor, the

   A. unloaders operate on head and crank end of both cylinders simultaneously
   B. intercooler pressure is the arithmetic average of inlet and discharge pressures
   C. unloaders act on the inlet valves
   D. unloaders commonly unload the high pressure cylinder first

   5.____

6. Air passing through a spray chamber in which the spray water is recirculated but not heated or cooled will

   A. be humidified at approximately constant wet bulb temperature
   B. always leave in a saturated condition
   C. be de-humidified
   D. leave the spray chamber at the same water vapor pressure

   6.____

7. When the solid absorbent silica-gel is used in an air conditioning system, the air passing over it

   A. will be humidified
   B. has its dry bulb temperature increased
   C. will have its wet bulb temperature decreased
   D. will reach a higher water vapor pressure

8. In the process of heating atmospheric air in an air conditioning apparatus, the

   A. absolute or specific humidity increases
   B. relative humidity remains constant
   C. absolute or specific humidity does not change
   D. water vapor pressure decreases

9. 100 pounds per minute of outside air at 90° F. dry bulb and 200 pounds per minute of recirculated air at 72° F. dry bulb are mixed in an air conditioning system.
   The resulting dry bulb temperature will be, in °F., MOST NEARLY

   A. 84   B. 78   C. 88   D. 81

10. In a compression refrigerating system, the principal useful refrigerating effect is obtained in the

    A. condenser   B. evaporator
    C. expansion valve   D. compressor

11. Recirculation of conditioned air in an air conditioned building is done MAINLY to

    A. reduce refrigeration tonnage required
    B. increase room entropy
    C. increase air specific humidity
    D. reduce room temperature below the dewpoint

12. *Sweating* of cold water pipes in a room is due to the

    A. surface of the pipe being below the wet bulb temperature of the room air
    B. surface of the pipe being below the dew point temperature of the room air
    C. air in the room exceeding 100% relative humidity
    D. specific humidity exceeding the relative humidity

13. In a two-stage air compressor, the intercooler is placed between the

    A. compressor and air receiver
    B. compressor and intake pipe
    C. after cooler and air receiver
    D. intake of the second stage and the discharge of the first stage

14. The quantity of heat required to change the stage (e.g., liquid to vapor, or solid to liquid) of a body within a change in temperature is USUALLY called

    A. specific heat   B. enthalpy
    C. latent heat   D. entropy

15. When a refrigeration machine is in operation under normal load, the refrigerant leaving the compressor is in a state of

    A. low pressure vapor   B. hot liquid
    C. high pressure vapor   D. cold liquid

15.____

16. In a commercial ammonia refrigerating system, the ammonia that has just passed through the expansion valve

    A. is partially vaporized
    B. has become highly superheated
    C. has a greater enthalpy than it had before entering the expansion valve
    D. is all in a liquid state

16.____

17. An ice making machine freezes 50 lbs. of water at 45° F. to ice at 25° F. (under atmospheric conditions) in one hour.
The cooling load, in tons, of refrigeration is MOST NEARLY

    A. 0.7   B. 1.4   C. 6.8   D. 13.6

17.____

18. The pressure drop through a ventilating duct is 3.8 inches of water when the air velocity is 32 feet per second.
The pressure drop, in inches of water, when the air velocity is reduced to 24 feet per second will be MOST NEARLY

    A. 6.8   B. 3.8   C. 3.0   D. 2.1

18.____

19. The three methods in common use in the design and sizing of air duct systems are known as

    A. abrupt enlargement, dynamic loss, maximum velocity
    B. turbulent loss, equal friction, static regain
    C. velocity reduction, equal friction, static regain
    D. velocity reduction, maximum velocity, dynamic loss

19.____

20. The actual amount of water vapor which atmospheric air can hold is governed by the

    A. pressure   B. temperature
    C. relative humidity   D. specific volume

20.____

21. A pitot tube inserted in a ventilating duct is USUALLY used to determine the _____ in the duct.

    A. velocity pressure
    B. total pressure
    C. barometric pressure
    D. static pressure in p.s.i. absolute

21.____

22. Wetness forming inside frame building walls is often due to water vapor migration into the wall. The vapor movement is usually from the warm air side to the cool air side.
The vapor USUALLY moves in this direction because the

    A. relative humidity of cool air is lower than the relative humidity of warm air
    B. partial pressure of the vapor is lower on the cool side than on the warm air side of the wall

22.____

C. warm air has a lower dewpoint temperature
D. specific humidity or humidity ratio is so much lower for the warm air than for the cool air

23. Of the following, the dividing point between the high pressure and low pressure side of a refrigeration system is the

    A. evaporator
    B. receiver
    C. condenser
    D. expansion valve

24. In operating a closed water circulating system, it is good practice to

    A. treat the water chemically for corrosion control
    B. drain and flush the system regularly to control corrosion
    C. leave the system undisturbed because it is sealed and needs no maintenance
    D. replace the pump shaft seals every three months

25. The function of an unloader on an electric motor-driven air compressor is to

    A. release the pressure in the cylinders in order to reduce the starting load
    B. reduce the speed of the motor when the maximum pressure is reached
    C. prevent excess pressure in the receiver
    D. drain the condensate from the cylinder head

26. The MOST highly toxic of the following refrigerants is

    A. sulphur dioxide
    B. ammonia
    C. methyl chloride
    D. freon 12

27. Of the following piping materials, the one which is NOT generally used for pneumatic temperature control systems is

    A. copper
    B. plastic
    C. steel
    D. galvanized iron

28. In accordance with recommended maintenance practice, thermostats used in a pneumatic temperature control system should be checked

    A. weekly
    B. bi-monthly
    C. monthly
    D. once a year

29. Of the following, the BEST method to use to determine the moisture level in a refrigeration system is to

    A. weigh the drier after it has been in the system for a period of time
    B. visually check the sight glass for particles of corrosion
    C. use a moisture indicator
    D. test a sample of lubricating oil with phosphorus pentoxide

30. A full-flow drier is USUALLY recommended to be used in a hermetic refrigeration compressor system to keep the system dry and to

    A. prevent the products of decomposition from getting into the evaporator in the event of a motor burn-out
    B. condense out liquid refrigerant during compressor off cycles and compressor start-up

C. prevent the compressor unit from decreasing in capacity
D. prevent the liquid from dumping into the compressor crankcase

31. The rating of a unit ventilator is USUALLY determined by a(n) 31._____

  A. anemometer
  B. hydrometer
  C. psychrometer
  D. ammeter

32. The STANDARD capacity rating conditions for any refrigeration compressor is _____ for the suction and _____ for the discharge. 32._____

  A. 5° F., 19.6 psig; 86° F., 154.5 psig
  B. 5° F., 9.6 psig; 96° F., 154.5 psig
  C. 10° F., 9.6 psig; 96° F., 144.5 psig
  D. 10° F., 19.6 psig; 96° F., 134.5 psig

33. Of the following, the MAIN purpose of a subcooler in a refrigerant piping system for a two-stage system is to 33._____

  A. reduce the total power requirements and total heat rejection to the second stage
  B. reduce total power requirements and return oil to the compressor
  C. improve the flow of evaporator gas per ton and increase the temperature
  D. increase the heat rejection per ton and avoid system shutdown

34. In large refrigeration systems, the USUAL location for charging the refrigeration system is into the 34._____

  A. suction line
  B. liquid line between the receiver shut-off valve and the expansion valve
  C. line between the condenser and the compressor
  D. line between the high pressure cut-off switch and the expansion valve

35. Assume that one of your assistants was near the Freon 11 refrigeration system when a liquid Freon line ruptured. Some of the liquid Freon 11 has gotten into your assis-tant's right eye.
Of the following actions, the one which you should NOT take is to 35._____

  A. immediately call for an eye specialist (medical doctor)
  B. gently and quickly rub the Freon 11 out of the eye
  C. use a boric-acid solution to clean out the Freon 11 from his eye
  D. wash the eye by gently blowing the Freon 11 out of his eye with air

KEY (CORRECT ANSWERS)

1.	D	16.	A
2.	C	17.	A
3.	D	18.	D
4.	B	19.	C
5.	C	20.	B
6.	A	21.	A
7.	B	22.	B
8.	C	23.	D
9.	B	24.	A
10.	B	25.	A
11.	A	26.	A
12.	B	27.	C
13.	D	28.	D
14.	C	29.	C
15.	C	30.	A

31. A
32. A
33. A
34. B
35. B

EXAMINATION SECTION
TEST 1

DIRECTIONS: Each question or incomplete statement is followed by several suggested answers or completions. Select the one that BEST answers the question or completes the statement. *PRINT THE LETTER OF THE CORRECT ANSWER IN THE SPACE AT THE RIGHT.*

1. A plant refrigerating unit has 600 pounds of refrigerant in it. The CFM from the exhaust blower should be

    A. 1275 B. 1450 C. 1100 D. 600

2. A rupture member can be substituted for a relief valve in a(n) _____ system.

    A. aqua ammonia
    B. sulphur dioxide
    C. carbon dioxide
    D. ammonia

3. Which of the following groups of refrigerants is in Group 3?

    A. CO_2
       F-12
       F-22
       Propane

    B. F-11
       F-113
       Ammonia
       Butane

    C. Ethane
       Butane
       F-12
       Carbon dioxide

    D. Butane
       Ethane
       Propane
       Ethylene

4. When withdrawing refrigerant from a system into containers, they cannot be filled more than _____%.

    A. 70 B. 75 C. 80 D. 85

5. When field testing Refrigerant 12, the high and low sides should be tested to _____#.

    A. 300-150 B. 235-140 C. 95-50 D. 1500-1000

6. In a refrigerating system with a gauge where the dial points to 100 psi, under normal operating conditions, the LAST number of the gauge should read

    A. 105 B. 110 C. 115 D. 120

7. The MAXIMUM pounds in a direct system, per 1,000 cubic feet of occupied space, for Refrigerant 12 is

    A. 31 B. 41 C. 51 D. 61

8. The metallic mixtures of alloys used to make a gas tight soldered joint should melt at _____ °F.

    A. 600
    B. 800° F and above 300
    C. 935
    D. 1000° F and above 400

9. A specification calls for the installation of a unit air conditioning system in the lobby of a building. This is to contain 30# Freon 12.
   In keeping with the rules, this system may

   A. be installed
   B. be installed, if the system is reduced to 20#
   C. not be installed; no unit can be placed in the lobby
   D. not be installed, as it contains a group 2 refrigerant

10. The minimum required rated discharge capacity of the pressure relief device or fusible plug for a refrigerant containing vessel shall be determined by the formula C = Fdl.
    What is C equal to?

    A. Feet per hour
    B. Refrigerant per minute
    C. Air in pounds per minute
    D. Amount of second

11. To pack tongue and groove, flanges on ammonia lines should be made of

    A. rubber   B. asbestos sheet
    C. tin   D. sheet lead

12. How many kinds of lubricants are used in a horizontal double-acting compressor?

    A. One   B. Two   C. Three   D. Four

13. Flash gas would be found in the

    A. receiver   B. condenser
    C. king valve   D. evaporator

14. The accepted method to test oil for moisture content is the dielectric test. This test imposes high voltage electric pressure on electrodes immersed in an oil sample. If any current flows, there is moisture present.
    The electrodes are spaced _____ inch(es), _____ volts.

    A. 1/2 to 1; 40,000   B. 1 to 2; 25,000
    C. 2 to 3; 22,000   D. 1 1/2 to 4; 33,000

15. Heat transfer takes place by
    I. evaporation
    II. convection
    III. conduction
    IV. radiation
    The CORRECT answer is:

    A. I, II   B. II, III, IV
    C. I, II, III   D. III, IV

16. A pan of an evaporative condenser 8 feet long, 4 feet wide, and 9 inches deep contains _____ gallons of water.

    A. 120   B. 180   C. 280   D. 204.5

17. A hermetically sealed unit is a unit with the

    A. motor and compressor, *both* enclosed in a sealed casing
    B. motor *only* sealed in a casing
    C. compressor *only* sealed in a casing
    D. carrier absorption system

18. Regarding centrifugal compressors, it is TRUE that

    A. only the main bearing and thrust need to be oiled
    B. refrigerant leaks into the oiling system are common
    C. they have no auxiliary oil pump
    D. the auxiliary oil pump is hand-operated

19. There are dummy tubes or a *Tell Tale* welded to the shell of a large accumulator in an industrial ammonia plant. The pipe extends through the insulation.
    Its purpose is to

    A. increase the capacity of the system
    B. facilitate taking ammonia samples
    C. check and mark the refrigerant level in the vessel
    D. make the accumulator physically stronger

20. Synchronous motors that are used for industrial refrigeration have

    A. AC and DC supplied to them
    B. constant speed
    C. ability to correct the power factor
    D. all of the above

21. An absorption system uses 100 pounds of steam per day.
    This is a _____ -ton plant.

    A. five   B. one   C. ten   D. fifty

22. The characteristics of ammonia include

    A. colorless gas   B. sharp odor
    C. lighter than air   D. all of the above

23. Where would you place an accumulator in the system?

    A. On the suction side of the compressor
    B. Just before the condenser on the discharge side of the system
    C. On the high side of the liquid line
    D. Before the king valve

24. Methyl chloride refrigerant is classified in Group

    A. 4   B. 3   C. 2   D. 1

25. A rotary booster compressor has _____ bearing(s).

    A. one   B. two   C. three   D. four

KEY (CORRECT ANSWERS)

1. B
2. C
3. D
4. B
5. B

6. D
7. A
8. D
9. A
10. C

11. D
12. B
13. D
14. B
15. B

16. A
17. A
18. A
19. C
20. D

21. A
22. D
23. A
24. C
25. B

TEST 2

DIRECTIONS: Each question or incomplete statement is followed by several suggested answers or completions. Select the one that BEST answers the question or completes the statement. *PRINT THE LETTER OF THE CORRECT ANSWER IN THE SPACE AT THE RIGHT.*

1. How many BTU's are removed to cool 2,000 bars of butter from 70° F to 36° F if the specific heat of butter is .87 and each bar weighs 1.5 pounds? 1.____

    A. 74,130 B. 51,000 C. 88,500 D. 104,731

2. A system with one compressor is using two evaporators of different temperatures, one with 35° F and the other with 20° F. 2.____
The back pressure valve would be located on the

    A. common suction line
    B. common liquid line
    C. suction line nearer to the lower temperature cooler
    D. suction line of the high temperature cooler

3. There are several refrigerants in the Freon group that are in common use. In connection with Freon 11, it can be stated that this refrigerant is widely used in air conditioning systems that have a _____ compressor. 3.____

    A. small reciprocating B. large reciprocating
    C. rotary D. large centrifugal

4. With the same compressor displacement, the refrigerant that will give the MOST refrigerating effect per pound circulated is 4.____

    A. Freon 12 B. ammonia C. butane D. Freon 11

5. The term *anhydrous* is used with a refrigerant to indicate the 5.____

    A. presence of ammonia B. presence of water
    C. absence of Freon D. absence of water

6. A *swirl* is a device used in a(n) _____ condenser. 6.____

    A. shell and coil B. closed shell and tube
    C. open shell and tube D. atmospheric

7. Carbon dioxide is in refrigerant Group 7.____

    A. 1 B. 2 C. 3 D. 6

8. In many direct refrigerant systems, thermal expansion valves with equalizer lines may be installed. 8.____
If the equalizer line became plugged, the effect on the cooling coil with a full load would be

    A. a starved coil B. a flooded coil
    C. 4% superheat D. 7% superheat

9. In a Freon 12 air conditioning system, the finned evaporator coil is wet. It can be CORRECTLY stated that

   A. the system is not operating efficiently
   B. there is a shortage of refrigerant
   C. there is an oversized expansion valve
   D. the system is operating efficiently

   9.___

10. In absorption systems, the ammonia pump transfers _____ from the _____.

    A. strong liquor; absorber to the generator
    B. ammonia gas; generator to the condenser
    C. weak liquor; generator to the absorber
    D. liquid ammonia; condenser to the receiver

    10.___

11. In an automatic Freon 12 system for air conditioning, you, as the original installer, have to make a tight pipe joint.
    You would use a

    A. serrated flange without a leak gasket
    B. threaded *streamline fitting* and white lead
    C. combination of solder, litharge, glycerine, and white lead
    D. *streamline fitting* and solder to copper piping

    11.___

12. The chemical in a dehydrator for a Freon or methyl chloride system is

    A. sawdust   B. silica gel
    C. aluminum   D. dichromate

    12.___

13. A brine cooler in a refrigeration cycle is between the

    A. evaporator and the compressor
    B. compressor and the receiver
    C. compressor and the condenser
    D. expansion valve and the compressor

    13.___

14. A piston design for a compressor without a cross-head is

    A. box   B. balanced   C. trunk   D. telescopic

    14.___

15. In an automatic Freon unit with a low pressure control (off and on type), upon starting, there is a pounding condition.
    This is due to

    A. a worn piston pin
    B. a slapping piston pin
    C. excessive oil in the compressor
    D. a worn crank bearing

    15.___

16. When the crosshead is properly aligned, the piston rod of a horizontal ammonia compressor is MOST likely to wear

    A. at the crosshead end   B. at the piston end
    C. at the middle of the rod   D. on the side

    16.___

17. In a carbon dioxide system, the condenser cooling water rises to 87° F. Could some of the refrigeration be used to cool the cooling water so that the gas could condense at a savings?
    The BEST response is:

    A. It is impractical because the water would freeze
    B. In general, it would be a very economical set-up
    C. Refrigeration loss would be greater, but the total would gain
    D. The cooling refrigeration gains, but the plant total would lose

17.____

18. Upon testing for ammonia leaks with red litmus paper, if ammonia is present, the color changes to

    A. green   B. blue   C. red   D. yellow

18.____

19. A horizontal shell and tube cooler is equipped with eliminators. The PRIMARY function of the eliminators is to

    A. prevent the carry-over of liquid refrigerant
    B. protect the tubes in the event of a freeze-up
    C. absorb noises and vibration impulses
    D. prevent oil from being carried into the cooler

19.____

20. A large cooler is equipped with ceiling-hung brine cooling coils. The insulated baffles are properly arranged along one side and underneath the cooling coils. These baffles are PRIMARILY used

    A. as drip pans when defrosting
    B. to get proper gravity circulation of air through the coils
    C. to help support the weight of the coils when they frost up
    D. to collect the brine in case of a leak in the coils

20.____

21. Anhydrous ammonia is MOST like water in

    A. odor
    B. color
    C. saturates at atmospheric pressure
    D. sublimes like water at 212° F and 14.69 pounds absolute

21.____

22. Carron oil (a liniment used for ammonia burns) is made up of equal parts of

    A. linseed oil and lime water
    B. vaseline and picric acid
    C. lanolin and vinegar
    D. sulphur dioxide and water

22.____

23. In an absorption type refrigerating plant, the weak liquor is very often used to

    A. precool the condenser water
    B. precool the liquid ammonia
    C. preheat the strong liquor
    D. preheat the steam

23.____

24. The degree of solubility in reference to a refrigerating oil is usually the LOWEST when using

    A. genetron 141
    B. methyl chloride
    C. Freon 12
    D. carbon dioxide

24.____

25. In a large plant, there is a synchronous motor. It could be said that

    A. the speed will vary
    B. in a weak field, current will be leading
    C. a strong field will make up for the lagging
    D. excitation will cause current to lag

25.____

KEY (CORRECT ANSWERS)

1.	B	11.	D
2.	D	12.	B
3.	D	13.	D
4.	B	14.	C
5.	D	15.	C
6.	C	16.	C
7.	A	17.	D
8.	B	18.	B
9.	D	19.	A
10.	A	20.	B

21. B
22. A
23. C
24. D
25. B

TEST 3

DIRECTIONS: Each question or incomplete statement is followed by several suggested answers or completions. Select the one that BEST answers the question or completes the statement. *PRINT THE LETTER OF THE CORRECT ANSWER IN THE SPACE AT THE RIGHT.*

1. In a given temperature of air, the ratio of vapor pressure to humidity is called   1.____

   A. absolute humidity
   B. relative humidity
   C. pressure
   D. partial pressure

2. A compressor that has two compression strokes and two suction strokes per cylinder per revolution of the crankshaft is a   2.____

   A. single-acting compressor
   B. double-acting compressor
   C. two stage compressor
   D. compressor in duplex

3. In the lubrication of a Freon refrigeration compressor,   3.____

   A. vegetable oil is preferred for best results
   B. Freon has the same degree of miscibility with oils as does ammonia
   C. a chemical action between the Freon and lubricating oil occurs
   D. the refrigerant mixes with the lubricating oil

4. A Freon refrigeration plant is being used in an air conditioning system to remove the sensible heat from the air in a two stage after cooler to a silica gel air dehydrating unit. If the outside surface of the coils in the after cooler were to operate wet, the probability is that the   4.____

   A. suction pressure is too high
   B. refrigerant is wet
   C. coils of the after cooler are not properly vented
   D. none of the above

5. The speed, in revolutions per minute, of a six pole synchronous motor rated at 80 HP, 400 volts, and 60 cycles is   5.____

   A. 480   B. 900   C. 1200   D. 1800

6. The capacity of an evaporative condenser INCREASES as _____ bulb temperature _____.   6.____

   A. wet; decreases
   B. wet; increases
   C. wet and dry; increases
   D. dry; increases

7. For a pressure testing of newly installed R-12 systems, it is BEST to use   7.____

   A. dry carbon dioxide with a trace of R-12 in it
   B. water in a hydrostatic test
   C. dry hydrogen with a trace of R-12 in it
   D. anhydrous ammonia

8. A dehydrator should be used in a(n) _____ system.

   A. sulphur dioxide
   B. Freon 12
   C. ammonia
   D. carbon dioxide

9. In the absorption system, the flow of ammonia gas in relation to the strong liquor in the analyzer is called _____ flow.

   A. cross   B. parallel   C. counter   D. diagonal

10. In an ice plant, the agitation air is precooled because it

    A. lessens the load on the ice field
    B. increases air pressure capacity
    C. prevents freezing of air lines
    D. decreases air pressure capacity

11. The one of the following that can be used to make up a threaded joint (NH_3) is

    A. red lead and shellac
    B. Red Indian shellac
    C. white lead
    D. litharge and glycerine

12. If Nessler's solution is added to a sample of brine, in the event of ammonia being present, the color of the solution in the brine will turn

    A. blue   B. red   C. yellow   D. pink

13. An ammonia system was working with 8" vacuum on the return line. The absolute pressure would be CLOSE to _____ #.

    A. 7   B. 22   C. 25   D. 10

14. A thermostatic expansion valve in a refrigeration system regulates the

    A. pressure of the evaporator
    B. pressure of the compressor
    C. flow of refrigerant to the precooler
    D. flow of refrigerant to the evaporator

15. In testing condenser water for carbon dioxide leaks, you would use

    A. Nessler's solution
    B. bromthymol blue
    C. a halide torch
    D. litmus paper

16. The purpose of the halide torch is

    A. to heat copper fitting for soldering
    B. a safety light
    C. to find carbon dioxide leaks
    D. to find Freon leaks

17. An oil lantern is used in the stuffing box

    A. to hold the seat tight and rigid
    B. as a guiding light
    C. as a seal
    D. as a space to hold oil

18. One of the effects of the presence of non-condensable gases in a refrigerating system is _____ pressure.   18._____

    A. high condensing
    B. low suction
    C. high suction
    D. low condensing

19. It is true that the greater the temperature differential between the water and the refrigerant gas, the more effective the condenser is.   19._____
    An operator, keeping this in mind, would

    A. raise the condenser pressure
    B. cut back on the inlet water
    C. raise the temperature of the incoming water
    D. reduce the power to the compressor (unit)

20. At a cost of .04 cents per KWH, what would be the cost per hour for a 100 HP motor running at 80% efficiency?   20._____

    A. $3.20   B. $3.70   C. $4.20   D. $4.90

21. In an air conditioning system having ducts, the evaporator coil has moisture on it during most days of the summer.   21._____
    This is due to

    A. not enough liquid refrigerant
    B. excessive liquid refrigerant
    C. the feeler bulb which requires movement to make frost
    D. generally a condition that is normal

22. Ammonia operates at higher pressures than Freon 12, but the higher temperatures and pressures required are offset by _____ volumetric displacement per ton.   22._____

    A. better
    B. worse
    C. the same
    D. none of the above

23. An oil interceptor placed in an ammonia plant of 300 tons is found   23._____

    A. so that it returns oil to the pump
    B. on the discharge line between the compressor and condenser
    C. lower than the compressor base
    D. before the pump and is used as an oil strainer

24. One ton of refrigeration equals   24._____

    A. 12,000 BTU per minute
    B. 1,200 BTU for 6 minutes
    C. 288,000 BTU per hour
    D. 144 BTU per minute

25. How many tons of ice would a 15 ton refrigeration unit make per day?   25._____

    A. 30   B. 15   C. 8   D. 5

KEY (CORRECT ANSWERS)

1. B
2. B
3. D
4. C
5. B

6. D
7. A
8. B
9. C
10. B

11. D
12. C
13. D
14. D
15. B

16. D
17. D
18. A
19. B
20. B

21. D
22. A
23. B
24. B
25. C

TEST 4

DIRECTIONS: Each question or incomplete statement is followed by several suggested answers or completions. Select the one that BEST answers the question or completes the statement. *PRINT THE LETTER OF THE CORRECT ANSWER IN THE SPACE AT THE RIGHT.*

1. In the absorption system, the weak liquid cooler is sometimes used to cool the 1.____

   A. liquid ammonia going to the evaporator
   B. strong liquid before it goes to the analyzer
   C. aqua ammonia before it goes to the condenser
   D. weak liquid before it goes to the absorber

2. In an ammonia flooded coil system, it is noticed that the evaporator tubes are dry and warm at the bottom and the upper coils are frosted. The reason for this is 2.____

   A. the evaporator is overloaded
   B. the evaporator is oil-logged
   C. the evaporator is underloaded
   D. this is normal operation for such a system

3. A thermostatic expansion valve has an external equalizer line. If the line became clogged while the system was operating, the evaporator would 3.____

   A. become flooded
   B. operate at 9 of superheat
   C. operate at full capacity
   D. starve

4. If the specific gravity of water is 1, then for a brine, it would be 4.____

   A. the same   B. greater   C. less   D. 1.44

5. In a large ammonia plant, the power factor reading on the panel board reads 90% or 90. This indicates that the power factor is 5.____

   A. good   B. bad   C. constant   D. irregular

6. _____ CANNOT be used with ammonia. 6.____

   A. Lead   B. Copper   C. Steel   D. Iron

7. A means to detect a carbon dioxide leak is a _____ test. 7.____

   A. white litmus paper
   B. red litmus paper
   C. blue litmus paper
   D. soapy water

8. The BEST evaporator to overcome flash gas is 8.____

   A. a direct expansion with a thermal expansion valve
   B. a coil with a bypass valve
   C. the flooded evaporator type
   D. one with a constant pressure valve

9. The _____ pump is the only moving part in the absorption system.

   A. steam
   B. water
   C. aqua ammonia
   D. compressed air

10. A system having less than 50# of refrigerant in it is usually stopped before purging of non-condensable gases. The reason for this is that

   A. it prevents the loss of large amounts of refrigerant
   B. the operator is present
   C. it saves time in the long run
   D. it is better because it takes longer

11. In a cold storage plant of 21 rooms with expansion coils in each, EVERY coil should have

   A. a strainer
   B. a common header
   C. an oil accumulator
   D. its own expansion valve

12. In a low temperature Freon 12 system, you would expect to find the booster compressor

   A. on the low pressure side of the system
   B. on the high side of the plant
   C. in a special room
   D. separate

13. With the same compressor displacement and the same suction pressure, which will give the MOST effective refrigeration per pound pumped?

   A. Freon 12
   B. Carrene
   C. Ammonia
   D. Carbon dioxide

14. If the liquid line becomes partly clogged between the receiver and the expansion valve, the result may be that the line

   A. between restriction and receiver will become hot
   B. between restriction and receiver will have 2" of frost
   C. above restriction will become hot
   D. above restriction will become frosted

15. Methyl chloride belongs to refrigerant group

   A. 1   B. 2   C. 3   D. 4

16. Assuming that all other conditions in a refrigeration system remain constant, the horsepower per ton of refrigeration will MOST likely _____ as the _____.

   A. increase; suction pressure increases
   B. increase; head pressure decreases
   C. increase; head pressure increases
   D. decrease; suction pressure decreases

17. The pump in the absorption system should PREFERABLY handle

   A. 50% gas and 50% liquid
   B. 100% liquid
   C. 100% gas
   D. none of the above

18. An employee received an ammonia burn near his eyes. You should apply _____ solution.   18._____

    A. 10% sulphuric acid
    B. 1% hydrochloric
    C. 2% boric acid
    D. 6% muriatic

19. To test for a leak in a CO_2 plant,   19._____

    A. pump NH_3 into the system and use Nessler's solution
    B. pump methyl chloride in and use litmus paper
    C. leave the CO_2 plant in operation and use a soapy water solution
    D. pump Freon into the system and use litmus paper

20. The CORRECT sequence of flow of refrigerant in the NH_3 compression system is   20._____

    A. compressor, scale trap, condenser, expansion valve, and evaporator
    B. compressor, oil trap, condenser, king valve, expansion valve, evaporator, and scale trap
    C. generator, condenser, expansion valve, evaporator, and absorber
    D. expansion valve, evaporator, condenser, oil trap, and condenser

21. Lithium bromide absorption systems, for use in air conditioning, have the LOWEST possible water temperature of _____ °F.   21._____

    A. 31   B. 33   C. 35   D. 38

22. The one of the following that could NOT be used in dehumidifying and cooling air in a modern air conditioning system is   22._____

    A. silica gel
    B. solution of calcium chloride
    C. zeolite method
    D. direct expansion refrigerating coil

23. To INCREASE the capacity of an absorption system, you would   23._____

    A. increase the steam pressure on the generator and pump
    B. increase the water in the condenser
    C. decrease the water in the absorber
    D. close the expansion valve

24. In changing a plant from Freon 12 to another refrigerant, which of the following would require the LEAST change in machinery?   24._____

    A. Ammonia
    B. Methyl chloride
    C. Carrene
    D. Carbon dioxide

25. In a calcium chloride brine tank of 1000 cubic feet, how many pounds of sodium dichromate would you use?   25._____

    A. 20   B. 40   C. 100   D. 200

KEY (CORRECT ANSWERS)

1.	D	11.	D
2.	B	12.	A
3.	A	13.	C
4.	B	14.	B
5.	A	15.	B
6.	B	16.	C
7.	D	17.	B
8.	C	18.	C
9.	C	19.	C
10.	A	20.	B

21. D
22. C
23. A
24. B
25. C

EXAMINATION SECTION
TEST 1

DIRECTIONS: Each question or incomplete statement is followed by several suggested answers or completions. Select the one that BEST answers the question or completes the statement. *PRINT THE LETTER OF THE CORRECT ANSWER IN THE SPACE AT THE RIGHT.*

Questions 1-6.

DIRECTIONS: Questions 1 through 6 are to be answered on the basis of the circuit diagram below. All switches are initially open.

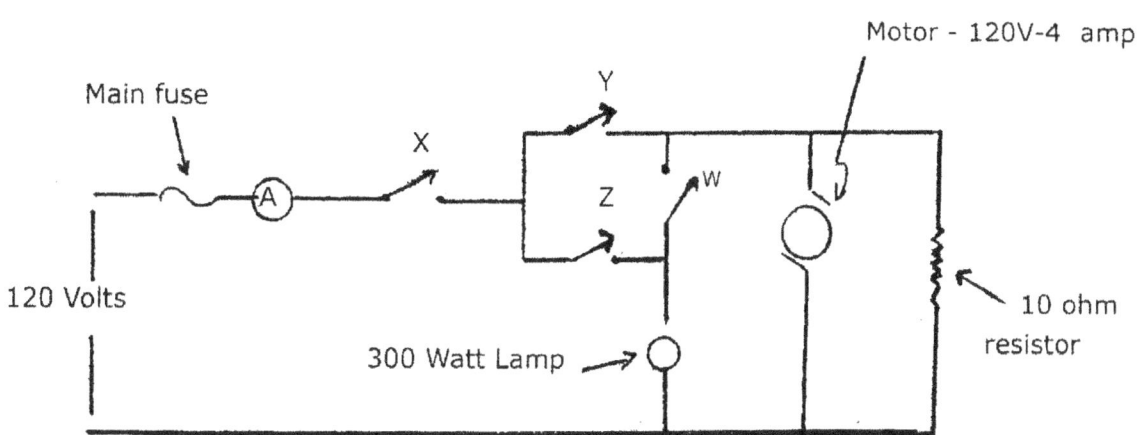

1. To light the 300 watt lamp, the following switches MUST be closed: 1.____

   A. X and Y   B. Y and Z   C. X and Z   D. X and W

2. If all of the switches W, X, Y, and Z are closed, the following will happen: 2.____

   A. The lamp will light and the motor will rotate
   B. The lamp will light and the motor will not rotate
   C. The lamp will not light and the motor will not rotate
   D. A short circuit will occur and the main fuse will blow

3. With 120 volts applied across the 10 ohm resistor, the current drawn by the resistor is _____ amp(s).   3.____

   A. 1/12   B. 1.2   C. 12   D. 1200

4. With 120 volts applied to the 10 ohm resistor, the power used by the resistor is _____ kw.   4.____

   A. 1.44   B. 1.2   C. .144   D. .12

5. The current drawn by the 300 watt lamp when lighted should be APPROXIMATELY _____ amps.   5.____

   A. 2.5   B. 3.6   C. 25   D. 36

75

6. In the circuit shown, the symbol A is used to indicate a (n)

   A. ammeter
   B. *and* circuit
   C. voltmeter
   D. wattmeter

7. Of the following materials, the BEST conductor of electricity is

   A. iron
   B. copper
   C. aluminum
   D. glass

8. The sum of 6'6", 5'9", and 2' 1 1/2" is

   A. 13'4 1/2"
   B. 13'6 1/2"
   C. 14'4 1/2"
   D. 14'6 1/2"

9.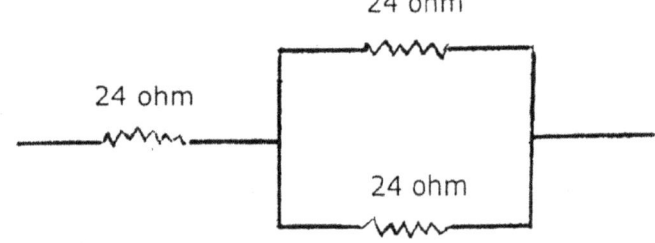

   The equivalent resistance of the three resistors shown in the sketch above is _____ ohms.

   A. 8
   B. 24
   C. 36
   D. 72

10.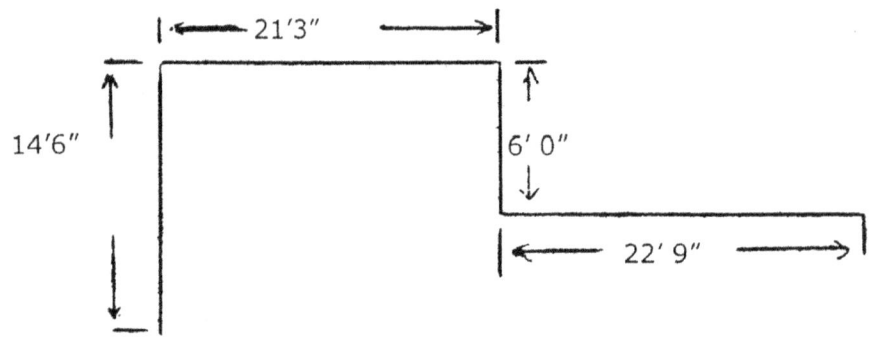

    The TOTAL length of electrical conduit that must be run along the path shown on the diagram above is

    A. 63'8"
    B. 64'6"
    C. 65'6"
    D. 66'8"

11. Of the following electrical devices, the one that is NOT normally used in direct current electrical circuits is a (n)

    A. circuit breaker
    B. double-pole switch
    C. transformer
    D. inverter

12. The number of 120-volt light bulbs that should NORMALLY be connected in series across a 600-volt electric line is

    A. 1
    B. 2
    C. 3
    D. 5

13. Of the following motors, the one that does NOT have any brushes is the _____ motor. 13.____

    A. d.c. shunt
    B. d.c. series
    C. squirrel cage induction
    D. compound

14. Of the following materials, the one that is COMMONLY used as an electric heating element in an electric heater is 14.____

    A. zinc
    B. brass
    C. terne plate
    D. nichrome

Questions 15-25.

DIRECTIONS: Questions 15 through 25 are to be answered on the basis of the instruments listed below. Each instrument is listed with an identifying number in front of it.

    1 - Hygrometer
    2 - Ammeter
    3 - Voltmeter
    4 - Wattmeter
    5 - Megger
    6 - Oscilloscope
    7 - Frequency meter
    8 - Micrometer
    9 - Vernier caliper
    10 - Wire gage
    11 - 6-foot folding rule
    12 - Architect's scale
    13 - Planimeter
    14 - Engineer's scale
    15 - Ohmmeter

15. The instrument that should be used to accurately measure the resistance of a 4,700 ohm resistor is Number 15.____

    A. 3   B. 4   C. 7   D. 15

16. To measure the current in an electrical circuit, the instrument that should be used is Number 16.____

    A. 2   B. 7   C. 8   D. 15

17. To measure the insulation resistance of a rubber-covered electrical cable, the instrument that should be used is Number 17.____

    A. 4   B. 5   C. 8   D. 15

18. An AC motor is hooked up to a power distribution box. In order to check the voltage at the motor terminals, the instrument that should be used is Number 18.____

    A. 2   B. 3   C. 4   D. 7

19. To measure the shaft diameter of a motor accurately to one-thousandth of an inch, the instrument that should be used is Number 19.____

    A. 8   B. 10   C. 11   D. 14

20. The instrument that should be used to determine whether 25 Hz. or 60 Hz. is present in an electrical circuit is Number 20.____

    A. 4   B. 5   C. 7   D. 8

21. Of the following, the PROPER instrument to use to determine the diameter of the conductor of a piece of electrical hook-up wire is Number

    A. 10   B. 11   C. 12   D. 14

22. The amount of electrical power being used in a balanced three-phase circuit should be measured with Number

    A. 2   B. 3   C. 4   D. 5

23. The electrical wave form at a given point in an electronic circuit can be observed with Number

    A. 2   B. 3   C. 6   D. 7

24. The PROPER instrument to use for measuring the width of a door is Number

    A. 11   B. 12   C. 13   D. 14

25. A one-inch hole with a tolerance of plus or minus three-thousandths is reamed in a steel block.
    The PROPER instrument to use to accurately check the diameter of the hole is Number

    A. 8   B. 9   C. 11   D. 14

KEY (CORRECT ANSWERS)

1. C
2. A
3. C
4. A
5. A

6. A
7. B
8. C
9. C
10. B

11. C
12. D
13. C
14. D
15. D

16. A
17. B
18. B
19. A
20. C

21. A
22. C
23. C
24. A
25. B

TEST 2

DIRECTIONS: Each question or incomplete statement is followed by several suggested answers or completions. Select the one that BEST answers the question or completes the statement. *PRINT THE LETTER OF THE CORRECT ANSWER IN THE SPACE AT THE RIGHT.*

1. The number of conductors required to connect a 3-phase delta connected heater bank to an electric power panel board is

    A. 2   B. 3   C. 4   D. 5

    1.____

2. Of the following, the wire size that is MOST commonly used for branch lighting circuits in homes is _____ A.W.G.

    A. #12   B. #8   C. #6   D. #4

    2.____

3. When installing electrical circuits, the tool that should be used to pull wire through a conduit is a

    A. mandrel
    B. snake
    C. rod
    D. pulling iron

    3.____

4. Of the following AC voltages, the LOWEST voltage that a neon test lamp can detect is _____ volts.

    A. 6   B. 12   C. 80   D. 120

    4.____

5. Of the following, the BEST procedure to use when storing tools that are subject to rusting is to

    A. apply a thin coating of soap onto the tools
    B. apply a light coating of oil to the tools
    C. wrap the tools in clean cheesecloth
    D. place the tools in a covered container

    5.____

6. If a 3 1/2 inch long nail is required to nail wood framing members together, the nail size to use should be

    A. 2d   B. 4d   C. 16d   D. 60d

    6.____

7. Of the four motors listed below, the one that can operate only on alternating current is a(n) _____ motor.

    A. series
    B. shunt
    C. compound
    D. induction

    7.____

8. The sum of 1/3 + 2/5 + 5/6 is

    A. 1 17/30   B. 1 3/5   C. 1 15/24   D. 1 5/6

    8.____

9. Of the following instruments, the one that should be used to measure the state of charge of a lead-acid storage battery is a(n)

    A. ammeter
    B. ohmmeter
    C. hydrometer
    D. thermometer

    9.____

10. If three 1 1/2 volt dry cell batteries are wired in series, the TOTAL voltage provided by the three batteries is _____ volts.

    A. 1.5   B. 3   C. 4.5   D. 6.0

11. Taking into account time and one-half payment for time over 40 hours of work, the gross pay of an employee who works 43 hours in a week at a rate of pay of $10.68 per hour is

    A. $427.20   B. $459.24   C. $475.26   D. $491.28

12. The sum of 0.365 + 3.941 + 10.676 + 0.784 is

    A. 13.766   B. 15.666   C. 15.756   D. 15.766

13. In order to transmit mechanical power between two rotating shafts at right angles to each other, two gears are used. Of the following, the type of gears that should be used are _____ gears.

    A. herringbone   B. spur
    C. bevel   D. rack and pinion

14. To properly ground the service electrical equipment in a building, a ground connection should be made to _____ the building.

    A. the waste or soil line leaving
    B. the vent line going to the exterior of
    C. any steel beam in
    D. the cold water line entering

15. The area of the triangle shown at the right is _____ square inches.
    A. 120
    B. 240
    C. 360
    D. 480

Questions 16-25.

DIRECTIONS: Questions 16 through 25 are to be answered on the basis of the tools shown on the next page. The tools are not shown to scale. Each tool is shown with an identifying number alongside it.

3 (#2)

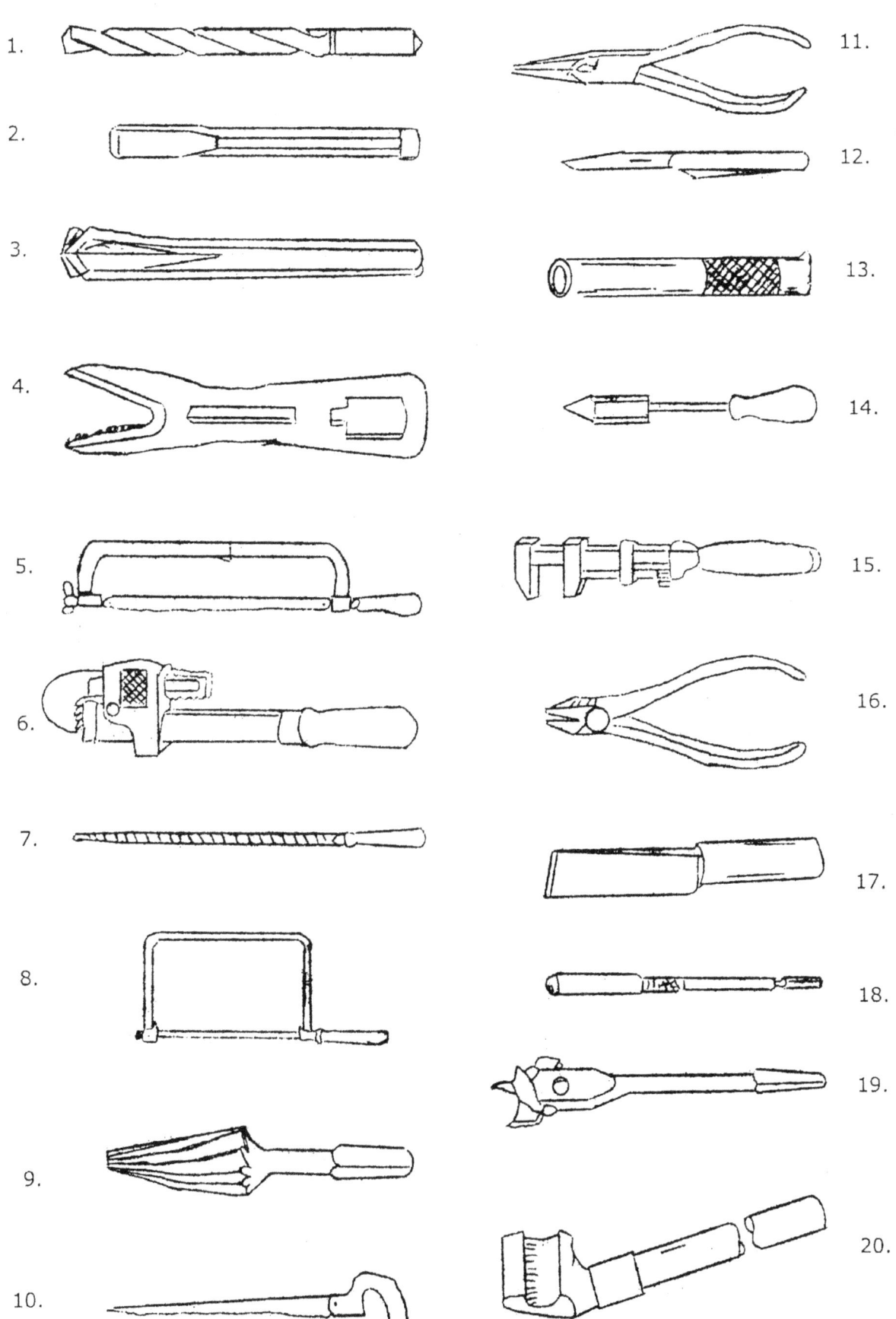

16. The tool that should be used for cutting thin wall steel conduit is Number   16._____
    A. 5   B. 8   C. 10   D. 16

17. The tool that should be used for cutting a 1 7/8 inch diameter hole in a wood joist is Number   17._____
    A. 3   B. 9   C. 14   D. 19

18. The tool that should be used for soldering splices in electrical wire is Number   18._____
    A. 3   B. 7   C. 13   D. 14

19. After cutting off a piece of 3/4 inch diameter electrical conduit, the tool that should be used for removing a burr from the inside of the conduit is Number   19._____
    A. 9   B. 11   C. 12   D. 14

20. The tool that should be used for turning a coupling onto a threaded conduit is Number   20._____
    A. 6   B. 11   C. 15   D. 16

21. The tool that should be used for cutting wood lathing in plaster walls is Number   21._____
    A. 5   B. 7   C. 10   D. 12

22. The tool that should be used for drilling a 3/8 inch diameter hole in a steel beam is Number   22._____
    A. 1   B. 2   C. 3   D. 9

23. Of the following, the BEST tool to use for stripping insulation from electrical hook-up wire is Number   23._____
    A. 11   B. 12   C. 15   D. 20

24. The tool that should be used for bending an electrical wire around a terminal post is Number   24._____
    A. 4   B. 11   C. 15   D. 16

25. The tool that should be used for cutting electrical hookup wire is Number   25._____
    A. 5   B. 12   C. 16   D. 17

KEY (CORRECT ANSWERS)

1.	B	11.	C
2.	A	12.	D
3.	B	13.	C
4.	C	14.	D
5.	B	15.	A
6.	C	16.	A
7.	D	17.	D
8.	A	18.	D
9.	C	19.	A
10.	C	20.	A

21. C
22. A
23. B
24. B
25. C

TEST 3

DIRECTIONS: Each question or incomplete statement is followed by several suggested answers or completions. Select the one that BEST answers the question or completes the statement. *PRINT THE LETTER OF THE CORRECT ANSWER IN THE SPACE AT THE RIGHT.*

1. An electric circuit has current flowing through it. The panel board switch feeding the circuit is opened, causing arcing across the switch contacts.
   Generally, this arcing is caused by

   A. a lack of energy storage in the circuit
   B. electrical energy stored by a capacitor
   C. electrical energy stored by a resistor
   D. magnetic energy induced by an inductance

2. MOST filter capacitors in radios have a capacity rating given in

   A. microvolts   B. milliamps
   C. millihenries   D. microfarads

3. Of the following, the electrical wire size that is COMMONLY used for telephone circuits is _____ A.W.G.

   A. #6   B. #10   C. #12   D. #22

Questions 4-9.

DIRECTIONS: Questions 4 through 9 are to be answered on the basis of the electrical circuit diagram shown below, where letters are used to identify various circuit components.

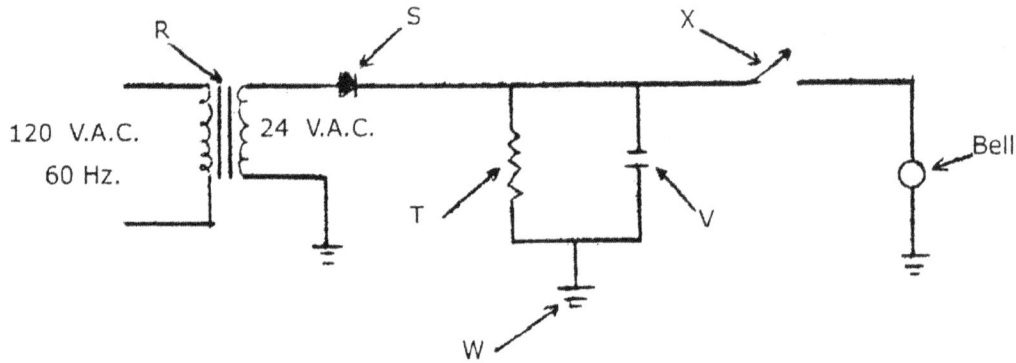

4. The device indicated by the letter R is a

   A. capacitor   B. converter
   C. resistor   D. transformer

5. The device indicated by the letter S is a

   A. transistor   B. diode
   C. thermistor   D. directional relay

6. The devices indicated by the letters T and V are used together to _____ components of the secondary current.

   A. reduce the AC
   B. reduce the DC
   C. transform the AC
   D. invert the AC

7. The letter W points to a standard electrical symbol for a

   A. wire
   B. ground
   C. terminal
   D. lightning arrestor

8. Closing switch X will apply the following type of voltage to the bell:

   A. 60 Hz. AC
   B. DC
   C. pulsating AC
   D. 120 Hz. AC

9. The circuit shown contains a _____ rectifier.

   A. mercury-arc
   B. full-wave
   C. bridge
   D. half-wave

10. A bolt specified as 1/4-28 means the following:
    The

    A. bolt is 1/4 inch in diameter and has 28 threads per inch
    B. bolt is 1/4 inch in diameter and is 2.8 inches long
    C. bolt is 1/4 inch long and has 28 threads
    D. threaded portion of the bolt is 1/4 inch long and has 28 threads per inch

11. When cutting 0.045-inch thickness sheet metal, it is BEST to use a hacksaw blade that has _____ teeth per inch.

    A. 7 B. 12 C. 18 D. 32

12. To accurately tighten a bolt to 28 foot-pounds, it is BEST to use a(n) _____ wrench.

    A. pipe B. open end C. box D. torque

13. When bending a 2-inch diameter conduit, the CORRECT tool to use is a

    A. hickey
    B. pipe wrench
    C. hydraulic bender
    D. stock and die

14. When soldering two #20 A.W.G. copper wires together to form a splice, the solder that SHOULD be used is _____ solder.

    A. acid-core
    B. solid-core
    C. rosin-core
    D. liquid

15. A bathroom heating unit draws 10 amperes at 115 volts.
    The hot resistance of the heating unit should be _____ ohms.

    A. .08 B. 8 C. 11.5 D. 1150

16. Of the following materials, the one that is NOT suitable as an electrical insulator is

    A. glass B. mica C. rubber D. platinum

17. An air conditioning unit is rated at 1000 watts. The unit is run for 10 hours per day, five days per week.
    If the cost for electrical energy is 5 cents per kilowatt-hour, the weekly cost for electricity should be

    A. 25¢ B. 50¢ C. $2.50 D. $25.00

18. If a fuse is protecting the circuit of a 15 ohm electric heater and it is designed to blow out at a current exceeding 10 amperes, the MAXIMUM voltage from among the following that should be applied across the terminals of the heater is _____ volts.

    A. 110 B. 120 C. 160 D. 600

19. Before opening a pneumatic hose connection, it is important to remove pressure from the hose line PRIMARILY to avoid

    A. losing air
    B. personal injury
    C. damage to the hose connection
    D. a build-up of pressure in the air compressor

20. If the scale on a shop drawing is 1/4 inch to the foot, then a part which measures 3 3/8 inches long on the drawing has an ACTUAL length of _____ feet _____ inches.

    A. 12; 6 B. 13; 6 C. 13; 9 D. 14; 9

21. The function that is USUALLY performed by a motor controller is to

    A. start and stop a motor
    B. protect a motor from a short circuit
    C. prevent bearing failure of a motor
    D. control the brush wear in a motor

22. Of the following galvanized sheet metal electrical outlet boxes, the one that is NOT a commonly used size is the _____ box.

    A. 4" square   B. 4" octagonal
    C. 4" x 2 1/8"   D. 4" x 1"

23. When soldering a transistor into a circuit, it is MOST important to protect the transistor from

    A. the application of an excess of rosin flux
    B. excessive heat
    C. the application of an excess of solder
    D. too much pressure

24. When installing BX type cable, it is important to protect the wires in the cable from the cut ends of the armored sheath.
    The APPROVED method of providing this protection is to

    A. use a fiber or plastic insulating bushing
    B. file the cut ends of the sheath smooth
    C. use a connector where the cable enters a junction box
    D. tie the wires into an Underwriter's knot

25. While lifting a heavy piece of equipment off the floor, a person should NOT

   A. twist his body
   B. grasp it firmly
   C. maintain a solid footing on the ground
   D. bend his knees

26. It is important that metal cabinets and panels that house electrical equipment should be grounded PRIMARILY in order to

   A. prevent short circuits from occurring
   B. keep all circuits at ground potential
   C. minimize shock hazards
   D. reduce the effects of electrolytic corrosion

27. A foreman explains a technical procedure to a new employee. If the employee does not understand the instructions he has received, it would be BEST if he were to

   A. follow the procedure as best he could
   B. ask the foreman to explain it to him again
   C. avoid following the procedure
   D. ask the foreman to give him other work

28. Of the following, the BEST connectors to use when mounting an electrical panel box directly onto a concrete wall are

   A. threaded studs   B. machine screws
   C. lag screws   D. expansion bolts

29. Of the following, the BEST instrument to use to measure the small gap between relay contacts is

   A. a micrometer   B. a feeler gage
   C. inside calipers   D. a plug gage

30. A POSSIBLE result of mounting a 40 ampere fuse in a fuse box for a circuit requiring a 20 ampere fuse is that the 40 ampere fuse may

   A. provide twice as much protection to the circuit from overloads
   B. blow more easily than the smaller fuse due to an overload
   C. cause serious damage to the circuit from an overload
   D. reduce power consumption in the circuit

KEY (CORRECT ANSWERS)

1.	D	16.	D
2.	D	17.	C
3.	D	18.	B
4.	D	19.	B
5.	B	20.	B
6.	A	21.	A
7.	B	22.	D
8.	B	23.	B
9.	D	24.	A
10.	A	25.	A
11.	D	26.	C
12.	D	27.	B
13.	C	28.	D
14.	C	29.	B
15.	C	30.	C

MECHANICAL APTITUDE TOOLS AND THEIR USE

EXAMINATION SECTION
TEST 1

Questions 1-16.

DIRECTIONS: Questions 1 through 16 refer to the tools shown below. The numbers in the answers refer to the numbers beneath the tools.
NOTE: These tools are NOT shown to scale

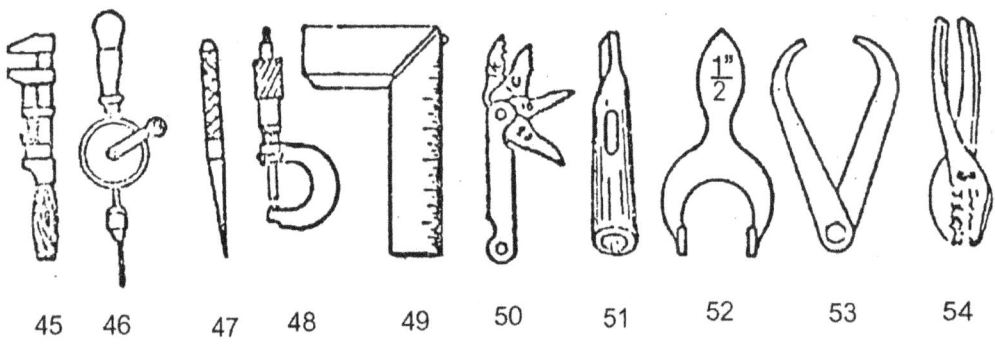

```
45   46   47   48   49   50   51   52   53   54
```

1. A 1" x 1" x 1/8" angle iron should be cut by using tool number

   A. 7   B. 12   C. 23   D. 42

2. To peen an iron rivet, you should use tool number

   A. 4   B. 7   C. 21   D. 43

3. The star "drill" is tool number

   A. 5   B. 10   C. 20   D. 22

4. To make holes in sheet metal for sheet metal screws, you should use tool number.

   A. 6   B. 10   C. 36   D. 46

5. To cut through a 3/8" diameter wire rope, you should use tool number

   A. 12   B. 23   C. 42   D. 54

6. To remove cutting burrs from the inside of a steel pipe, you should use tool number

   A. 5   B. 11   C. 14   D. 20

7. The depth of a bored hole may be measured MOST accurately with tool number

   A. 8   B. 16   C. 26   D. 41

8. If the marking on the blade of tool number 7 reads:12"-32", the 32 refers to the

   A. length   B. thickness   C. weight
   D. number of teeth per inch

9. If tool number 6 bears the mark "5", it should be used to drill holes having a diameter of

   A. 5/32"   B. 5/16"   C. 5/8"   D. 5"

10. To determine MOST quickly the number of threads per inch on a bolt, you should use tool number

    A. 8   B. 16   C. 26   D. 50

11. Wood screws, located in positions where the headroom does not permit the use of an ordinary screwdriver, may be removed by using tool number

    A. 17   B. 28   C. 35   D. 46

12. To remove a broken-off piece of 1/2" diameter pipe from a fitting, you should use tool number

    A. 5   B. 11   C. 20   D. 36

13. The outside diameter of a bushing may be measured MOST accurately with tool number

    A. 8   B. 26   C. 33   D. 43

14. To re-thread a stud hole in the casting of an elevator motor, you should use tool number

    A. 5   B. 20   C. 22   D. 36

15. To enlarge slightly a bored hole in a steel plate, you should use tool number

    A. 5   B. 11   C. 20   D. 36

16. The term "16 oz." should be applied to tool number

    A. 1   B. 12   C. 21   D. 42

KEYS (CORRECT ANSWERS)

1.	A	9.	B
2.	C	10.	D
3.	B	11.	C
4.	D	12.	C
5.	B	13.	C
6.	B	14.	D
7.	B	15.	A
8.	D	16.	C

TEST 2

Questions 1-11.

DIRECTIONS: Questions 1 through 11 refer to the instruments listed below. Each instrument is listed with an identifying number in front of it.

1 - Hygrometer	6 - Oscilloscope	11 - 6-foot folding rule
2 - Ammeter	7 - Frequency meter	12 - Architect's scale
3 - Voltmeter	8 - Micrometer	13 - Planimeter
4 - Wattmeter	9 - Vernier calliper	14 - Engineer's scale
5 - Megger	10 - Wire gage	15 - Ohmmeter

1. The instrument that should be used to *accurately* measure the resistance of a 4,700-ohm resistor is number

   A. 3   B. 4   C. 7   D. 15

2. To measure the current in an electrical circuit, the instrument that should be used is number

   A. 2   B. 7   C. 8   D. 15

3. To measure the insulation resistance of a rubber-covered electrical cable, the instrument that should be used is number

   A. 4   B. 5   C. 8   D. 15

4. An AC motor is hooked up to a power distribution box. In order to check the voltage at the motor terminals, the instrument that should be used is number

   A. 2   B. 3   C. 4   D. 7

5. To measure the shaft diameter of a motor *accurately* to one-thousandth of an inch, the instrument that should be used is number

   A. 8   B. 10   C. 11   D. 14

6. The instrument that should be used to determine whether 25 Hz. or 60 Hz. is present in an electrical circuit is number

   A. 4   B. 5   C. 7   D. 8

7. Of the following, the *proper* instrument to use to determine the diameter of the conductor of a piece of electrical hookup wire is number

   A. 10   B. 11   C. 12   D. 14

8. The amount of electrical power being used in a balanced three-phase circuit should be measured with number

   A. 2   B. 3   C. 4   D. 5

9. The electrical wave form at a given point in an electronic circuit can be observed with number

   A. 2   B. 3   C. 6   D. 7

10. The *proper* instrument to use for measuring the width of a door is number   10._____

    A. 11   B. 12   C. 13   D. 14

11. A one-inch hole with a tolerance of plus or minus three-thousandths is reamed in a steel   11._____
    block. The *proper* instrument to accurately check the diameter of the hole is number

    A. 8   B. 9   C. 11   D. 14

12. An oilstone is LEAST likely to be used correctly to sharpen a   12._____

    A. scraper   B. chisel   C. knife   D. saw

13. To cut the ends of a number of lengths of wood at an angle of 45 degrees, it would be   13._____
    BEST to use a

    A. mitre-box   B. protractor   C. triangle   D. wooden rule

14. A gouge is a tool used for   14._____

    A. planing wood smooth   B. grinding metal
    C. drilling steel   D. chiseling wood

15. Holes are usually countersunk when installing   15._____

    A. carriage bolts   B. lag screws
    C. flat-head screws   D. square nuts

16. A tool that is *generally* used to slightly elongate a round hole in scrap-iron is a   16._____

    A. rat-tail file   B. reamer   C. drill   D. rasp

17. When the term "10-24" is used to specify a machine screw, the number 24 refers to the   17._____

    A. number of screws per pound   B. diameter of the screw
    C. length of the screw   D. number of threads per inch

18. If you were unable to tighten a nut by means of a ratchet wrench because, although the   18._____
    nut turned on with the forward movement of the wrench, it turned off with the backward
    movement, you should

    A. make the nut hand-tight before using the wrench
    B. reverse the ratchet action
    C. put a few drops of oil on the wrench
    D. use a different socket in the handle

19. If you were installing a long wood screw and found you were unable to drive this screw   19._____
    more than three-quarters of its length by the use of a properly-fitting straight-handled
    screwdriver, the *proper* SUBSEQUENT action would be for you to

    A. take out the screw and put soap on it
    B. change to the use of a screwdriver-bit and brace
    C. take out the screw and drill a shorter hole before redriving
    D. use a pair of pliers on the blade of the screwdriver

20. Good practice requres that the end of a pipe to be installed in a plumbing system be reamed to remove the inside burr after it has been cut to length. The *purpose* of this reaming is to

    A. restore the original inside diameter of the pipe at the end
    B. remove loose rust
    C. make the threading of the pipe easier
    D. finish the pipe accurately to length

20.____

KEYS (CORRECT ANSWERS)

1.	D	11.	B
2.	A	12.	D
3.	B	13.	A
4.	B	14.	D
5.	A	15.	C
6.	C	16.	A
7.	A	17.	D
8.	C	18.	A
9.	C	19.	A
10.	A	20.	A

READING COMPREHENSION
UNDERSTANDING AND INTERPRETING WRITTEN MATERIAL
EXAMINATION SECTION
TEST 1

DIRECTIONS: Each question or incomplete statement is followed by several suggested answers or completions. Select the one that BEST answers the question or completes the statement. *PRINT THE LETTER OF THE CORRECT ANSWER IN THE SPACE AT THE RIGHT.*

Questions 1-2.

DIRECTIONS: Questions 1 and 2 are to be answered SOLELY on the basis of the following paragraph.

When fixing an upper sash cord, you must also remove the lower sash. To do this, the parting strip between the sash must be removed. Now remove the cover from the weight box channel, cut off the cord as before, and pull it over the pulleys. Pull your new cord over the pulleys and down into the channel where it may be fastened to the weight. The cord for an upper sash is cut off 1" or 2" below the pulley with the weight resting on the floor of the pocket and the cord held taut. These measurements allow for slight stretching of the cord. When the cord is cut to length, it can be pulled up over the pulley and tied with a single common knot in the end to fit into the socket in the sash groove. If the knot protrudes beyond the face of the sash, tap it gently to flatten. In this way, it will not become frayed from constant rubbing against the groove.

1. When repairing the upper sash cord, the FIRST thing to do is to
   A. remove the lower sash
   B. cut the existing sash cord
   C. remove the parting strip
   D. measure the length of new cord necessary

1._____

2. According to the above paragraph, the rope may become frayed if the
   A. pulley is too small   B. knot sticks out
   C. cord is too long   D. weight is too heavy

2._____

Questions 3-4.

DIRECTIONS: Questions 3 and 4 are to be answered SOLELY on the basis of the following paragraph.

Repeated burning of the same area should be avoided. Burning should not be done on impervious, shallow, unstable, or highly erodible soils, or on steep slopes—especially in areas subject to heavy rains or rapid snowmelt. When existing vegetation is likely to be killed or seriously weakened by the fire, measures should be taken to assure prompt revegetation of the burned area. Burns should be limited to relatively small proportions of a watershed unit so that the stream channels will be able to carry any increased flows with a minimum of damage.

3. According to the above paragraph, planned burning should be limited to small areas of the watershed because
   A. the fire can be better controlled
   B. existing vegetation will be less likely to be killed
   C. plants will grow quicker in small areas
   D. there will be less likelihood of damaging floods

4. According to the above paragraph, burning USUALLY should be done on soils that
   A. readily absorb moisture
   B. have been burnt before
   C. exist as a thin layer over rock
   D. can be flooded by nearby streams

Questions 5-11.

DIRECTIONS: Questions 5 through 11 are to be answered SOLELY on the basis of the following paragraph.

FUSE INFORMATION

Badly bent or distorted fuse clips cannot be permitted. Sometimes, the distortion or bending is so slight that it escapes notice, yet it may be the cause for fuse failures through the heat that is developed by the poor contact. Occasionally, the proper spring tension of the fuse clips has been destroyed by overheating from loose wire connections to the clips. Proper contact surfaces must be maintained to avoid faulty operation of the fuse. Maintenance men should remove oxides that form on the copper and brass contacts, check the clip pressure, and make sure that contact surfaces are not deformed or bent in any way. When removing oxides, use a well-worn file and remove only the oxide film. Do not use sandpaper or emery cloth as hard particles may come off and become embedded in the contact surfaces. All wire connections to the fuse holders should be carefully inspected to see that they are tight.

5. Fuse failure because of poor clip contact or loose connections is due to the resulting
   A. excessive voltage   B. increased current
   C. lowered resistance   D. heating effect

6. Oxides should be removed from fuse contacts by using
   A. a dull file   B. emery cloth
   C. fine sandpaper   D. a sharp file

7. One result of loose wire connections at the terminal of a fuse clip is stated in the above paragraph to be
   A. loss of tension in the wire
   B. welding of the fuse to the clip
   C. distortion of the clip
   D. loss of tension of the clip

8. Simple reasoning will show that the oxide film referred to is undesirable CHIEFLY because it
   A. looks dull
   B. makes removal of the fuse difficult
   C. weakens the clips
   D. introduces undesirable resistance

   8._____

9. Fuse clips that are bent very slightly
   A. should be replaced with new clips
   B. should be carefully filed
   C. may result in blowing of the fuse
   D. may prevent the fuse from blowing

   9._____

10. From the fuse information paragraph, it would be reasonable to conclude that fuse clips
    A. are difficult to maintain
    B. must be given proper maintenance
    C. require more attention than other electrical equipment
    D. are unreliable

    10._____

11. A safe practical way of checking the tightness of the wire connection to the fuse clips of a live 120-volt lighting circuit is to
    A. feel the connection with your hand to see if it is warm
    B. try tightening with an insulated screwdriver or socket wrench
    C. see if the circuit works
    D. measure the resistance with an ohmmeter

    11._____

Questions 12-13.

DIRECTIONS: Questions 12 through 13 are to be answered SOLELY on the basis of the following paragraph.

For cast iron pipe lines, the middle ring or sleeve shall have *beveled* ends and shall be high quality cast iron. The middle ring shall have a minimum wall thickness of 3/8" for pipe up to 8", 7/16" for pipe 10" to 30", and 1/2" for pipe over 30", nominal diameter. Minimum length of middle ring shall be 5" for pipe up to 10", 6" for pipe 10" to 30", and 10" for pipe 30" nominal diameter and larger. The middle ring shall not have a center pipe stop, unless otherwise specified.

12. As used in the above paragraph, the word *beveled* means MOST NEARLY
    A. straight   B. slanted   C. curved   D. rounded

    12._____

13. In accordance with the above paragraph, the middle ring of a 24" nominal diameter pipe would have a minimum wall thickness and length of _____ thick and _____ long.
    A. 3/8"; 5:   B. 3/8"; 6"
    C. 7/16"; 6"   D. 1/2"; 6"

    13._____

Questions 14-17.

DIRECTIONS: Questions 14 through 17 are to be answered SOLELY on the basis of the following paragraph.

Operators spotting loads with long booms and working around men need the smooth, easy operation and positive control of uniform pressure swing clutches. There are no jerks or grabs with these large disc-type clutches because there is always even pressure over the entire clutch lining surface. In the conventional band-type swing clutch, the pressure varies between dead and live ends of the band. The uniform pressure swing clutch has excellent provision for heat dissipation. The driving elements, which are always rotating, have a great number of fins cast in them. This gives them an impeller or blower action for cooling, resulting in longer life and freedom from frequent adjustment.

14. According to the above paragraph, it may be said that conventional band-type swing clutches have
    A. even pressure on the clutch lining
    B. larger contact area
    C. smaller contact area
    D. uneven pressure on the clutch lining

15. According to the above paragraph, machines equipped with uniform pressure swing clutches will
    A. give better service under all conditions
    B. require no clutch adjustment
    C. give positive control of hoist
    D. provide better control of swing

16. According to the above paragraph, it may be said that the rotation of the driving elements of the uniform pressure swing clutch is ALWAYS
    A. continuous   B. constant
    C. varying   D. uncertain

17. According to the above paragraph, freedom from frequent adjustment is due to the
    A. operator's smooth, easy operation
    B. positive control of the clutch
    C. cooling effect of the rotating fins
    D. larger contact area of the bigger clutch

Questions 18-22.

DIRECTIONS: Questions 18 through 22 are to be answered SOLELY on the basis of the following paragraphs.

Exhaust valve clearance adjustment on diesel engines is very important for proper operation of the engine. Insufficient clearance between the exhaust valve stem and the rocker arm causes a loss of compression and, after a while, burning of the valves and valve seat inserts. On the other hand, too much valve clearance will result in noisy operation of the engine.

Exhaust valves that are maintained in good operating condition will result in efficient combustion in the engine. Valve seats must be true and unpitted, and valve stems must work smoothly within the valve guides. Long valve life will result from proper maintenance and operation of the engine.

Engine operating temperatures should be maintained between 160°F and 185°F. Low operating temperatures result in incomplete combustion and the deposit of fuel lacquers on valves.

18. According to the above paragraphs, too much valve clearance will cause the engine to operate   18._____
    A. slowly   B. noisily   C. smoothly   D. cold

19. On the basis of the information given in the above paragraphs, operating temperatures of a diesel engine should be between   19._____
    A. 125°F and 130°F   B. 140°F and 150°F
    C. 160°F and 185°F   D. 190°F and 205°F

20. According to the above paragraphs, the deposit of fuel lacquers on valves is caused by   20._____
    A. high operating temperatures
    B. insufficient valve clearance
    C. low operating temperatures
    D. efficient combustion

21. According to the above paragraphs, for efficient operation of the engine, valve seats must   21._____
    A. have sufficient clearance
    B. be true and unpitted
    C. operate at low temperatures
    D. be adjusted regularly

22. According to the above paragraphs, a loss of compression is due to insufficient clearance between the exhaust valve stem and the   22._____
    A. rocker arm   B. valve seat
    C. valve seat inserts   D. valve guides

Questions 23-25.

DIRECTIONS: Questions 23 through 25 are to be answered SOLELY on the basis of the following excerpt:

A SPECIFICATION FOR ELECTRIC WORK FOR THE CITY

Breakers shall be equipped with magnetic blowout coils...Handles of breakers shall be trip-free...Breakers shall be designed to carry 100% of trip rating continuously; to have inverse time delay tripping above 100% of trip rating...

23. According to the above paragraph, the breaker shall have provision for   23._____
    A. resetting   B. arc quenching
    C. adjusting trip time   D. adjusting trip rating

24. According to the above paragraph, the breaker   24._____
    A. shall trip easily at exactly 100% of trip rating
    B. shall trip instantly at a little more than 100% of trip rating
    C. should be constructed so that it shall not be possible to prevent it from opening on overload or short circuit by holding the handle in the ON position
    D. shall not trip prematurely at 100% of trip rating

25. According to the above paragraph, the breaker shall trip
    A. instantaneously as soon as 100% of trip rating is reached
    B. instantaneously as soon as 100% of trip rating is exceeded
    C. more quickly the greater the current, once 100% of trip rating is exceeded
    D. after a predetermined fixed time lapse, once 100% of trip rating is reached

KEY (CORRECT ANSWERS)

1.	C	11.	B
2.	B	12.	B
3.	D	13.	C
4.	A	14.	D
5.	D	15.	D
6.	A	16.	A
7.	D	17.	C
8.	D	18.	B
9.	C	19.	C
10.	B	20.	C

21.	B
22.	A
23.	B
24.	C
25.	C

TEST 2

DIRECTIONS: Each question or incomplete statement is followed by several suggested answers or completions. Select the one that BEST answers the question or completes the statement. *PRINT THE LETTER OF THE CORRECT ANSWER IN THE SPACE AT THE RIGHT.*

Questions 1-4.

DIRECTIONS: Questions 1 through 4 are to be answered SOLELY on the basis of the following paragraph.

    A low pressure hot water boiler shall include a relief valve or valves of a capacity such that with the heat generating equipment operating at maximum, the pressure cannot rise more than 20 percent above the maximum allowable working pressure (set pressure) if that is 30 p.s.i. gage or less, nor more than 10 percent if it is more than 30 p.s.i. gage. The difference between the set pressure and the pressure at which the valve is relieving is known as *over-pressure or accumulation.* If the steam relieving capacity in pounds per hour is calculated, it shall be determined by dividing by 1,000 the maximum BTU output at the boiler nozzle obtainable from the heat generating equipment, or by multiplying the square feet of heating surface by five.

1. In accordance with the above paragraph, the capacity of a relief valve should be computed on the basis of
    A. size of boiler
    B. maximum rated capacity of generating equipment
    C. average output of the generating equipment
    D. minimum capacity of generating equipment

1._____

2. In accordance with the above paragraph, with a set pressure of 30 p.s.i. gage, the overpressure should not be more than _____ p.s.i.
    A. 3   B. 6   C. 33   D. 36

2._____

3. In accordance with the above paragraph, a relief valve should start relieving at a pressure equal to the
    A. set pressure
    B. over pressure
    C. over pressure minus set pressure
    D. set pressure plus over pressure

3._____

4. In accordance with the above paragraph, the steam relieving capacity can be computed by
    A. *multiplying* the maximum BTU output by 5
    B. *dividing* the pounds of steam per hour by 1,000
    C. *dividing* the maximum BTU output by the square feet of heating surface
    D. *dividing* the maximum BTU output by 1,000

4._____

Questions 5-8.

DIRECTIONS: Questions 5 through 8 are to be answered SOLELY on the basis of the following paragraph.

Air conditioning units requiring a minimum rate of flow of water in excess of one-half (1/2) gallon per minute shall be metered. Air conditioning equipment with a refrigeration unit which has a definite rate of capacity in tons or fractions thereof, the charge will be at the rate of $30 per annum per ton capacity from the date installed to the date when the supply is metered. Such units, when equipped with an approved water-conserving device, shall be charged at the rate of $4.50 per annum per ton capacity from the date installed to the date when the supply is metered.

5. A man who was in the market for air conditioning equipment was considering three different units. Unit 1 required a flow of 28 gallons of water per hour; Unit 2 required 30 gallons of water per hour; Unit 3 required 32 gallons of water per hour. The man asked the salesman which units would require the installation of a water meter. According to the above passage, the salesman SHOULD answer:
   A. All three units require meters
   B. Units 2 and 3 require meters
   C. Unit 3 only requires a meter
   D. None of the units require a meter

6. Suppose that air conditioning equipment with a refrigeration unit of 10 tons was put in operation on October 1; and in the following year on July 1, a meter was installed. According to the above passage, the charge for this period would be _____ the annual rate.
   A. twice   B. equal to
   C. three-fourths   D. one-fourth

7. The charge for air conditioning equipment which has no refrigeration unit
   A. is $30 per year
   B. is $25.50 per year
   C. is $4.50 per year
   D. cannot be determined from the above passage

8. The charge for air conditioning equipment with a seven-ton refrigeration unit equipped with an approved water-conserving device
   A. is $4.50 per year
   B. is $25.50 per year
   C. is $31.50 per year
   D. cannot be determined from the above passage

Questions 9-14.

DIRECTIONS: Questions 9 through 14 are to be answered SOLELY on the basis of the following paragraph.

The city makes unremitting efforts to keep the water free from pollution. An inspectional force under a sanitary expert is engaged in patrolling the watersheds to see that the department's sanitary regulations are observed. Samples taken daily from various points in the water supply system are examined and analyzed at the three laboratories maintained by the department. All water before delivery to the distribution mains is treated with chlorine to destroy bacteria. In addition, some water is aerated to free it from gases and, in some cases, from microscopic organisms. Generally, microscopic organisms which develop in the reservoirs and at times impart an unpleasant taste and odor to the water, though in no sense harmful to health, are destroyed by treatment with copper sulfate and by chlorine dosage. None of the supplies is filtered, but the quality of the water supplied by the city is excellent for all purposes, and it is clear and wholesome.

9. According to the above paragraph, microscopic organisms are removed from the water supplied to the city by means of 9._____
   A. chlorine alone
   B. chlorine, aeration, and filtration
   C. chlorine, aeration, filtration, and sampling
   D. copper sulfate, chlorine, and aeration

10. Microscopic organisms in the water supply GENERALLY are 10._____
    A. a health menace   B. impossible to detect
    C. not harmful to health   D. not destroyed in the water

11. The MAIN function of the inspectional force, as described in the above paragraph, is to 11._____
    A. take samples of water for analysis
    B. enforce sanitary regulations
    C. add chlorine to the water supply
    D. inspect water-use meters

12. According to the above paragraph, chlorine is added to water before entering the 12._____
    A. watersheds   B. reservoirs
    C. distribution mains   D. run-off areas

13. Of the following suggested headings or titles for the above paragraph, the one that BEST tells what the paragraph is about is 13._____
    A. QUALITY OF WATER   B. CHLORINATION OF WATER
    C. TESTING OF WATER   D. BACTERIA IN WATER

14. The MOST likely reason for taking samples of water for examination and analysis from various points in the water supply system is: 14._____
    A. The testing points are convenient to the department's laboratories
    B. Water from one part of the system may be made undrinkable by a local condition
    C. The samples can be distributed equally among the three laboratories
    D. The hardness or softness of water varies from place to place

Questions 15-17.

DIRECTIONS: Questions 15 through 17 are to be answered SOLELY on the basis of the following paragraph.

A building measuring 200' x 100' at the street is set back 20' on all sides at the 15th floor, and an additional 10' on all sides at the 30th floor. The building is 35 stories high.

15. The floor area of the 16th floor is MOST NEARLY _____ sq. ft. 15._____
    A. 20,000 B. 14,400 C. 9,600 D. 7,500

16. The floor area of the 35th floor is MOST NEARLY _____ sq. ft. 16._____
    A. 20,000 B. 13,900 C. 7,500 D. 5,600

17. The floor area of the 16th floor, compared to the floor area of the 2nd floor, is MOST NEARLY _____ as much. 17._____
    A. three-fourths (3/4)   B. two-thirds (2/3)
    C. one-half (1/2)   D. four-tenths (4/10)

Question 18.

DIRECTIONS: Question 18 is to be answered SOLELY on the basis of the following paragraph.

Experience has shown that, in general, a result of the installation of meters on services not previously metered is to reduce the amount of water consumed, but is not necessarily to reduce the peak load on plumbing systems. The permissible head loss through meters at their rated maximum flow is 20 p.s.i. The installation of a meter may therefore appreciably lower the pressures available in fixtures on a plumbing system.

18. According to the above paragraph, a water meter may 18._____
    A. limit the flow in the plumbing system of 20 p.s.i.
    B. reduce the peak load on the plumbing system
    C. increase the overall amount of water consumed
    D. reduce the pressure in the plumbing system

Question 19.

DIRECTIONS: Question 19 is to be answered SOLELY on the basis of the following paragraph.

Spring comes without trumpets to a city. The asphalt is a wilderness that does not quicken overnight; winds blow gritty with cinders instead of merry with the smells of earth and fertilizer. Women wear their gardens on their hats. But spring is a season in the city, and it has its own harbingers, constant as daffodils. Shop windows change their colors, people walk more slowly on the streets, what one can see of the sky has a bluer tone. Pulitzer prizes awake and sing and matinee tickets go-a-begging. But gayer than any of these are the carousels, which are already in sheltered places, beginning to turn with the sound of springtime itself. They are the earliest and the truest and the oldest of all the urban signs.

19. In the passage above, the word *harbingers* means 19._____
    A. storms   B. truths   C. virtues   D. forerunners

Questions 20-22.

DIRECTIONS: Questions 20 through 22 are to be answered SOLELY on the basis of the following paragraph.

Gas heaters include manually operated, automatic, and instantaneous heaters. Some heaters are equipped with a thermostat which controls the fuel supply so that when the water falls below a predetermined temperature, the fuel is automatically turned on. In some types, the hot-water storage tank is well-insulated to economize the use of fuel. Instantaneous heaters are arranged so that the opening of a faucet on the hot-water pipe will increase the flow of fuel, which is ignited by a continuously burning pilot light to heat the water to from 120° to 130°F. The possibility that the pilot light will die out offers a source of danger in the use of automatic appliances which depend on a pilot light. Gas and oil heaters are dangerous, and they should be designed to prevent the accumulation, in a confined space within the heater, of a large volume of an explosive mixture.

20. According to the above passage, the opening of a hot-water faucet on a hot-water pipe connected to an instantaneous hot-water heater will the pilot light.
    A. *increase* the temperature of
    B. *increase* the flow of fuel to
    C. *decrease* the flow of fuel to
    D. *have a marked effect* on

21. According to the above passage, the fuel is automatically turned on in a heater equipped with a thermostat whenever
    A. the water temperature drops below 120°F
    B. the pilot light is lit
    C. the water temperature drops below some predetermined temperature
    D. a hot water supply is opened

22. According to the above passage, some hot-water storage tanks are well-insulated to
    A. accelerate the burning of the fuel
    B. maintain the water temperature between 120° and 130°F
    C. prevent the pilot light from being extinguished
    D. minimize the expenditure of fuel

Question 23.

DIRECTIONS: Question 23 is to be answered SOLELY on the basis of the following paragraph.

Breakage of the piston under high-speed operation has been the commonest fault of disc piston meters. Various techniques are adopted to prevent this, such as *throttling* the meter, cutting away the edge of the piston, or reinforcing it, but these are simply makeshifts.

23. As used in the above paragraph, the word *throttling* means MOST NEARLY
    A. enlarging   B. choking
    C. harnessing   D. dismantling

Questions 24-25.

DIRECTIONS: Questions 24 and 25 are to be answered SOLELY on the basis of the following paragraph.

One of the most common and objectionable difficulties occurring in a drainage system is trap seal loss. This failure can be attributed directly to inadequate ventilation of the trap and the subsequent negative and positive pressures which occur. A trap seal may be lost either by siphonage and/or back pressure. Loss of the trap seal by siphonage is the result of a negative pressure in the drainage system. The seal content of the trap is forced by siphonage into the waste piping of the drainage system through exertion of atmospheric pressure on the fixture side of the trap seal.

24. According to the above paragraph, a positive pressure is a direct result of 24._____
    A. siphonage
    B. unbalanced trap seal
    C. poor ventilation
    D. atmospheric pressure

25. According to the above paragraph, the water in the trap is forced into the drain pipe by 25._____
    A. atmospheric pressure
    B. back pressure
    C. negative pressure
    D. back pressure on fixture side of seal

KEY (CORRECT ANSWERS)

1. B
2. B
3. D
4. D
5. C

6. C
7. D
8. C
9. D
10. C

11. B
12. C
13. A
14. B
15. C

16. D
17. C
18. D
19. B
20. B

21. C
22. D
23. B
24. C
25. A

ABSTRACT REASONING

COMMENTARY

Since intelligence exists in many forms or phases and the theory of differential aptitudes is now firmly established in testing, other manifestations and measurements of intelligence than verbal or purely arithmetical must be identified and measured.

Classification inventory, or figure classification, involves the aptitude of form perception, i.e., the ability to perceive pertinent detail in objects or in pictorial or graphic material. It involves making visual comparisons and discriminations and discerning slight differences in shapes and shading figures and widths and lengths of lines.

Leading examples of presentation are the figure analogy and the figure classification. The section that follows presents progressive and varied samplings of this type of question.

SAMPLE QUESTIONS

DIRECTIONS: In each of these sample questions, look at the symbols in the first two boxes. Something about the three symbols in the first box makes them alike; something about the two symbols in the other box with the question mark makes them alike. Look for some characteristic that is common to all symbols in the same box, yet makes them different from the symbols in the other box. Among the five answer choices, find the symbol that can BEST be substituted for the question mark, because it is *like* the symbols in the second box, and, for the same reason, different from those in the first box.

1.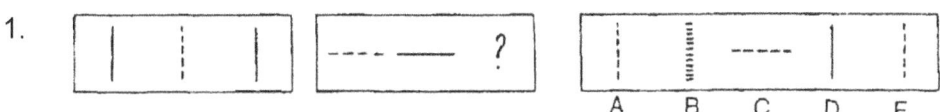

In sample question 1, all the symbols in the first box are vertical lines. The second box has two lines, one broken and one solid. Their *likeness* to each other consists in their being horizontal; and their being horizontal makes them *different* from the vertical lines in the other box. The answer must be the only one of the five lettered choices that is a horizontal line, ether broken or solid. Therefore, the CORRECT answer is C.

2.

The CORRECT answer is A.

EXAMINATION SECTION
TEST 1

DIRECTIONS: In each of these questions, look at the symbols in the first two boxes. Something about the three symbols in the first box makes them alike; something about the two symbols in the other box with the question mark makes them alike. Look for some characteristic that is common to all symbols in the same box, yet makes them different from the symbols in the other box. Among the five answer choices, find the symbol that can BEST be substituted for the question mark, because it is *like* the symbols in the second box, and, for the same reason, different from those in the first box. PRINT THE LETTER OF THE CORRECT ANSWER IN THE SPACE AT THE RIGHT.

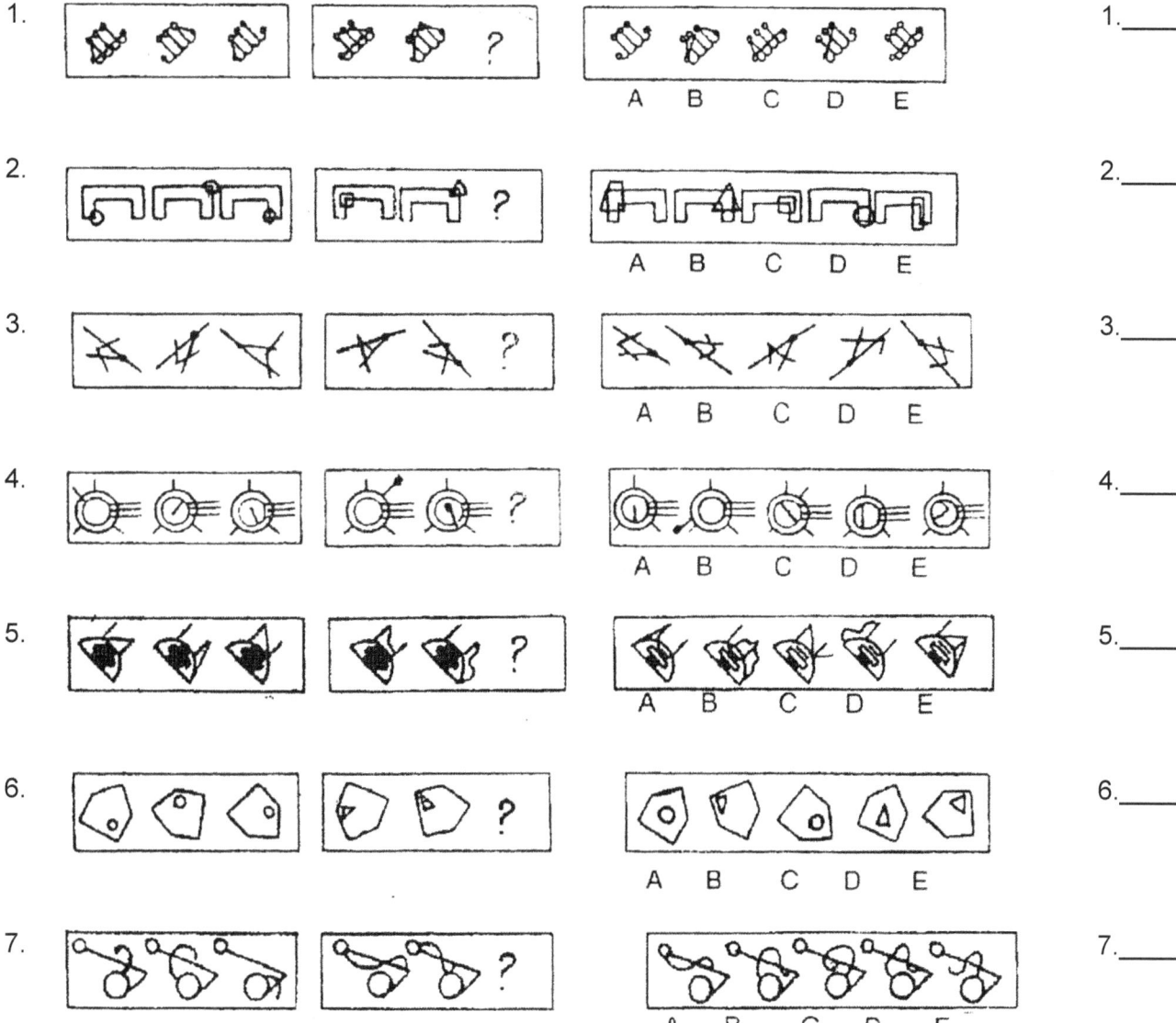

2 (#1)

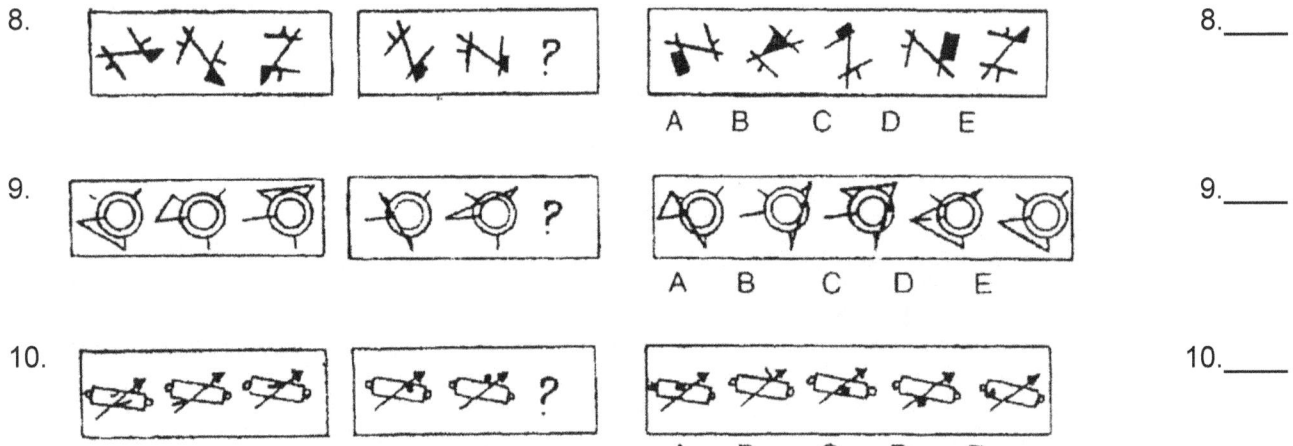

KEY (CORRECT ANSWERS)

1.	B	6.	B
2.	C	7.	A
3.	C	8.	C
4.	B	9.	B
5.	D	10.	D

TEST 2

DIRECTIONS: In each of these questions, look at the symbols in the first two boxes. Something about the three symbols in the first box makes them alike; something about the two symbols in the other box with the question mark makes them alike. Look for some characteristic that is common to all symbols in the same box, yet makes them different from the symbols in the other box. Among the five answer choices, find the symbol that can BEST be substituted for the question mark, because it is *like* the symbols in the second box, and, for the same reason, different from those in the first box. *PRINT THE LETTER OF THE CORRECT ANSWER IN THE SPACE AT THE RIGHT.*

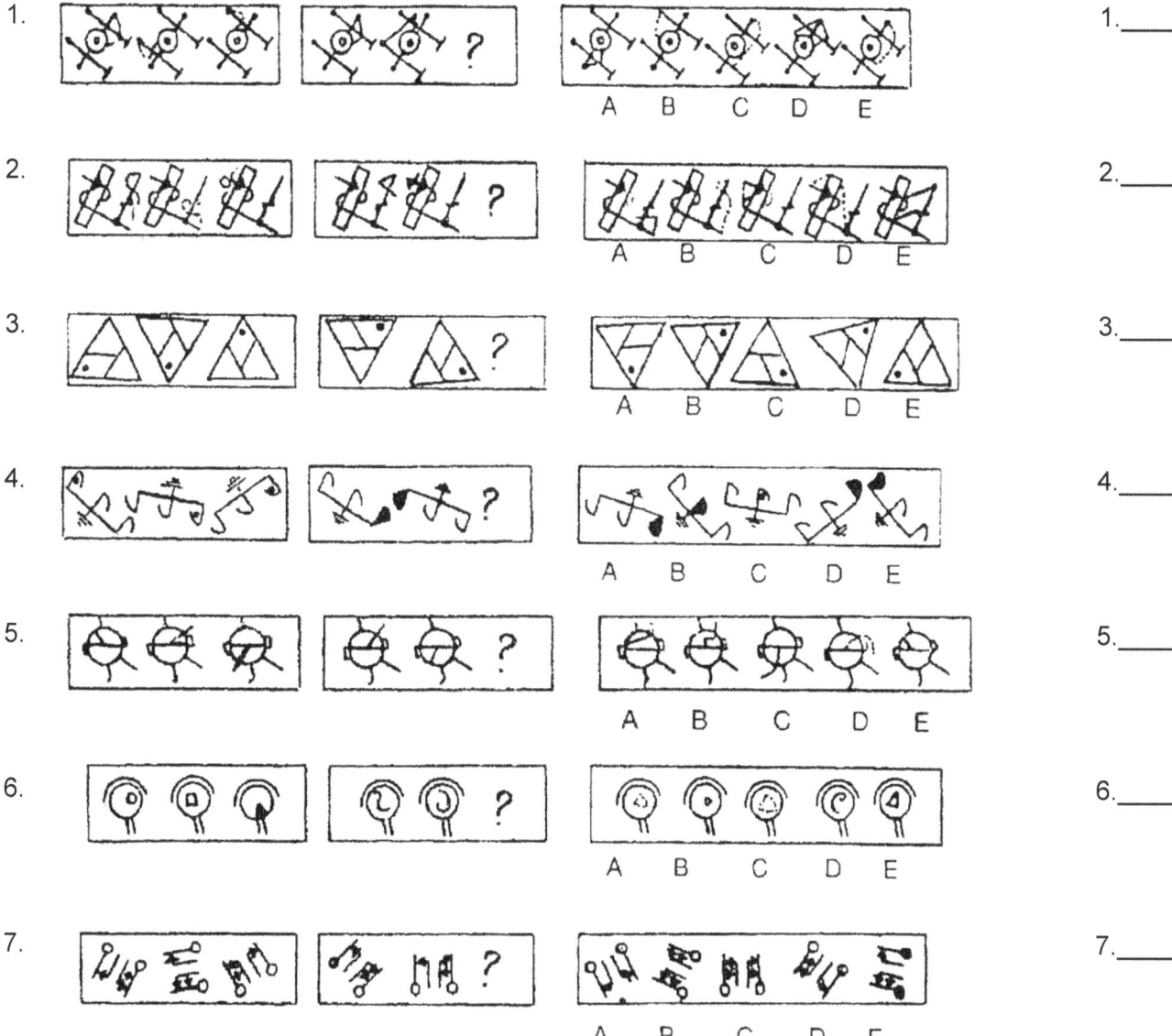

2 (#2)

8.
9.
10.

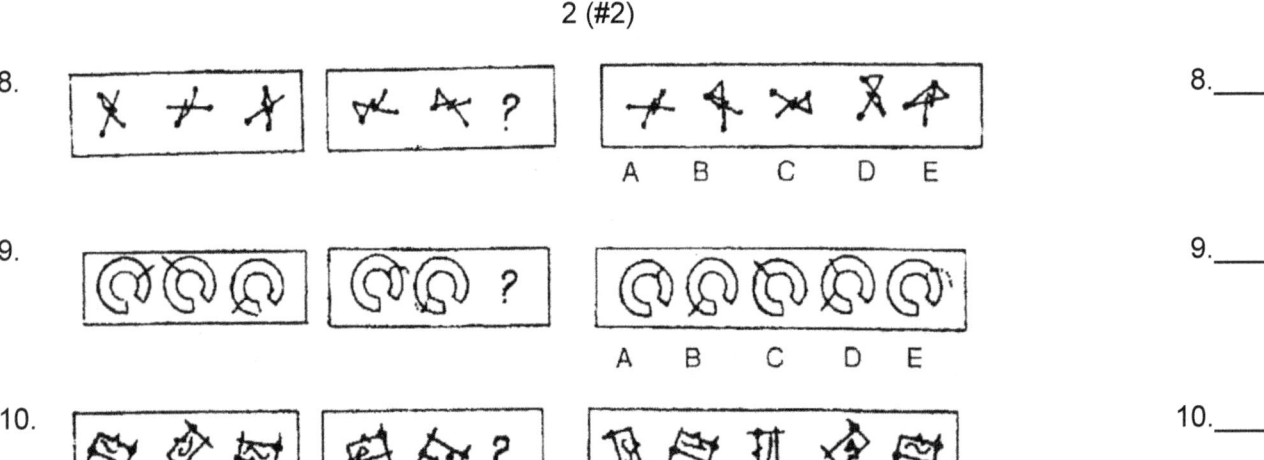

8. ___
9. ___
10. ___

KEY (CORRECT ANSWERS)

1.	A	6.	D
2.	A	7.	D
3.	A	8.	C
4.	D	9.	E
5.	E	10.	D

TEST 3

DIRECTIONS: In each of these questions, look at the symbols in the first two boxes. Something about the three symbols in the first box makes them alike; something about the two symbols in the other box with the question mark makes them alike. Look for some characteristic that is common to all symbols in the same box, yet makes them different from the symbols in the other box. Among the five answer choices, find the symbol that can BEST be substituted for the question mark, because it is *like* the symbols in the second box, and, for the same reason, different from those in the first box. *PRINT THE LETTER OF THE CORRECT ANSWER IN THE SPACE AT THE RIGHT.*

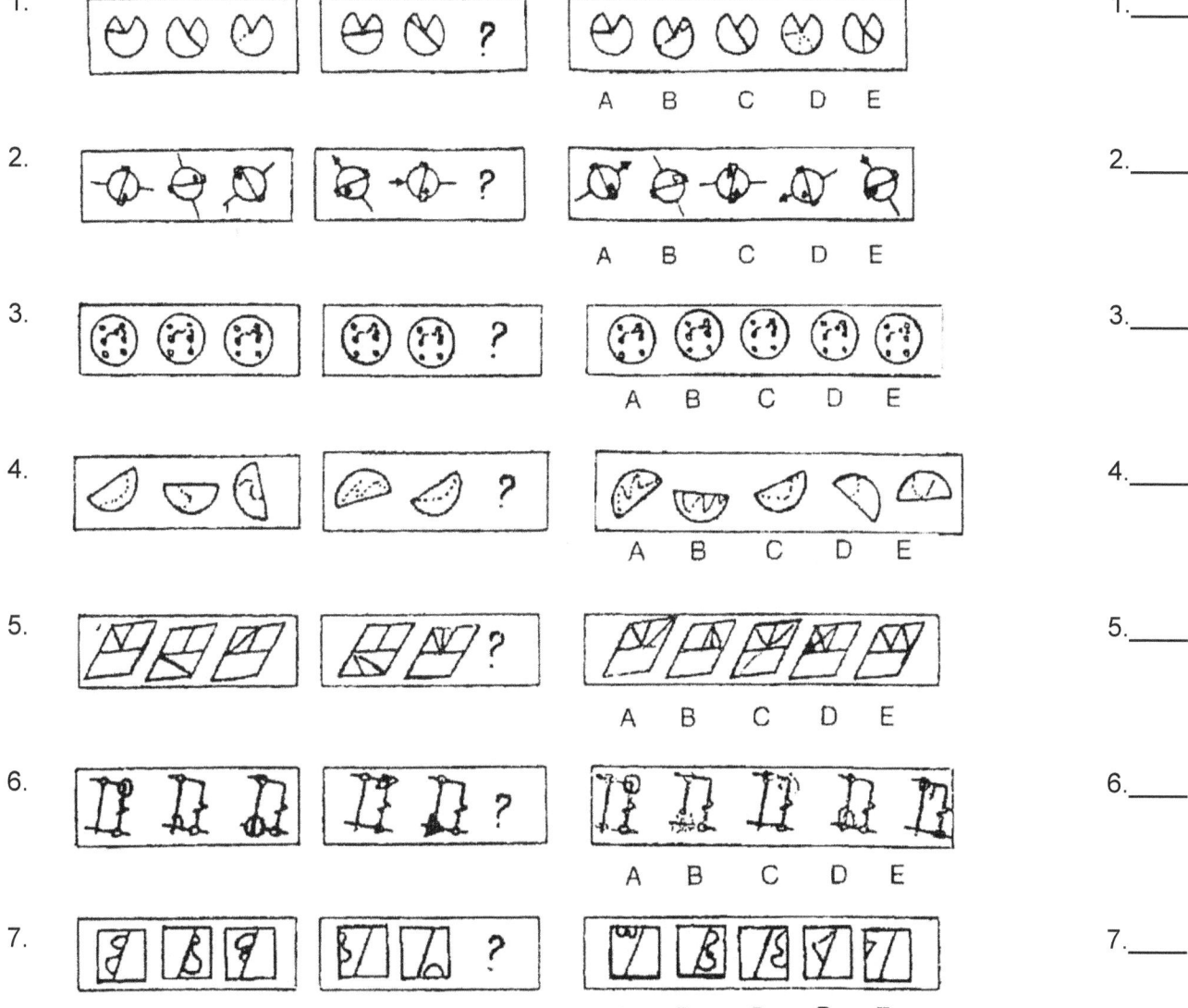

2 (#3)

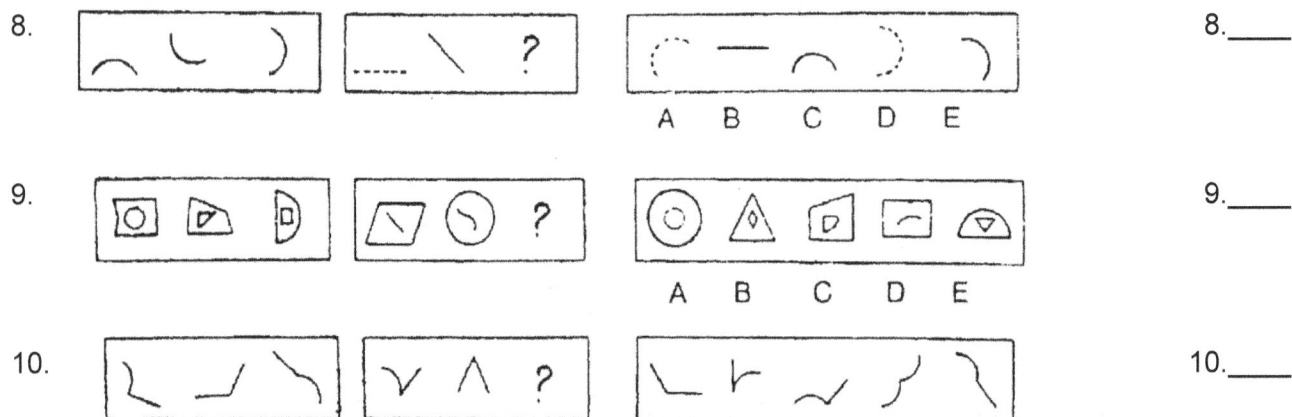

KEY (CORRECT ANSWERS)

1.	B	6.	C
2.	E	7.	C
3.	C	8.	B
4.	A	9.	D
5.	B	10.	B

SPATIAL RELATIONS
EXAMINATION SECTION
TEST 1

DIRECTIONS: In each of Questions 1 to 11 the front and top views of an object are given. Of the views labeled 1, 2, 3, and 4, select the one that CORRECTLY represents the right side view of each object for third angle projection.

1.   1.____

A. 1   B. 2   C. 3   D. 4

2.   2.____

A. 1   B. 2   C. 3   D. 4

3.   3.____

A. 1   B. 2   C. 3   D. 4

115

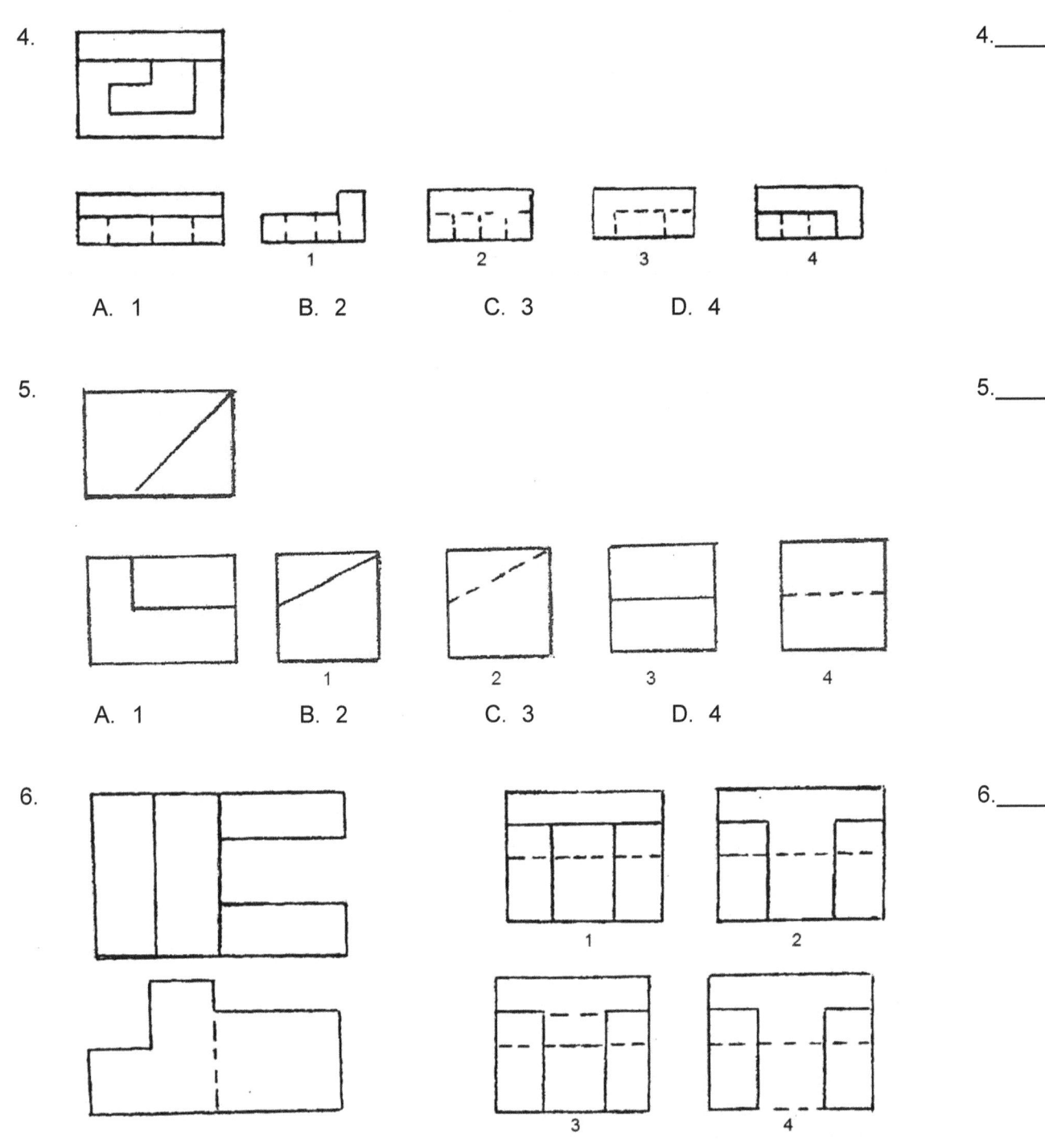

4.

A. 1   B. 2   C. 3   D. 4

5.

A. 1   B. 2   C. 3   D. 4

6.

A. 1   B. 2   C. 3.   D. 4

3 (#1)

7.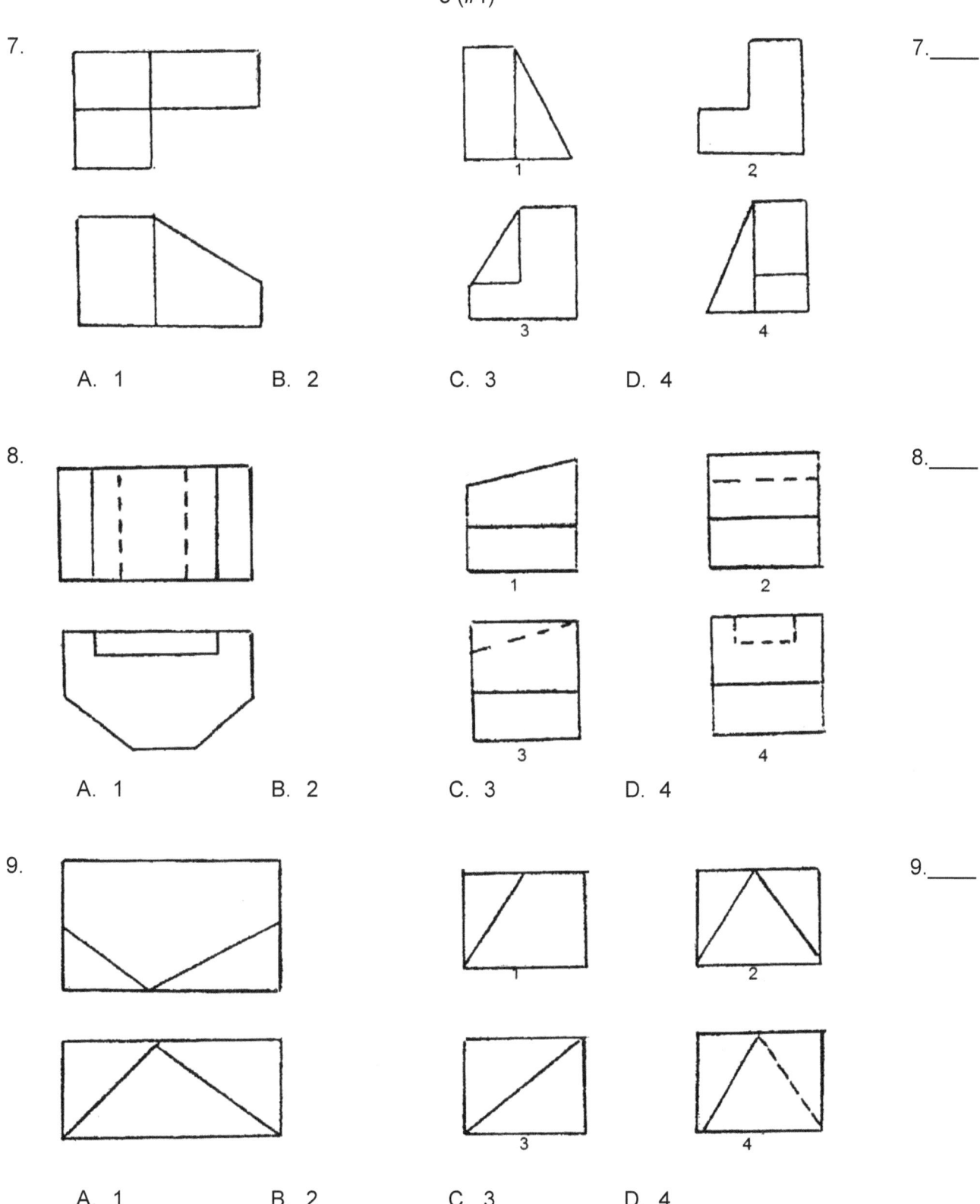

A. 1   B. 2   C. 3   D. 4

7.____

8.

A. 1   B. 2   C. 3   D. 4

8.____

9.

A. 1   B. 2   C. 3   D. 4

9.____

10.

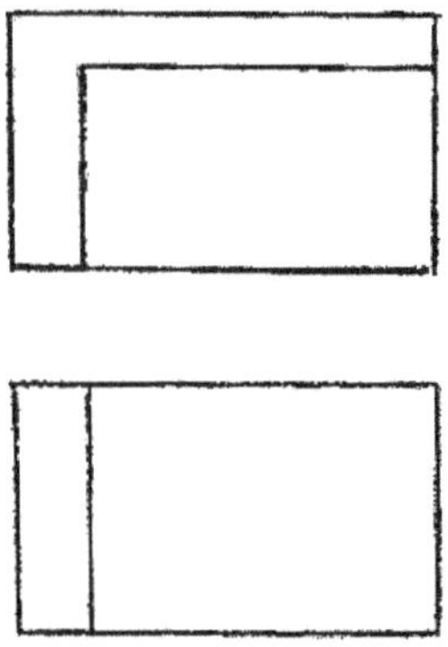

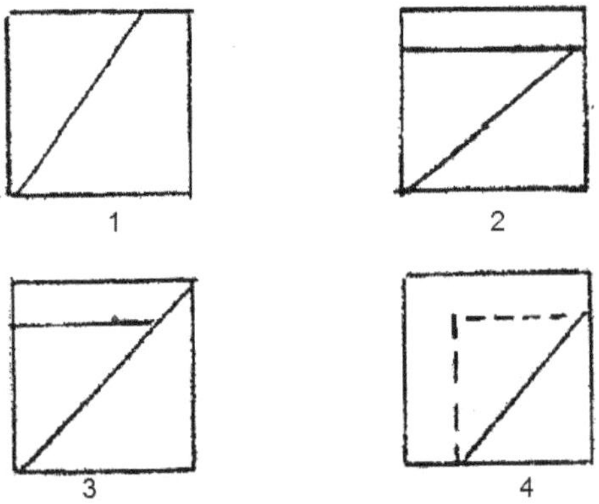

A. 1   B. 2   C. 3   D. 4

10.____

11.

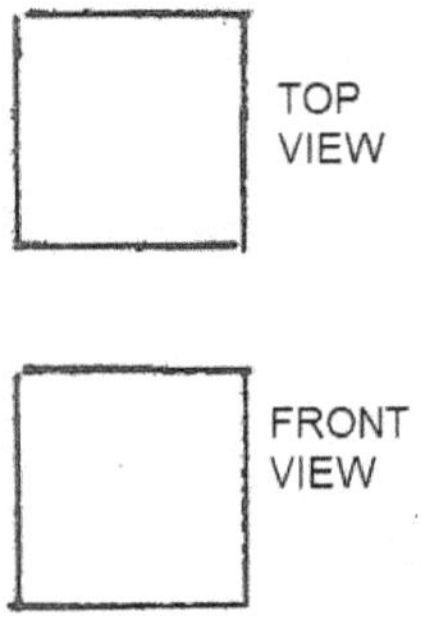

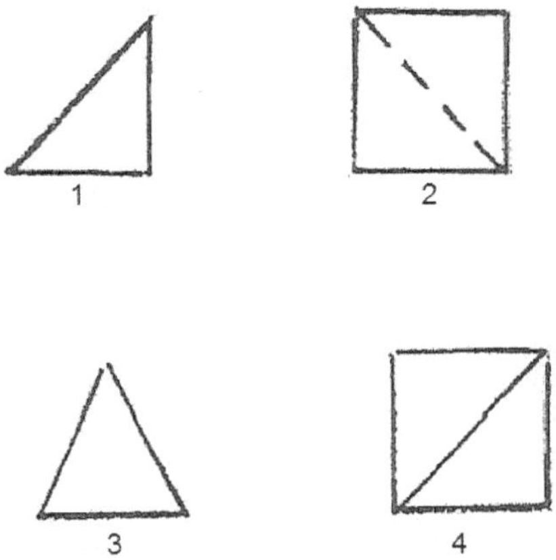

TOP VIEW

FRONT VIEW

A. 1   B. 2   C. 3   D. 4

11.____

Questions 12-16.

DIRECTIONS: In each of Questions 12 to 25 inclusive, two views of an object are given. Of the views labeled 1, 2, 3, and 4, select the one that CORRECTLY represents the right side view of each object.

12.

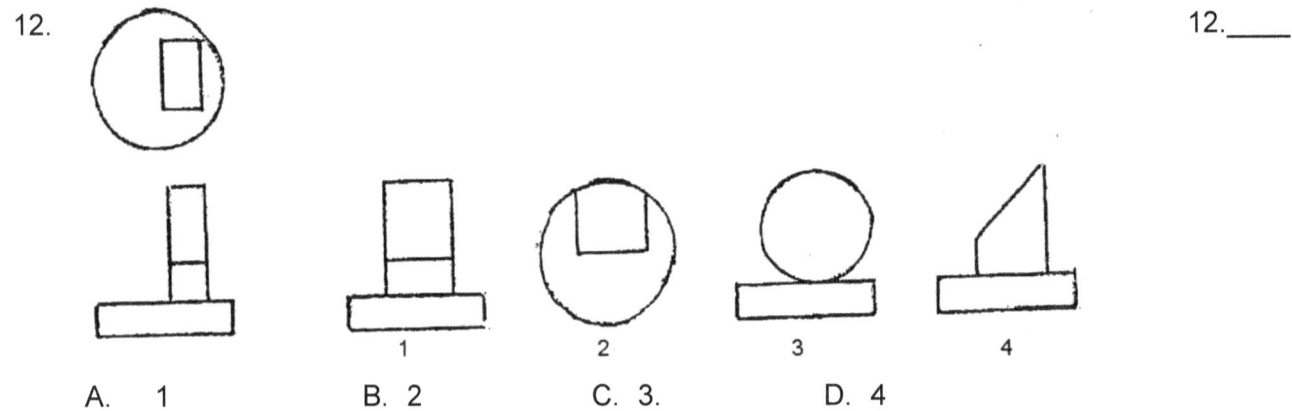

A. 1   B. 2   C. 3.   D. 4

12.____

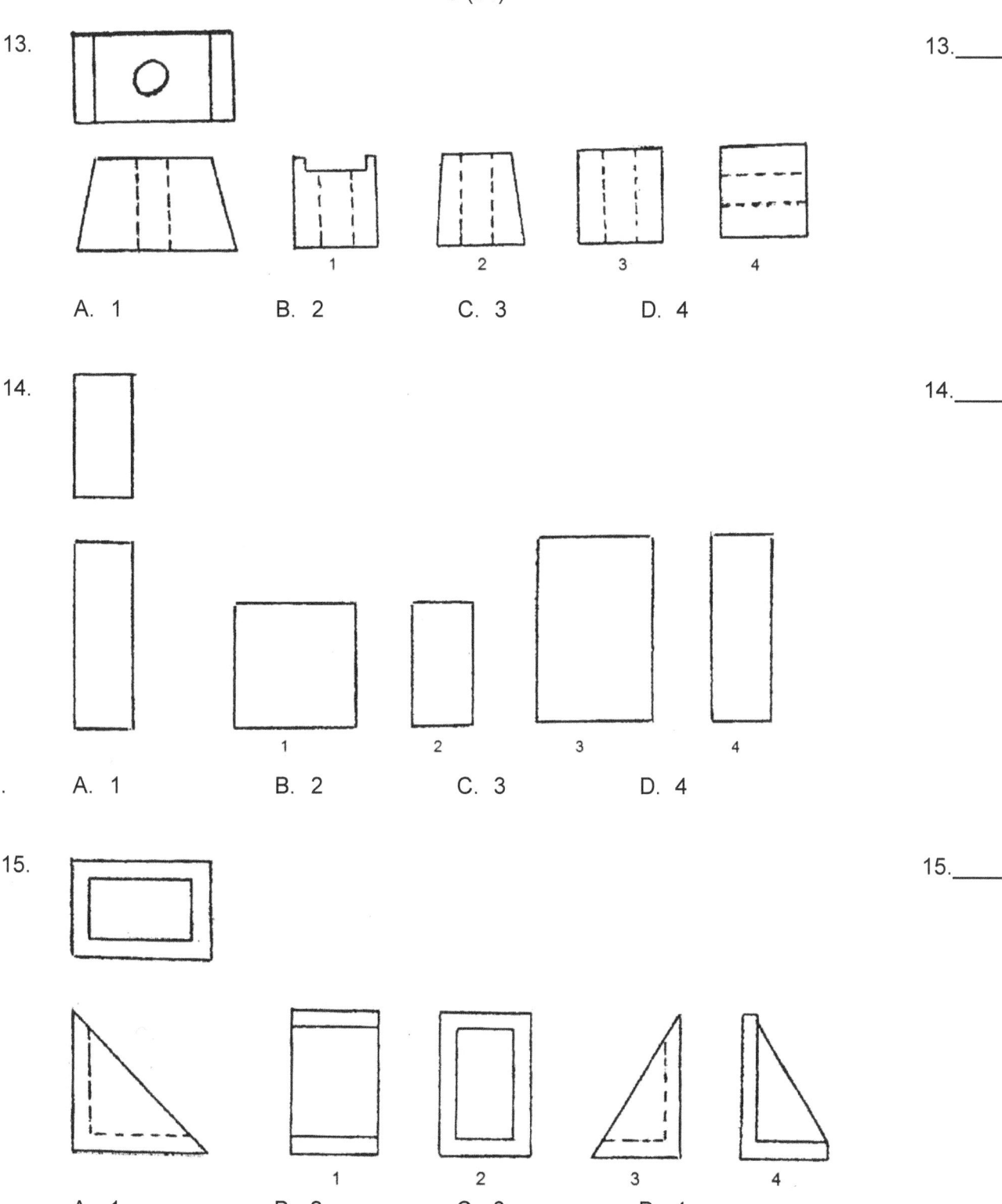

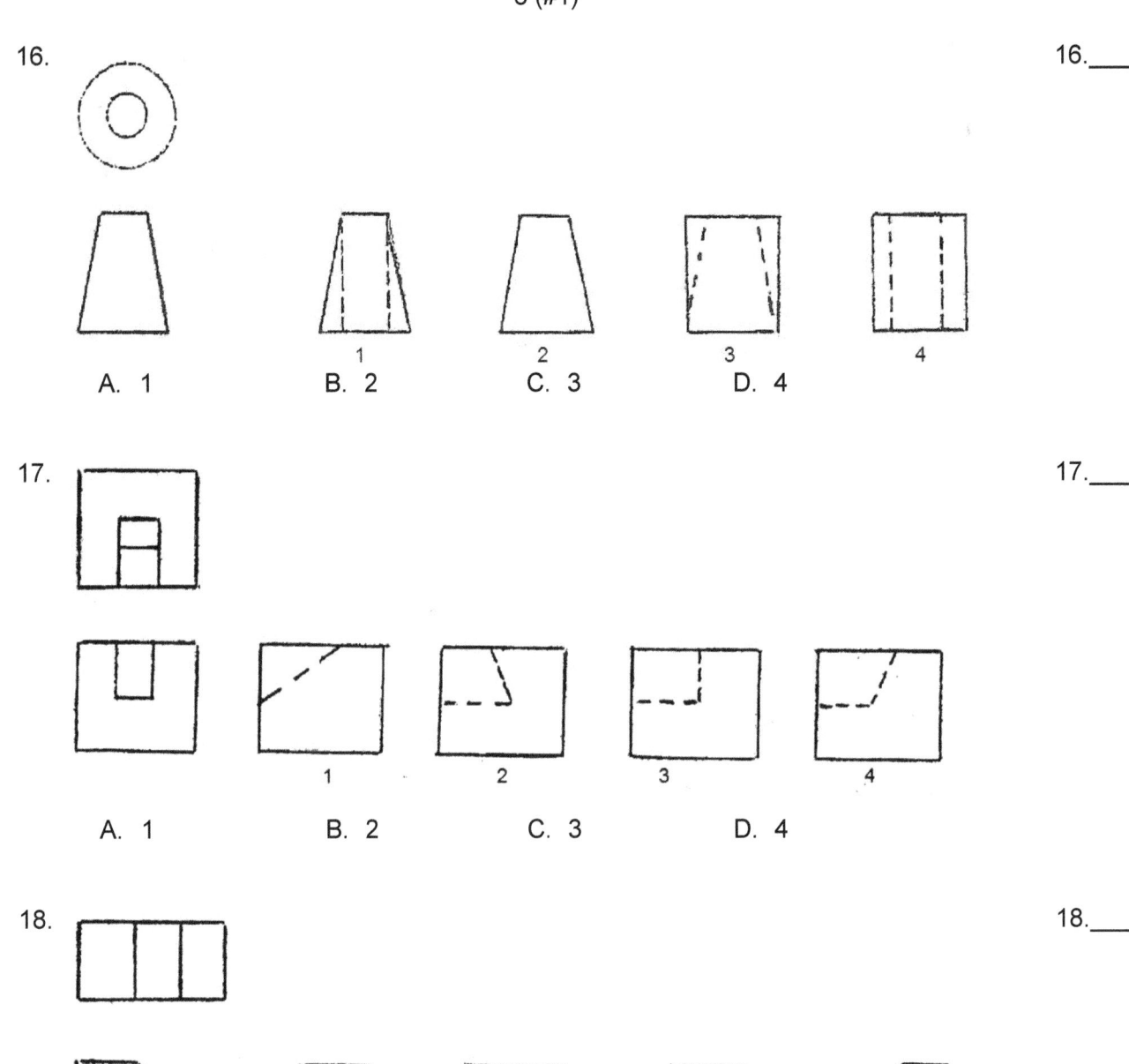

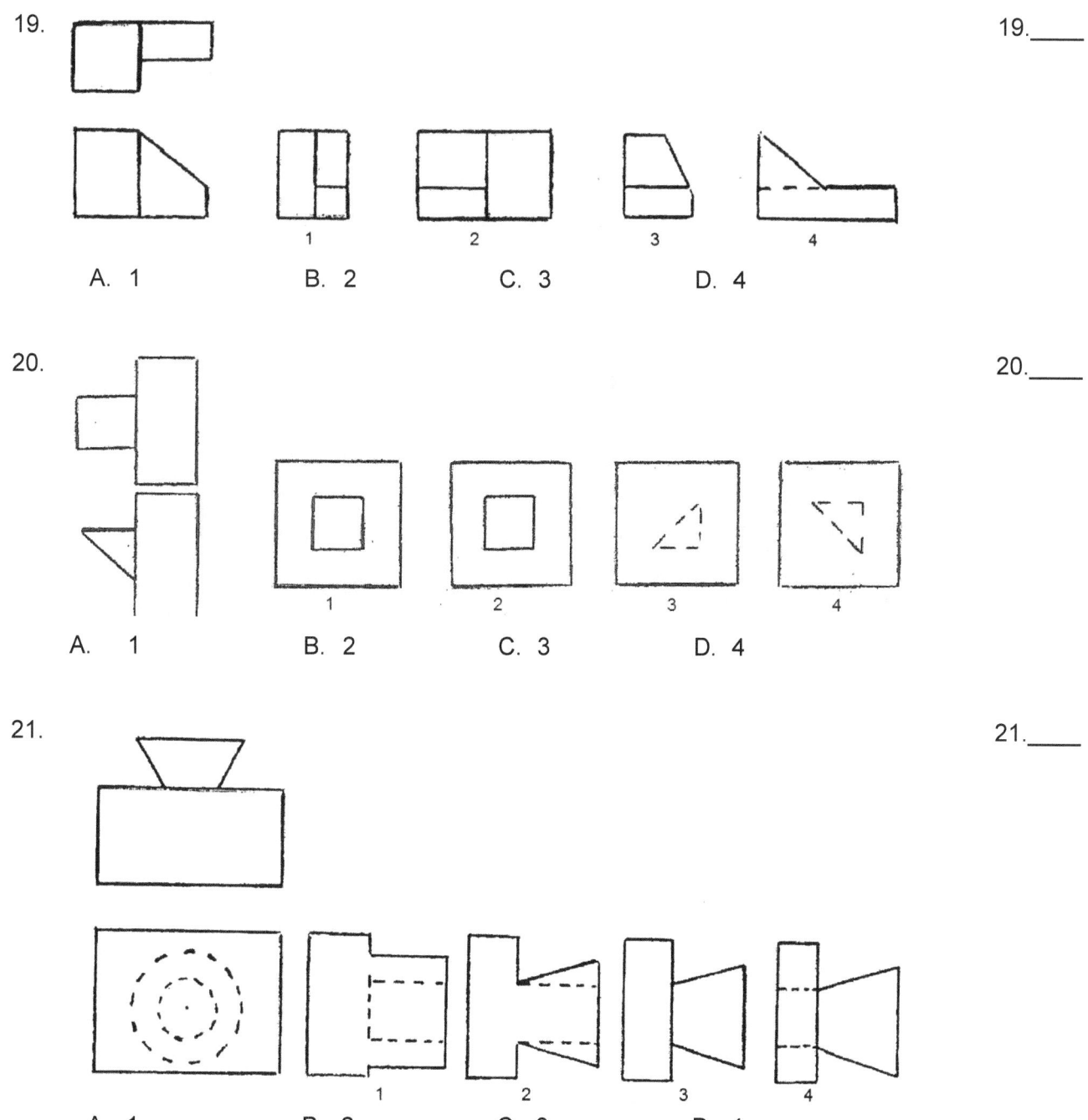

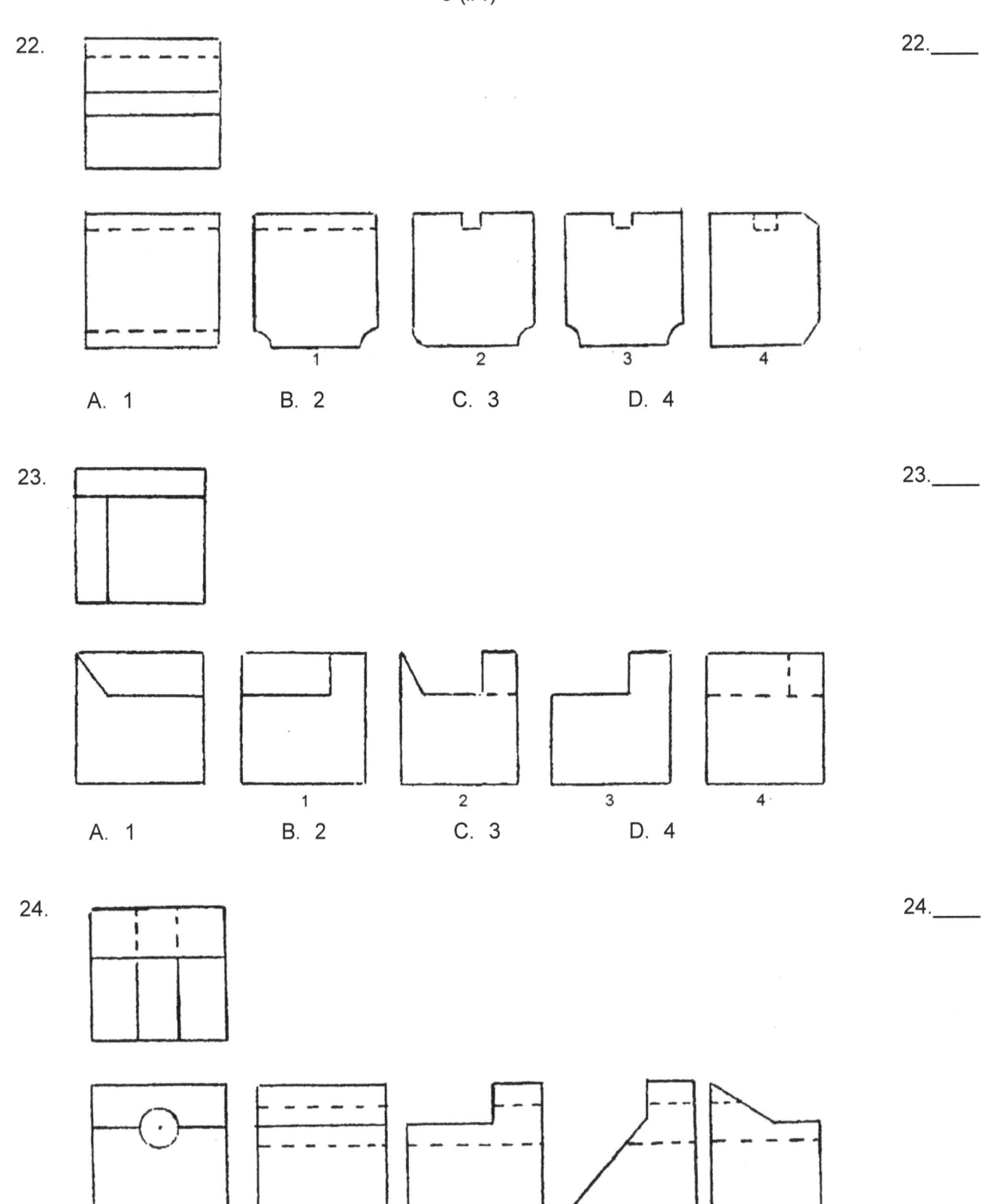

22.

A. 1   B. 2   C. 3   D. 4

22.____

23.

A. 1   B. 2   C. 3   D. 4

23.____

24.

24.____

25.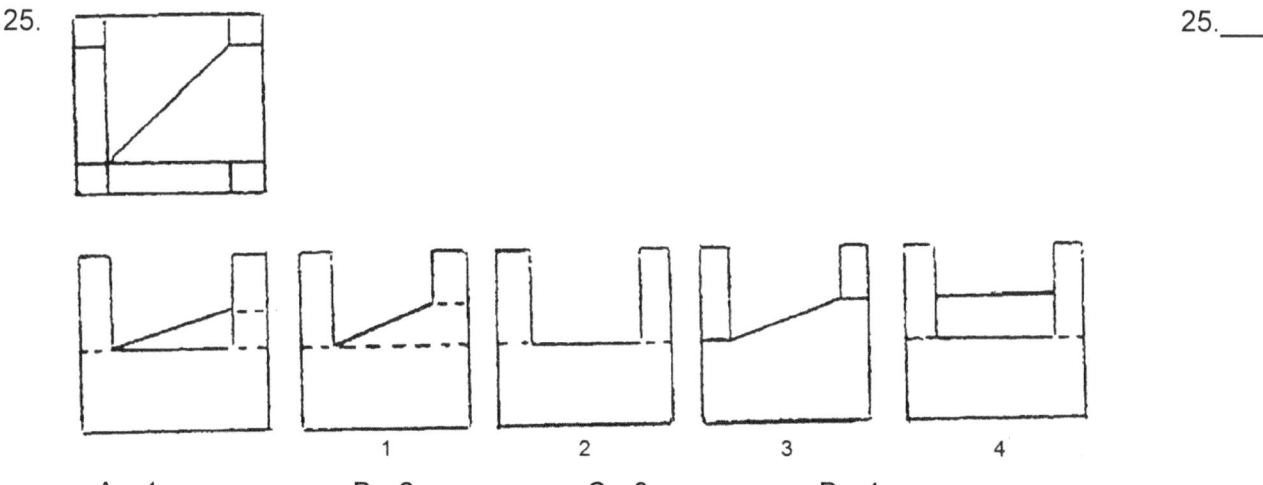

A. 1   B. 2   C. 3   D. 4

Questions 26-30.

DIRECTIONS: In Questions 26 through 30 which follow, the plan and front elevation of an object are shown on the left, and on the right are shown four figures, one of which and only one represents the right side elevation. Mark in the space at the right the letter which represents the right side elevation. In the sample below, which figure correctly represents the right side elevation?

SAMPLE QUESTION

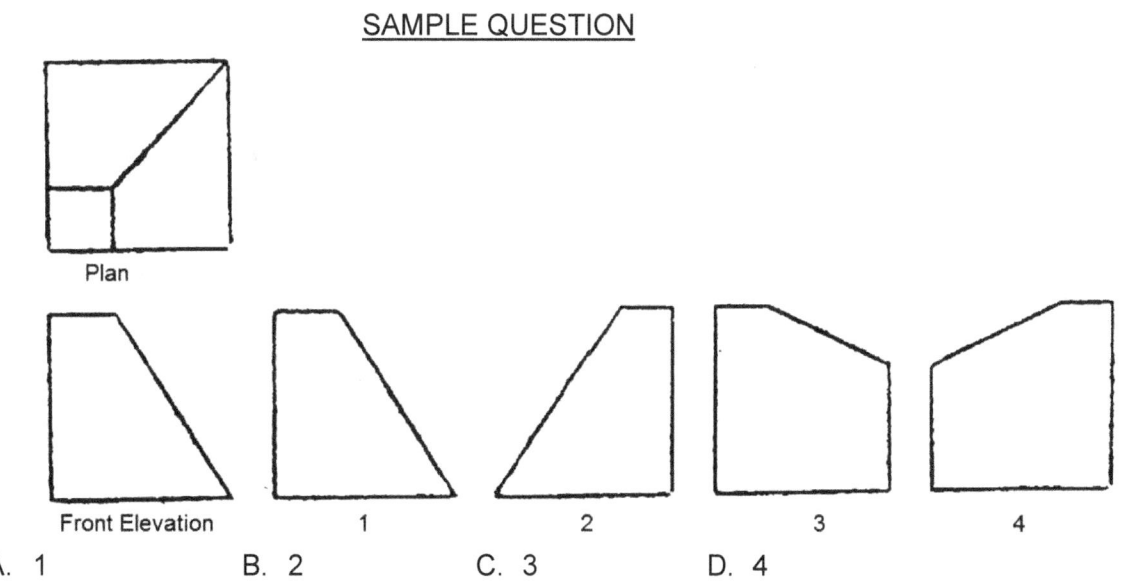

A. 1   B. 2   C. 3   D. 4

The correct answer is A.

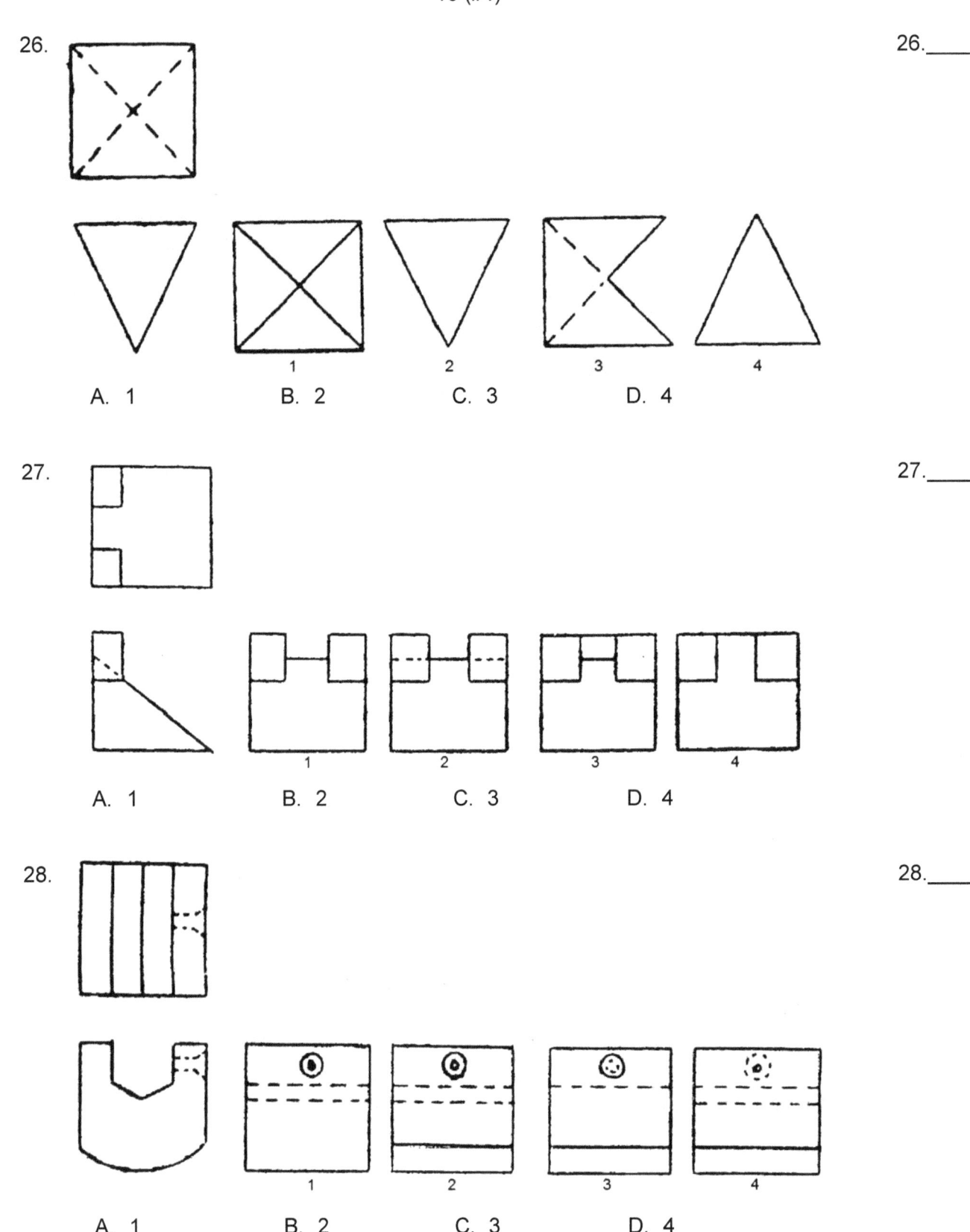

29.

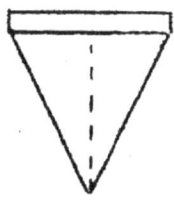 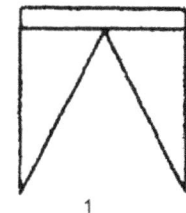 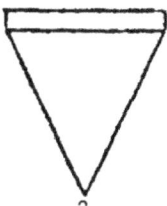 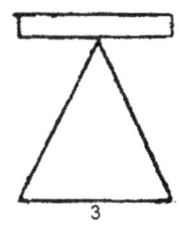 

A. 1　　　B. 2　　　C. 3　　　D. 4

29.____

30.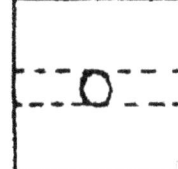

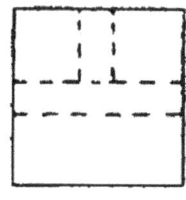 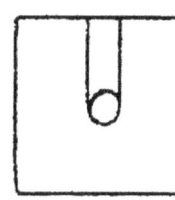 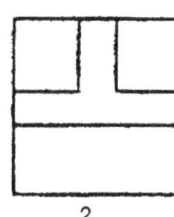 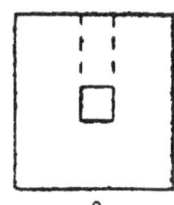 

A. 1　　　B. 2　　　C. 3　　　D. 4

30.____

KEY (CORRECT ANSWERS)

1.	B	11.	A	21.	C
2.	D	12.	D	22.	B
3.	A	13.	C	23.	A
4.	A	14.	C	24.	B
5.	C	15.	B	25.	A
6.	B	16.	B	26.	B
7.	D	17.	D	27.	A
8.	C	18.	C	28.	B
9.	A	19.	A	29.	A
10.	A	20.	B	30.	C

TEST 2

Questions 1-10.

DIRECTIONS: Questions 1 through 10 deal with relationships between sets of figures. For each question, select that choice (A, or B, or C, or D) which has the SAME relationship to Figure 3 that Figure 2 has to Figure 1.

SAMPLE: Study Figures 1 and 2 in the Sample. Notice that Figure 1 has been turned clockwise 1/4 of a turn to get Figure 2. Taking Figure 3 and turning it clockwise 1/4 of a turn, we get choice A, the correct answer.

2 (#2)

Questions 11-16.

DIRECTIONS: Questions 11 through 16 show the top view of an object in the first column, the front view of the same object in the second column and four drawings in the third column, one of which correctly represents the RIGHT side of the object. Select the CORRECT right side view.

As a guide, the first one is an illustrative example, the correct answer of which is C.

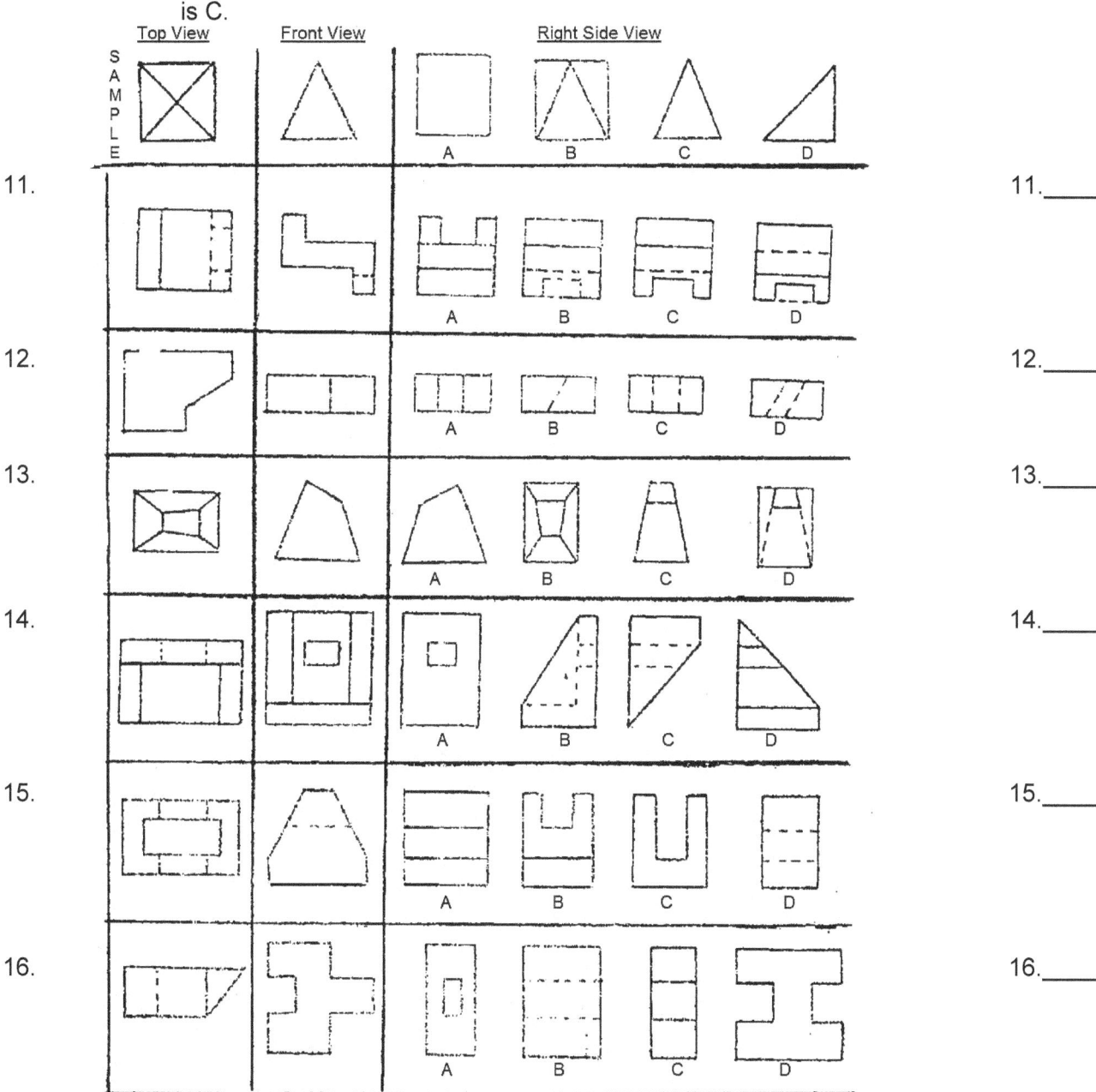

11. _____
12. _____
13. _____
14. _____
15. _____
16. _____

Questions 17-20.

DIRECTIONS: In each of the following groups of drawings, the top view and front elevation of an object are shown on the left. At the right are four drawings, one of which represents the end elevation of the object as seen from the right. Select the drawing which represents the correct end elevation and print the letter in the space at the right.

The first group is shown as an example only.
The correct answer in this group is C.

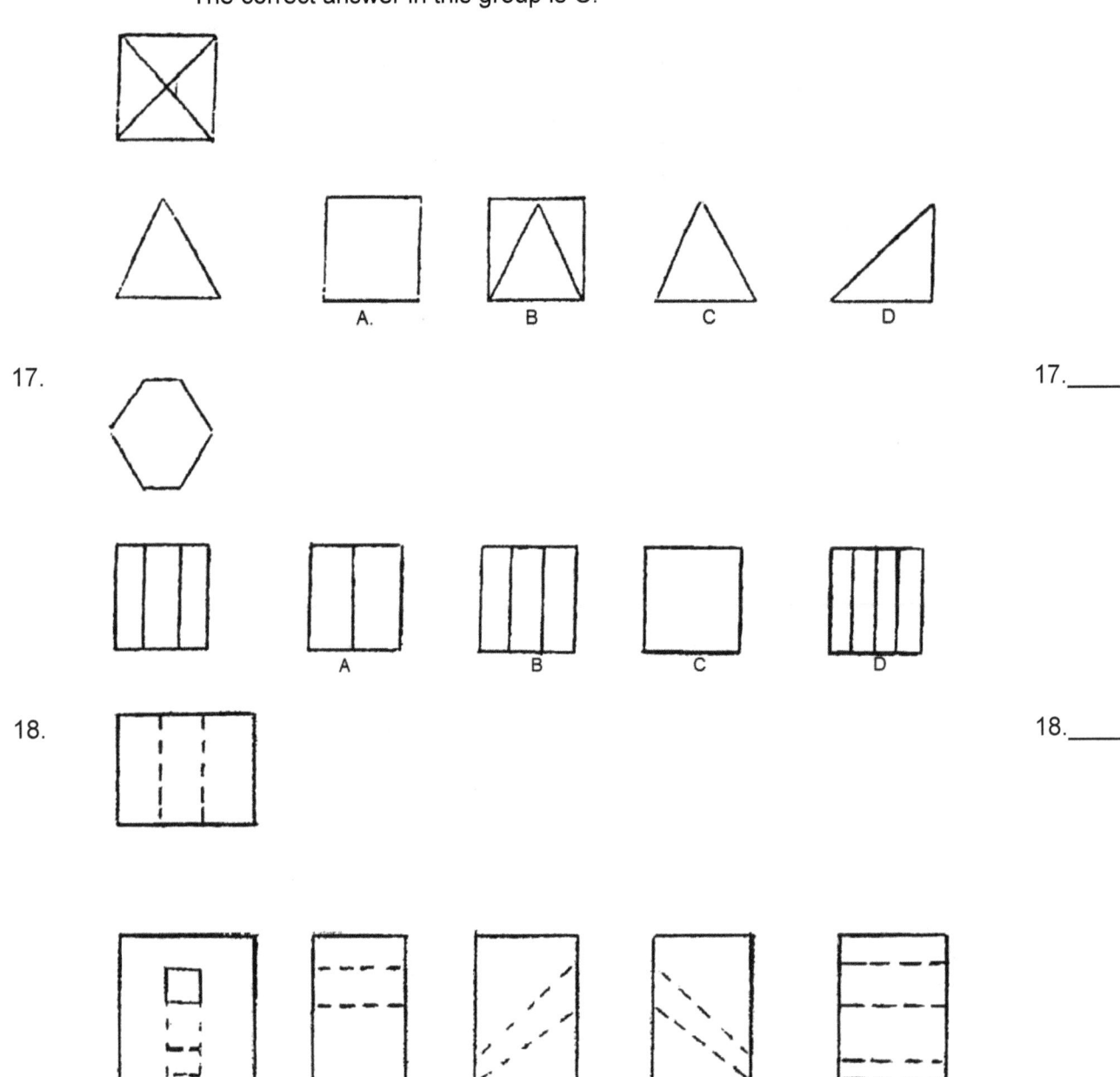

17. _____

18. _____

19.

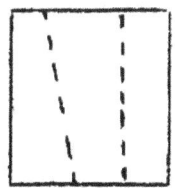  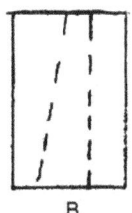 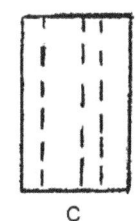 
A B C D

20.

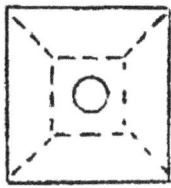 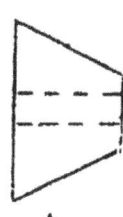 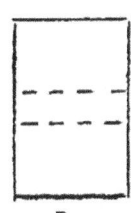  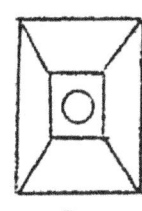
A B C D

KEY (CORRECT ANSWERS)

1.	C	6.	C	11.	C	16.	C
2.	B	7.	A	12.	A	17.	A
3.	D	8.	B	13.	C	18.	C
4.	A	9.	B	14.	B	18.	D
5.	B	10.	D	15.	B	19.	A

FOLLOWING ORAL DIRECTIONS

COMMENTARY

A large part of any job is listening to the supervisor and following his instructions. Since it is important that each employee do exactly as he is instructed, this test is used to make sure that each applicant can and will listen carefully and follow through without extra supervision.

The directions in the test are not hard to follow, but you must listen carefully and do exactly what you are told to do.

In order to do this practice section, you must have a friend who will read the directions to you. *Do not read the material in this section yourself; if you do, you will lose the value of this practice.*

DESCRIPTION OF THE TEST

FOLLOWING ORAL DIRECTIONS - SAMPLE QUESTIONS

The directions are to be read at the rate of 80 words per minute. Since not everybody speaks at this speed, your friend should practice reading the 1-minute practice that follows until he can read it in exactly 1 minute whenever he wants to. He will also need a watch with a second hand. Give the 1-Minute Practice box to your friend to use. (Each friend who is helping you will have to use it to practice, so don't throw it away.)

FOR THE PERSON WHO WILL READ THE FOLLOWING ORAL DIRECTIONS TEST TO YOU

The directions should be read at about 80 words per minute. Practice reading aloud the material in the box below until you can do it in exactly 1 minute. This will give you a feel for the way you should read the test material.

1-MINUTE PRACTICE
(This is for practice in reading aloud. It is not the sample test.)

> Look at line 20 in your work booklet. There are two circles and two boxes of different sizes with numbers in them. If 7 is less than 3 and if 2 is smaller than 4, write a G in the larger circle. Otherwise write B as in baker in the smaller box. Now on your Code Sheet darken the space for the number-letter combination in the box or circle.

When your friend reads the directions to you, listen carefully and do what he says. If you fall behind and miss a direction, don't get
excited. Let that one go and listen for the next one. Since B and D sound very much alike, he will say "B as in baker" when he means B and "D as in dog" when he means D.

He will tell you some things to do with the 5 sample questions below. Then, when he tells you to darken a box on the Sample Answer Sheet, use the one on this page.

SAMPLE QUESTIONS

SAMPLE QUESTIONS

QUESTION 1. 5 ____

QUESTION 2. 1 6 4 3 7

QUESTION 3. D B A E C

QUESTION 4. (8__) (5__) (2__) (9__) (10__)

QUESTION 5. (7__) [6__] (1__) [12__]

SAMPLE ANSWER SHEET

DIRECTIONS to be read. (The words in parentheses should *not* be read aloud. They tell you how long you should pause at the various spots. You should time the pauses with a watch with a second hand. The instruction "Pause slightly" means that you should stop long enough to take a breath.) You should not repeat any directions.

QUESTIONS ON THE SAMPLE

You are to follow the instructions that I read to you. I cannot repeat them.

Look at the Sample Questions. Question 1 has a number and a line beside it. On the line write an A.(Pause 2 seconds.) Now on the Sample Answer Sheet, find number 5 (pause 2 seconds) and darken the box for the letter you just wrote on the line. (Pause 5 seconds.)

Look at Question 2. (Pause slightly.) Draw a line under the third number. (Pause 2 seconds.) Now on the Sample Answer Sheet, find the number under which you just drew a line and darken box B as in baker for that number. (Pause 5 seconds.)

132

Look at the letters in Question 3. (Pause slightly.) Draw a line under the third letter in the line. (Pause 2 seconds.) Now on your . answer sheet, find number 9 (pause 2 seconds) and darken the box for the letter under which you drew a line. (Pause 5 seconds.)

Look at the five circles in Question 4. (Pause slightly.) Each circle has a number and a line in it. Write D as in dog on the blank in the last circle. (Pause 2 seconds.) Now on the Sample Answer Sheet, darken the space for the number-letter combination that is in the circle you just wrote in. (Pause 5 seconds.)

Look at Question 5. (Pause slightly.) There are two circles and two boxes of different sizes with numbers in them. (Pause slightly.) If 4 is more than 2 and if 5 is less than 3, write A in the smaller circle. (Pause slightly.) Otherwise write C in the larger box. (Pause 2 seconds.) Now on the Sample Answer Sheet, darken the space for the number-letter combination in the box or circle in which you just wrote. (Pause 5 seconds.)

Now look at the Sample Answer Sheet. (Pause slightly.) You should have darkened spaces 4B, 5A, 9A, 10D, and 12C on the Sample Answer Sheet.

SUGGESTIONS FOR DOING THE TEST OF FOLLOWING ORAL DIRECTIONS

* Listen carefully to the directions.
* Do exactly what the examiner tells you to do.
* Do not try to get ahead of the examiner.
* If you missed an instruction, wait for the next one.
* Make sure that you darken ONLY one box for each number on the answer sheet.

EXAMINATION SECTION
TEST 1

NOTE: In the examinations the examiner will read aloud directions for you to follow. A sample of directions is given below. The directions are not the same as the directions in the test, but they are somewhat alike. You should have a sheet of lined paper and a pencil as well as the Answer Sheet before you begin.

DIRECTIONS:
1. Fold your lined paper into 4 columns. (Pause for examinee to do this.)
2. In the first column, on the first line, write the number 4. (Pause)
3. On the second line in the same column, write the number 15.
4. Next line, write 12. (Pause)
5. Now go to column 2.
6. Write 35 on the first line (Pause), 26 on the next line, (Pause), and 38 on the third line. (Pause)
7. In column 3, write 11 on the first line (Pause), 18 on the next line (Pause) and 6 last.
8. In column 4, write 16 on the first line next to 4, (Pause), 32 next (Pause) and 19 last.
9. The first number in the first column is 4.
10. Write the letter C next to 4, so it reads 4C. (Pause)
11. The first number in the second column is 35.
12. Write the same letter next to it, so it reads 35C. (Pause)
13. Write C next to the other numbers on the first line, so they read 11C (Pause) and 16C. (Pause)
14. Write the letter A next to each number on the second line, so they read 15A, 26A, etc. (Pause)
15. Write the letter B as in Boy next to each number on the third line. (Pause)
16. Now, take the Answer Sheet you cut out.
17. It has numbers from 1 to 40, and letter spaces.
18. You will mark one space for certain numbers.
19. See how D has been marked for number 1.
20. You will make the same kind of black mark where I tell you. (Pause)
21. Mark 2E. That is, make a black mark at space E for number 2. (Pause)
22. Mark 9C. (Pause)
23. Mark 26C. (Pause)
24. Mark B as in Boy for 15, 16, and 20. (Pause)
25. Mark E for 12, 29, 34, and 39- (Pause)
26. Remember you should *NOT* have more than one mark for any number.
27. If I call a *SECOND* letter for a number where you already have a letter, do *NOT* mark the new letter. Instead, mark the letter A for the number below it.
28. Now I call 2D . You should *1301* mark 2D, because you have already marked 2E. Instead, mark A for the next number.
29. The next number to 2 is 3. So, you should mark 3A. (Pause)
30. Remember to mark A for the *NEXT* number to the one I call if I call a number where you already have a mark.
31. Now I call 28C. (Pause)
32. Next, 9B. (Pause)
33. 17C. (Pause)
34. 12D. (Pause)

35. 26E and 29D. (Pause)
36. Now, take the sheet of lined paper on which you wrote letters and, numbers. (Pause)
37. You will mark the space on your answer sheet for each number and letter you wrote. For example, the first is 4C, so you will mark 4C on your answer sheet.
38. Do *NOT* start until I tell you.
39. Remember: if you have a mark *ALREADY MADE* for a number, do *NOT* mark another letter. If there is already a mark for a number, make *NO* new mark at all.
40. Start to mark, now!

KEY (CORRECT ANSWERS)

1.	11. C	21.	31.
2. E	12. E	22.	32. A
3. A	13. A	23.	33.
4. C	14.	24.	34. E
5.	15. B	25.	35. C
6. B	16. B	26. C	36.
7.	17. C	27. A	37.
8.	18. A	28. C	38. B
9. C	19. B	29. E	39. E
10. A	20. B	30. A	40.

NOTE: ANY OTHER MARK COUNTS AS WRONG. YOU LOSE CREDIT FOR EACH WRONG MARK.

TEST 2

DIRECTIONS: In the test that follows the examiner will read directions aloud and you will mark your -answer sheet as directed.

1. "Mark E for 82, 83, 85, (slight pause) 78, and 102. (Pause)
2. "Mark C for 107, 110, and 103. (Pause)
3. "Mark D as in dog for 101, 110, (slight pause) 76, and 85. (Pause)

"For the next set of questions, mark space E and also mark the letter I call, unless E is already marked. If E is already marked for that number, do not make any mark for that number.

4. "Mark B as in boy for 106, 78, (slight pause) 80, and 84 . (Pause)
5. "Mark A for 108, 104, 83, and 109. (Pause)
6. "Mark C for 79, 102, (slight pause) and 77."

KEY (CORRECT ANSWERS)

76.	D	86.		96.		106.	B, E
77.	C, E	87.		97.		107.	C
78.	E	88.		98.		108.	A, E
79.	C, E	89.		99.		109.	A, E
80.	B, E	90.		100.		110.	C, D
81.		91.		101.	D		
82.	E	92.		102.	E		
83.	E	93.		103.	C		
84.	B, E	94.		104.	A, E		
85.	D, E	95.		105.			

NOTE: ANY OTHER MARK COUNTS AS WRONG. YOU LOSE CREDIT FOR EACH WRONG MARK.

TEST 3

DIRECTIONS:
1. "Mark B as in boy for 29, 12, 17, 38, 8 . (Pause)
2. "Mark D as in dog for 13, 6, 24, 5. (Pause)
3. "Mark A for 40, 27, 1, 15, 9. (Pause)
4. "Mark E for 13, 39, 31, 4, and 10. (Pause)

"For the next set of questions, mark space E and also mark the letter I call, unless E is already marked. If E is already marked for that number, do *NOT* make any mark for that number.

5. "Mark D as in dog for 12, 9, 19, 23, 2. (Pause)
6. "Mark C for 31, 37, 4, 39. (Pause)
7. "Mark B as in boy for 21, 16, 7, 10, and 26."

KEY (CORRECT ANSWERS)

1. A	11.	21. B, E	31. E
2. D, E	12. B, D, E	22.	32.
3.	13. D, E	23. D, E	33.
4. E	14.	24. D	34.
5. D	15. A	25.	35.
6. D	16. B, E	26. B, E	36.
7. B, E	17. B	27. A	37. C, E
8. B	18.	28.	38. B
9. A, D, E	19. D, E	29. B	39. E
10. E	20.	30.	40. A

NOTE: ANY OTHER MARK COUNTS AS WRONG. YOU LOSE CREDIT FOR EACH WRONG MARK.

TEST 4

DIRECTIONS:
1. "Mark A for 59, 33, 44, 66, and 75- (Pause)
2. "Mark B as in boy for 69, 42, 31, and 72. (Pause)
3. "Mark E for 35, 64, 58, 47, and 61. (Pause)

"For the next set of questions, mark space B and also mark the letter I call, unless B is already marked. If B is already marked for that number, do *NOT* mark the new letter. Instead, mark the letter B for the number below it .

4. "Mark D as in dog for 32, 41, 70, and 63. (Pause)
5. "Mark C for 44, 48, 37, 74, and 37 (Pause)
6. "Mark E for 72, 67, 60, 42, and 46. (Pause)
7. "Mark A for 34, 56, 67, 38, and 71."

KEY (CORRECT ANSWERS)

31.	B	46.	B, E	61.	E		
32.	B, D	47.	E	62.			
33.	A	48.	B, C	63.	B, D		
34.	A, B	49.		64.	E		
35.	E	50.		65.			
36.		51.		66.	A		
37.	B, C	52.		67.	B, E		
38.	B	53.		68.	B		
39.	B	54.		69.	B		
40.		55.		70.	B, D		
41.	B, D	56.	A, B	71.	A, B		
42.	B	57.		72.	B		
43.	B	58.	E	73.	B		
44.	A, B, C	59.	A	74.	B, C		
45.		60.	B, E	75.	A		

NOTE: ANY OTHER MARK COUNTS AS WRONG. YOU LOSE CREDIT FOR EACH WRONG MARK.

TEST 5

DIRECTIONS:
1. "Mark C for 73, 96, 84, and 80. (Pause)
2. "Mark D as in dog for 68, 88, 99, 91, 78, and 67. (Pause)
3. "Mark E for 70, 93, 82, 75, and 92. (Pause)
4. "Mark B as in boy for 87, 69, 77, 98, and 71. (Pause)

"For the next set of questions, mark space C and also mark the letter I call, unless C is already marked. If C is already marked for that number, do *NOT* mark the new letter. Instead mark the letter A for the number below it.

5. "Mark D as in dog for 72, 89, 92, and 84. (Pause)
6. "Mark A for 66, 95, 77, and 73. (Pause)
7. "Mark B as in boy for 75, 83, 88, 90, 96, 100, and 94."

KEY (CORRECT ANSWERS)

66. A, C	76.	86.	96. C
67. D	77. A, B, C	87. B	97. A
68. D	78. D	88. B, C, D	98. B
69. B	79. C, D	89. C, D	99. D
70. E	80. C	90. B, C	100. B, C
71. B	81.	91. D	
72. C, D	82. C, D, E	92. E	
73. C	83. B, C	93. E	
74. A	84. C	94. B, C	
75. B, C, E	85. A	95. A, C	

NOTE: ANY OTHER MARK COUNTS AS WRONG. YOU LOSE CREDIT FOR EACH WRONG MARK.

TEST 6

DIRECTIONS:
1. "Mark E for 50, 37, 19, 24, and 11. (Pause)
2. "Mark B as in boy for 16, 22, 40, and 31. (Pause)
3. "Mark D as in dog for 24, 40, 49, 33,' and 17. (Pause)

"For the next set of questions, mark space D as in dog and also mark the letter I call, unless D is already marked. If D is already marked for that number, do *NOT* mark the new letter. Instead mark the letter E for the number above it.

4. "Mark C for 12, 21, 42, and 29. (Pause)
5. "Mark A for 19, 49, 24, 15, 47, and 40. (Pause)
6. "Mark E for 41, 34, 29, and 17."

KEY (CORRECT ANSWERS)

10.	20.	30.	40. B, D
11. E	21. C, D	31. B	41. D, E
12. C, D	22. B	32.	42. C, D
13.	23. E	33. D	43.
14.	24. D, E	34. D, E	44.
15. A, D	25.	35.	45.
16. B, E	26.	36.	46.
17. D	27.	37. E	47. A, D
18.	28. E	38.	48. E
19. A, D, E	29. C, D	39. E	49. D
			50. E

NOTE: ANY OTHER MARK COUNTS AS WRONG. YOU LOSE CREDIT FOR EACH WRONG MARK.

TEST 7

DIRECTIONS:
1. "Mark D as in dog for 79, 51, 69, 42, and 64.(Pause)
2. "Mark A for 44, 62, 51, 59, 50, 42, 76, and 67. (Pause)
3. "Mark C for 64, 73, 80, 49, 55, and 62. (Pause)

"For the next set of questions, mark space A and also the letter I call, unless A is already marked. If A is already marked for that number, do NOT mark the new letter. Instead mark the letter E for that number.

4. "Mark E for 74, 68, 41, 77, and 58. (Pause)
5. "Mark B as in boy for 67, 60, 78, 44, and 76. (Pause)
6. "Mark C for 60, 51, 48, 69, 56, 66, and 79."

KEY (CORRECT ANSWERS)

41. A, E	51. A, D, E	61.	71.	
42. A, D	52.	62. A, C	72.	
43.	53.	63.	73. C	
44. A, E	54.	64. C, D	74. A, E	
45.	55. C	65.	75.	
46.	56. A, C	66. A, C	76. A, E	
47.	57.	67. A, E	77. A, E	
48. A, C	58. A, E	68. A, E	78. A, B	
49. C	59. A	69. A, C, D	79. A, C, D	
50. A	60. A, B, E	70.	80. C	

NOTE: ANY OTHER MARK COUNTS AS WRONG. YOU LOSE CREDIT FOR EACH WRONG MARK.

TEST 8

DIRECTIONS:
1. "Mark C for 37, 8, 29, 23, and 46. (Pause)
2. "Mark E for 50, 4 0, 28, 3, and 29. (Pause)
3. "Mark B as in boy for 38, 26, 23, 45, 47, and 35- (Pause)

"For the next set of questions, mark space C and also the letter I call, unless C... is already marked. If C is already marked for that number, do *NOT* mark the new letter. Instead mark the letter B for the number that is two below it.V-

4. "Mark D as in dog for 48, 14, 8, 23, 33, 18, and 34. (Pause)
5. "Mark A for 42, 2, 16, 43, and 29. (Pause)
6. "Mark E for 4, 41, 48, and 15."

KEY (CORRECT ANSWERS)

1.		16.	A, C	31.	B	46.	C
2.	A, C	17.		32.		47.	B
3.	E	18.	C, D	33.	C, D	48.	C, D
4.	C, E	19.		34.	C, D	49.	
5.		20.		35.	B	50.	B, E
6.		21.		36.			
7.		22.		37.	C		
8.	C	23.	B, C	38.	B		
9.		24.		39.			
10.	B	25.	B	40.	E		
11.		26.	B	41.	C, E		
12.		27.		42.	A, C		
13.		28.	E	43.	A, C		
14.	C, D	29.	C, E	44.			
15.	C, E	30.		45.	B		

NOTE: ANY OTHER MARK COUNTS AS WRONG. YOU LOSE CREDIT FOR EACH WRONG MARK.

TEST 9

DIRECTIONS:
1. "Mark A for 87, 56, 95, 98, 99, 54, 63, and 59. (Pause)
2. "Mark D as in dog for 84, 100, 57, 68, 87, and 60. (Pause)
3. "Mark C for 70, 52, 69, 96, 78, 84, 58, 53, 68, and 76. (Pause)

"For the next set of questions, mark space A and also mark the letter I call, unless A is already marked. If A is already marked for that number, do *NOT* mark the new letter. Instead mark the letter E for the number that is two above it.

4. "Mark B as in boy for 89, 51, 66, 73, 62, and 98. (Pause)
5. "Mark E for 55, 71, 90, 87, 65, 99, and 66. (Pause)
6. "Mark D as in dog for 75, 91, 80, 54, 89, and 95."

KEY (CORRECT ANSWERS)

51.	A, B	66.	A, B	81.		96.	C, E
52.	C, E	67.		82.		97.	E
53.	C	68.	C, D	83.		98.	A
54.	A	69.	C	84.	C, D	99.	A
55.	A, E	70.	C	85.	E	100.	D
56.	A	71.	A, E	86.			
57.	D	72.		87.	A, D, E		
58.	C	73.	A, B	88.			
59.	A	74.		89.	A, B		
60.	D	75.	A, D	90.	A, E		
61.		76.	C	91.	A, D		
62.	A, B	77.		92.			
63.	A	78.	C	93.	E		
64.	E	79.		94.			
65.	A, E	80.	A, D	95.	A		

NOTE: ANY OTHER MARK COUNTS AS WRONG. YOU LOSE CREDIT FOR EACH WRONG MARK.

TEST 10

DIRECTIONS:
1. "Mark E for 87, 12, 93, 29, 9, 94, 16, .33, 21, 59, 67, 43, and 17. (Pause)
2. "Mark C for 82, 7, 63, 37, 97, 55, 39, 5, 47, and 25 (Pause)
3. "Mark B as in boy for 89, 66, 77, 35, 92, 18, 54, 13, 71, and 30. (Pause)

"For the next set of questions, mark space E and also mark the letter I call unless E is already marked. If E is already marked for that number, do *NOT* mark the new letter. Instead mark the letter D for the number that is three above it and the letter A for the number that is three below it.

4. "Mark A for 91, 62, 14, 87, and 33. (Pause)
5. "Mark B as in boy for 51, 11, 98, 51, 68, and 9. (Pause)
6. Mark C for 56, 4l, 28, 94, 43, and 29."

KEY (CORRECT ANSWERS)

#	Ans	#	Ans	#	Ans	#	Ans
1.		26.	D	51.	D, E	76.	
2.		27.		52.		77.	B
3.		28.	C, E	53.		78.	
4.		29.	E	54.	A, B	79.	
5.	C	30.	B, D	55.	C	80.	
6.	D	31.		56.	C, E	81.	
7.	C	32.	A	57.		82.	C
8.		33.	E	58.		83.	
9.	E	34.		59.	E	84.	D
10.		35.	B	60.		85.	
11.	D, E	36.	A	61.		86.	
12.	A, E	37.	C	62.	A, E	87.	E
13.	B	38.		63.	C	88.	
14.	A, E	39.	C	64.		89.	B
15.		40.	D	65.		90.	A
16.	E	41.	C, E	66.	B	91.	A, D, E
17.	E	42.		67.	E	92.	B
18.	B	43.	E	68.	D, E	93.	E
19.		44.		69.		94.	E
20.		45.		70.		95.	
21.	E	46.	A	71.	B	96.	
22.		47.	C	72.		97.	A, C
23.		48.	D	73.		98.	D, E
24.		49.		74.		99.	
25.	C	50.		75.		100.	

NOTE: ANY OTHER MARK COUNTS AS WRONG. YOU LOSE CREDIT FOR EACH WRONG MARK.

HEATING AND ENVIRONMENTAL CONTROL

CONTENTS

		Page
I.	Introduction	1
II.	Definitions	1
III.	Fuels	3
IV.	Central Heating Units	6
V.	Fuel-Burning Procedures and Automatic Firing Equipment	9
VI.	Refractory	11
VII.	Heating Systems	11
VIII.	Domestic Hot Water Jack Stoves (Coal Stoves)	23
IX.	Hazardous Installations	23

HEATING AND ENVIRONMENTAL CONTROL

I. Introduction

The function of a heating system is to provide for human comfort. The variables to be controlled are temperature, air motion, and relative humidity. Temperature must be maintained uniformly throughout the heated area. Field experience indicates a variation from 6 to 10 degrees F from floor to ceiling. The adequacy of the heating device and the tightness of the structure or room determine the degree of personal comfort within the dwelling.

Coal, wood, oil, gas, and electricity are the main sources of heat energy. Heating systems commonly used are steam, hot water, and hot air. The housing inspector should have a knowledge of the various heating fuels and systems to be able to determine their adequacy and safety in operation. To cover fully all aspects of the heating system, the entire area and physical components of the system must be considered.

II. Definitions

A **Anti-flooding Control** — A safety control that shuts off fuel and ignition when excessive fuel accumulates in the appliance.

B **Appliance:**
 1 **High-heat** — a unit that operates with flue entrance temperature of combustion products above 1,500°F.
 2 **Medium heat** — same as high-heat, except above 600°F.
 3 **Low heat** — same as high heat, except below 600°F.

C **Boiler:**
 1 **High pressure** – a boiler furnishing pressure at 15 psi or more.
 2 **Low pressure** — (hot water or steam) — a boiler furnishing steam at a pressure less than 15 psi or hot water not more than 30 psi.

D **Burner** — A device that provides the mixing of fuel, air, and ignition in a combustion chamber.

E **Chimney** — A vertical shaft containing one or more passageways.
 1 **Factory-built chimney** — a tested and accredited flue for venting gas appliances, incinerators and solid or liquid fuel-burning appliances.
 2 **Masonry chimney** — a field-constructed chimney built of masonry and lined with terra cotta flue or firebrick.
 3 **Metal chimney** — a field-constructed chimney of metal.
 4 **Chimney Connector** — A pipe or breeching that connects the heating appliance to the chimney.

F **Clearance** — The distance separating the appliance, chimney connector, plenum, and flue from the nearest surface of combustible material.

G **Central Heating System** — A boiler or furnace, flue connected, installed as an integral part of the structure and designed to supply heat adequately for the structure.

H **Controls:**
 1 **High-low limit control** — an automatic control that responds to liquid level changes and pressure or temperature changes and that limits operation of the appliance to be controlled.

2. **Primary safety control** — the automatic safety control intended to prevent abnormal discharge of fuel at the burner in case of ignition failure or flame failure.

3. **Combustion safety control** — a primary safety control that responds to flame properties, sensing the presence of flame and causing fuel to be shut off in event of flame failure.

I. **Convector** — A convector is a radiator that supplies a maximum amount of heat by convection, using many closely-spaced metal fins fitted onto pipes that carry hot water or steam and thereby heat the circulating air.

J. **Conversion** — a boiler or furnace, flue connected, originally designed for solid fuel but converted for liquid or gas fuel.

K. **Damper** — a valve for regulating draft. Generally located on the exhaust side of the combustion chamber, usually in the chimney connector.

L. **Draft Hood** — a device placed in and made a part of the vent connector (chimney connector or smoke pipe) from an appliance, or in the appliance itself, that is designed to (a) ensure the ready escape of the products of combustion in the event of no draft, back-draft, or stoppage beyond the draft hood; (b) prevent backdraft from entering the appliance; (c) neutralize the effect of stack action of the chimney flue upon appliance operation.

M. **Draft Regulator** — a device that functions to maintain a desired draft in oil-fired appliances by automatically reducing the chimney draft to the desired value. Sometimes this device is referred to, in the field, as air-balance, air-stat, or flue velocity control.

N. **Fuel Oil** — a liquid mixture or compound derived from petroleum that does not emit flammable vapor below a temperature of 125°F.

O. **Heat** — the warming of a building, apartment, or room by a stove, furnace, or electricity.

P. **Heating Plant** — the furnace, boiler, or the other heating devices used to generate steam, hot water, or hot air, which then is circulated through a distribution system. It uses coal, gas, oil, or wood as its source of heat.

Q. **Limit Control** — a thermostatic device installed in the duct system to shut off the supply of heat at a predetermined temperature of the circulated air.

R. **Oil Burner** — a device for burning oil in heating appliances such as boilers, furnaces, water heaters, and ranges. A burner of this type may be a pressure-atomizing gun type, a horizontal or vertical rotary type, or a mechanical or natural draft-vaporizing type.

S. **Oil Stove** — a flue-connected, self-contained, self-supporting oil-burning range or room heater equipped with an integral tank not exceeding 10 gallons; it may be designed to be connected to a separate oil supply tank.

T. **Plenum Chamber** — an air compartment to which one or more distributing air ducts are connected.

U. **Pump, Automatic Oil** — a device that automatically pumps oil from the supply tank and delivers it in specific quantities to an oil-burning appliance. The pump or device is designed to stop pumping automatically in case of a breakage of the oil supply line.

V. **Radiant Heat** — a method of heating a building by means of electric coils, hot water, or steam pipes installed in the floors, walls, or ceilings.

W **Register** — a grille-covered opening in a floor or wall through which hot or cold air can be introduced into a room. It may or may not be arranged to permit closing of the grille.

X **Room Heater** — a self-contained, free-standing heating appliance intended for installation in the space being heated and not intended for duct connection (space heater).

Y **Smoke Detector** — a device installed in the plenum chamber or in the main supply air duct of an air-conditioning system to shut off the blower automatically and close a fire damper in the presence of smoke.

Z **Tank** — a separate tank connected, directly or by pump, to an oil-burning appliance.

AA **Thimble** — a term applied to a metal or terra cotta lining for a chimney or furnace pipe.

BB **Valve — Main Shut-off Valve** — a manually operated valve in an oil line for the purpose of turning on or off the oil supply to the burner.

CC **Vent System** — the gas vent or chimney and vent connector, if used, assembled to form a continuous, unobstructed passageway from the gas appliance to the outside atmosphere for the purpose of removing vent gases.

III. Fuels

A Coal

Classification and composition — the four types of coal are: anthracite, bituminous, sub-bituminous, and lignitic.

Coal is prepared in many sizes and combinations of sizes. The combustible portions of the coal are fixed carbons, volatile matter (hydrocarbons), and small amounts of sulfur. In combination with these are non-combustible elements composed of moisture and impurities that form ash. The various types differ in heat content. The heat content is determined by analysis and is expressed in British Thermal Units (BTU) per pound. The type and size of coal used are determined by the availability and by the equipment in which it is burned.

The type and size of coal must be proper for the particular heating unit; that is, the furnace grate and flue size must be designed for the particular type of coal. Excessive coal gas can be generated through improper firing as a result of improper fuel or improper furnace design, or both.

The owner should be questioned about his procedure for adding coal to his furnace. It should be explained that a period of time must be allowed to pass before damping to prevent the release of excessive coal gas. This should also be done before damping for the night or other periods when full draft is not required.

Improper coal furnace operation can result in an extremely hazardous and unhealthful occupancy — the inspector should be able to offer helpful operational procedures. Ventilation of the area surrounding the furnace is very important in order to prevent heat buildup and to supply air for combustion.

B Fuel Oil

Fuel oils are derived from petroleum, which consists primarily of compounds of hydrogen and carbon (hydrocarbons) and smaller amounts of nitrogen and sulfur.

Classification of fuel oils Domestic fuel oils are controlled by rigid specifications. Six grades of fuel oil arc generally used in healing systems; the lighter two grades arc used primarily for domestic heating.

These grades are:

1 **Grade Number 1** — A volatile, distillate oil for use in burners that prepare fuel for burning solely by vaporization (oil-fired space heaters).

2 **Grade Number 2** — A moderate-weight, volatile, distillate oil used for burners that prepare oil for burning by a combination of vaporization and atomization. This grade of oil is commonly used in domestic heating furnaces.

3 **Grade Number 3** — A low-viscosity, distillate oil used in burners wherein fuel and air are prepared for burning solely by atomization.

4 **Grade Number 4** — A medium-viscosity oil used in burners without preheating. (Small industrial or apartment house applications.)

5 **Grade Number 5** — A medium-viscosity oil used in burners with preheaters that require an oil of lower viscosity than Grade Number 6. (Industrial or apartment house application.)

6 **Grade Number 6** — A high-viscosity oil for use in burners with preheating facilities adequate for handling oil of high viscosity. (Industrial applications.)

7 **Heat content** — Heating values of oil vary from approximately 152,000 BTU per gallon for Number 6 oil to 136,000 BTU per gallon for Number 1.

Oil is more widely used today than coal and provides a more automatic source of heat and comfort. It also requires more complicated systems and controls.

If the oil supply is used within the basement or cellar area, certain basic regulations must be followed (see Figure 1). No more than two 275-gallon tanks may be installed above ground in the lowest story of any one building. The tank shall not be closer than 7 feet horizontally to any boiler, furnace, stove, or exposed flame. Fuel oil lines should be embedded in a concrete or cement floor or protected against damage if they run across the floor. Bach tank must have a shutoff valve that will stop the flow from each tank if a leak develops in the line to or in the burner itself.

The tank or tanks must be vented to the outside, and a gauge showing the quantity of oil in the tank or tanks must be tight and operative. Tanks must be off the floor and on a stable base to prevent settlement or movement that may rupture the connections.

A buried outside tank installation is shown in Figure 2.

C Gas

Commercial gas fuels are colorless gases. Some have a characteristic pungent odor, while others are odorless and cannot be detected by smell. Although gas fuels are easily handled in heating equipment, their presence in air in appreciable quantities becomes a serious health hazard. Gases diffuse readily in the air, making explosive mixtures possible. (A proportion of combustible gas and air that is ignited burns with such a high velocity that an explosive force is created.) Because of these characteristics of gas fuels, precautions must be taken to prevent leaks, and care must be exercised when gas-fired equipment is lit.

Classification of gas - Gas is broadly classified as natural or manufactured.

1. **Manufactured Gas** — This gas as distributed is usually a combination of certain proportions of gases produced by two or more processes as obtained from coke, coal, and petroleum. Its BTU value per cubic foot is generally closely regulated, and costs are determined on a guaran-

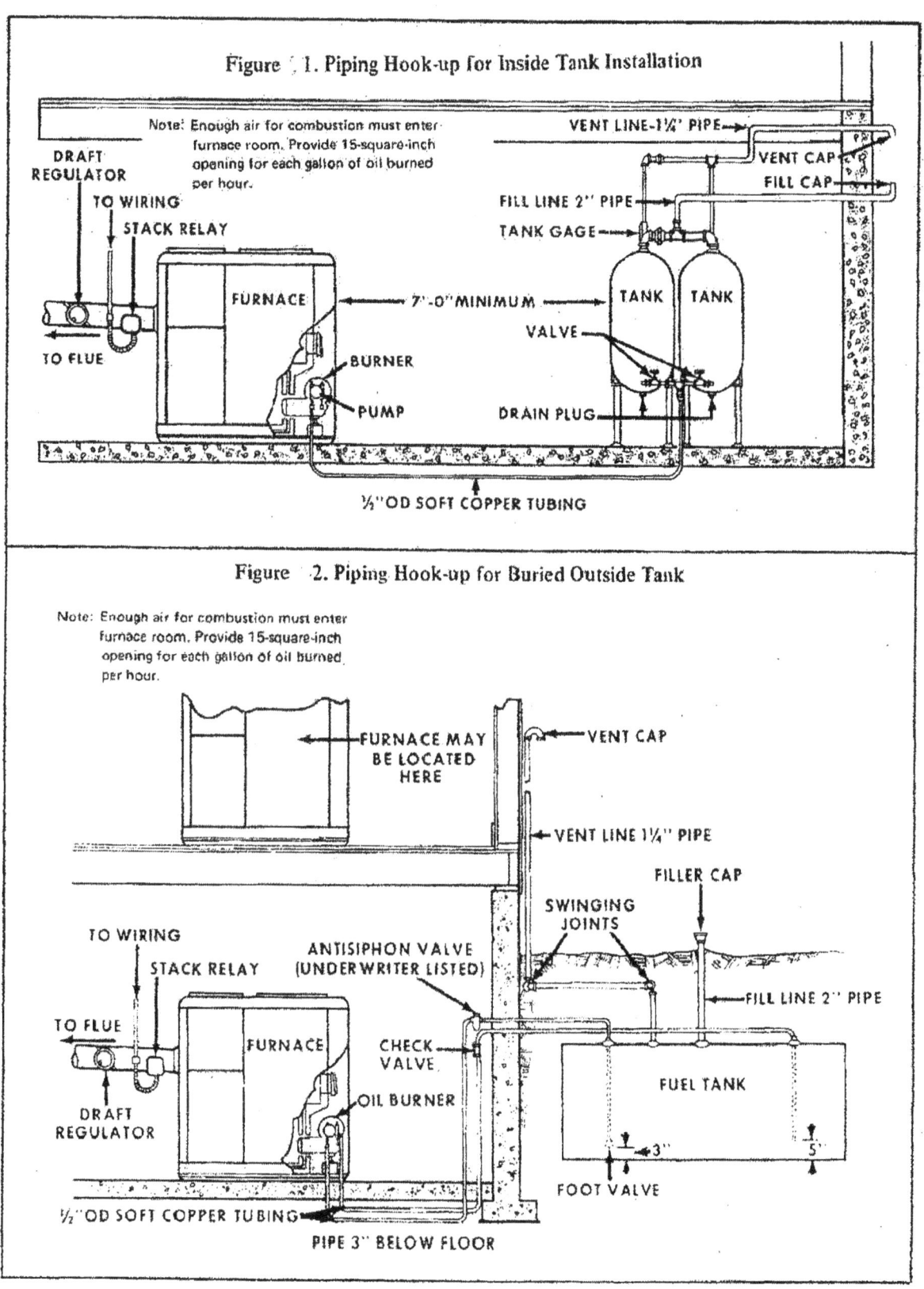

Figure 1. Piping Hook-up for Inside Tank Installation

Figure 2. Piping Hook-up for Buried Outside Tank

teed BTU basis, usually 520 to 540 per cubic foot.

2. **Natural Gas** — This gas is a mixture of several combustible and inert gases. It is one of the richest gases and is obtained from wells ordinarily located in petroleum-producing areas. The heat content may vary from 700 to 1,300 BTU's per cubic foot with a generally accepted average figure of 1,000 BTU's per cubic foot. Natural gases are distributed through pipe lines to point of utilization and are often mixed with manufactured gas to maintain a guaranteed BTU content.

3. **Liquified Petroleum Gas** — Principal products of liquified petroleum gas are butane and propane. Butane and propane are derived from natural gas or petroleum refinery gas and are chemically classified as hydrocarbon gases.

Specifically, butane and propane are on the borderline between a liquid and a gaseous state. At ordinary atmospheric pressure butane is a gas above 33°F and propane a gas at -42°F. These gases are mixed to produce commercial gas suitable for various climatic conditions. Butane and propane are heavier than air. The heat content of butane is 3,274 BTU's per cubic foot while that of propane is 2,519.

The gas burner should be equipped with an automatic cutoff in case the flame fails. Shutoff valves should be located within 1 foot of the burner connection and on the output side of the meter.

CAUTION — Liquified petroleum gas is heavier than air; therefore, the gas will accumulate at the bottom of confined areas. If a leak should develop, care should be taken to ventilate the appliance before lighting.

D Electricity

Electricity is gaining popularity in many regions, particularly where costs are competitive with other sources of heat energy. With an electric system, the housing inspector should rely mainly on the electrical inspector for proper installation. There are a few items, however, to be concerned with to ensure safe use of the equipment. Check to see that the units are accredited testing agency approved and installed according to the manufacturer's specifications. Most convector-type units are required to be installed at least 2 inches above the floor level, not only to ensure that proper convection currents are established through the unit, but also to allow sufficient air insulation from any combustible flooring material. The housing inspector should check for curtains that extend too close to the unit or loose, long pile rugs that are too close. A distance of 6 inches on the floor and 12 inches on the walls should separate rug or curtains from the appliance.

Radiant heating plastered into the ceiling or wall is technical in nature and not a part of the housing inspector's competence. He should, however, be knowledgeable about the system used. These systems are relatively new. If wires are bared in the plastering they should be treated as open and exposed wiring.

IV. Central Heating Units

The boiler should be placed in a separate room whenever possible; in new construction this is usually required. In most housing inspections, however, we are dealing with existing conditions; therefore, we must adapt the situation as closely as possible to acceptable safety standards. In many old buildings the furnace is located in the center of the cellar or basement, and this location does not lend itself for practical conversion to a boiler room.

A Boiler Location

Consider the physical requirements for a boiler room.

1. Ventilation — More circulating air is required for the boiler room than for a habitable room, in order to reduce the heat buildup caused by the boiler or furnace as well as to supply oxygen for combustion.

2. Fire Protection Rating — As specified by various codes (fire code, building code, and insurance underwriters) the fire regulations must be strictly adhered to in areas surrounding the boiler or furnace. This minimum dimension from which a boiler or furnace is to be spaced from a wall or ceiling is shown in Figure 3.

Many times the enclosure of the furnace or boiler creates a problem of providing adequate air supply and ventilation for the room. Where codes and local authority permit, it may be more practical to place the furnace or boiler in an open area. The ceiling above the furnace should be fire protected to a distance of 3 feet beyond all furnace or boiler appurtenances and this area should be free of all storage material. The furnace or boiler should be set on a firm foundation of concrete if located in the cellar or basement. If the codes permit furnace installations on the first floor, then the building code must be consulted for proper setting and location.

B Heating Boilers

Boilers may be classified according to several kinds of characteristics. The material may be cast iron or steel. Their construction may be section, portable, fire-tube, water-tube, or special. Domestic heating boilers are generally of low-pressure type with a maximum working pressure of 15 pounds per square inch for steam and 30 pounds per square inch for hot water.

All boilers have a combustion chamber for burning fuel. Automatic fuel-firing devices help supply the fuel and control the combustion. Handfiring is accomplished by the provision of a grate, ash pit, and controllable drafts to admit air under the fuel bed and over it through slots in the firing door. A check draft is required at the smoke pipe connection to control chimney draft. The gas passes from the combustion chamber to the flue, passages (smoke pipe) designed for maximum possible transfer of heat from the gas. Provisions must be made for cleaning flue passages.

The term boiler is applied to the single heat source that can supply either steam or hot-water (boiler is often called a heater).

Cast iron boilers are generally classified as:
1. Square or rectangular boilers with vertical sections.
2. Round, square, or rectangular boilers with horizontal pancake sections.

Cast iron boilers are usually shipped in sections and assembled at the site.

C Steel Boilers

Most steel boilers are assembled units with welded steel construction and are called portable boilers. Larger boilers are installed in refractory brick settings built on the site. Above the combustion chamber a group of tubes is suspended, usually horizontally, between two headers. If flue gases pass through the tubes and water surrounds them, the boiler is designated as the fire-tube type. When water flows through the tubes, it is termed water-tube. Fire-tube is the predominant type.

D Heating Furnaces

Heating furnaces are the heat sources used when air is the heat-carrying medium. When air circulates because of the different densities of the heated and cooled air, the furnace is a gravity type. A fan may be included for the air circulation; this type is called a mechanical warm-air furnace. Furnaces may be of cast iron or steel and burn various types of fuel.

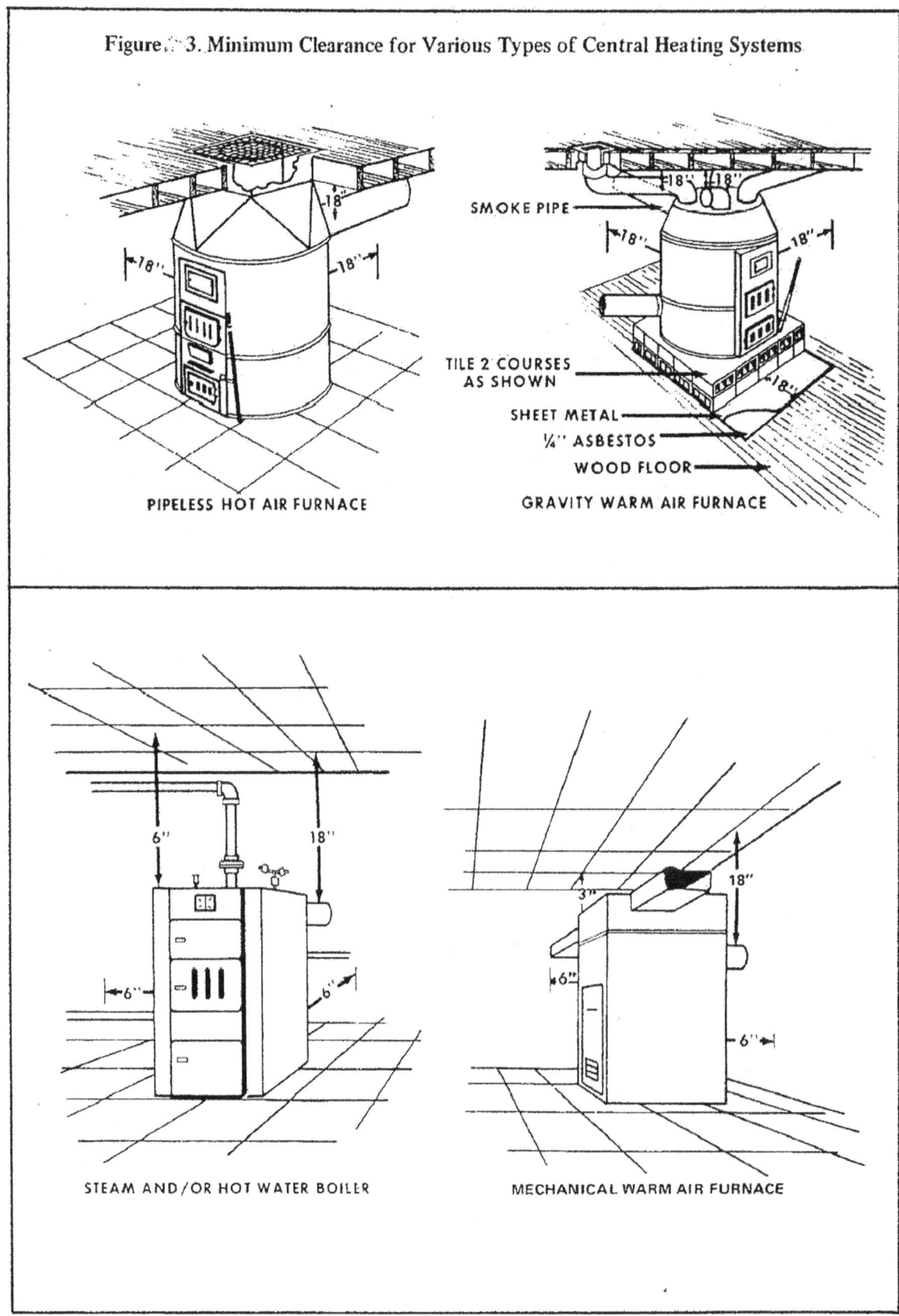

Figure 3. Minimum Clearance for Various Types of Central Heating Systems

V. Fuel-Burning Procedures and Automatic Firing Equipment

A Coal — Many localities throughout the nation still use coal as a heating fuel.

1. **Hand Stoking** - In many older furnaces, the coal is stoked or fed into the fire box by hand.

2. **Automatic Stokers** - The single-retort, underfeed-type bituminous coal stoker is the most commonly used domestic-type steam or hot water boiler (see Figure 4). The stoker consists of a coal hopper, a screw for conveying coal from hopper to retort, a fan that supplies air for combustion, a transmission for driving coalfeed and fan, and an electric motor for supplying power. The air for combustion is admitted to the fuel through tuyeres at the top of the retort. The stoker feeds coal to the furnace intermittently in accordance with the temperature or pressure demands.

B Oil Burners — Oil burners are broadly designated as distillate, domestic, and commercial or industrial. Distillate burners are usually found in oil-fired space heaters. Domestic oil burners are usually power driven and are used in domestic heating plants. Commercial or industrial burners are used in larger central-heating plants for steam or power generation.

1. **Domestic Oil Burners** — These vaporize and atomize the oil, and deliver a predetermined quantity of oil and air to the combustion chambers. Domestic oil burners operate automatically to maintain a desired temperature.

   a. **Gun-type burners** — These burners atomize the oil either by oil pressure or by low-pressure air forced through a nozzle.

The oil system pressure atomizing burner (see Figure 5) consists of a strainer, pump, pressure-regulating valve, shutoff valve, and atomizing nozzle. The air system consists of a power-drive fan and an air tube that surrounds the nozzle and electrode assembly. The fan and oil pump are generally connected directly to the motor. Oil pressures normally used are about 100 pounds per square inch, but pressures con-

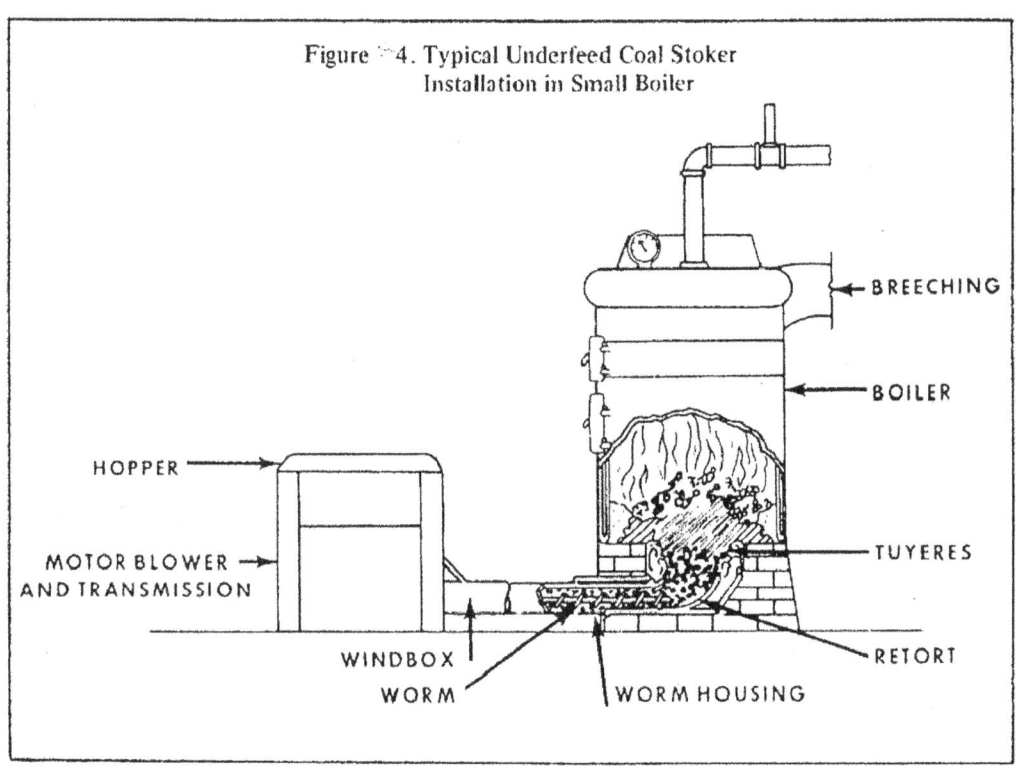

Figure 4. Typical Underfeed Coal Stoker Installation in Small Boiler

siderably in excess of this are sometimes used.

The form and parts of low-pressure air-atomizing burners (see Figure 5), are similar to high-pressure atomizing burners except for addition of a small air pump, and a different way of delivering air and oil to the nozzle or orifice.

b **Vertical rotary burners** - The atomizing-type burner, sometimes known as a radiant or suspended-flame burner, atomizes oil by throwing it from the circumference of a rapidly rotating motor-driven cup. The burner is installed so that the driving parts are protected from the heat of the flame by a hearth of refractory material at about the grate elevation. Oil is fed by pump or gravity, while the draft is mechanical or a combination of natural and mechanical.

c **Horizontal rotary burners** These were originally designed for commercial and industrial use but are available in sizes suitable for domestic use. In this burner, oil is atomized by being thrown in a

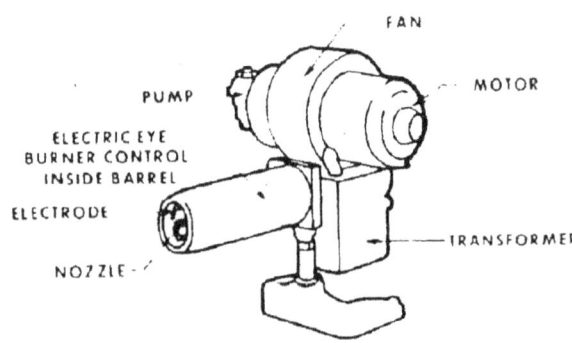

Figure 5. Cut-Away of Typical High-Pressure Gun-Burner

conical spray from a rapidly rotating cup. Horizontal rotary burners employ electric-gas or gas-pilot ignition and operate with a wide range of fuels, primarily with Numbers 1 and 2 fuel oil. Primary safety controls for burner operation are. necessary. An anti-flooding device must be a part of the system so that, if ignition in the burner should fail, the oil will not continue to flow. Likewise, a stack control is necessary to shut off the burner if the stack temperatures become excessive. A reset button on the older stack control units releases if excessive (predetermined) temperatures are exceeded and thus cuts off all power to the burner. This button must be reset before starting can be attempted. The newer models now use electric eye-type control on the burner itself.

2 **Ignition** — On the basis of the method employed to ignite fuels, burners are divided into five groups as follows:

a **Electric** — A high-voltage electric spark is made in the path of an oil and air mixture and this causes ignition. This electric spark may be continuous or may be in operation only long enough to ignite the oil. Electric ignition is almost universally used. Electrodes are located near the nozzles (see Figure 5) but not in the path of the oil spray.

b **Gas pilot** — A small gas pilot light that burns continuously is frequently used. Gas pilots usually have expanding gas valves that automatically increase flame size when motor circuit starts. After a fixed interval, the flame reverts to normal size.

c. **Electric gas** — An electric spark ignites a gas jet, which in turn ignites the oil air mixture.

d **Oil pilot** — A small oil flame is used.

e **Manual** — A burning wick or torch is placed in the combustion space through peepholes and thus ignites the charge. Operator should stand to one side of the fire door to guard against injury from chance explosion.

VI. Refractory

The refractory lining or material should be an insulating fireproof brick-like substance. Never use ordinary firebrick. The insulating brick should be set on end so as to build a 2 inch-thick wall in the pot. Size and shape of the refractory pot vary from furnace to furnace (see Figure 6 for various shapes). The shape can be either round or square, whichever is more convenient to build. It is important to use a special cement having properties similar to that of the insulating refractory-type brick.

VII. Heating Systems

A Steam Heating Systems - Steam heating systems are classified according to the pipe arrangement, accessories used, method of returning the con-densate to the boiler, method of expelling air from the system, or the type of control employed. The successful operation of a steam heating system consists of generating steam in sufficient quantity to equalize building heat loss at maximum efficiency, expelling entrapped air, and returning all condensate to the boiler rapidly. Steam cannot enter a space filled with air or water at pressure equal to the steam pressure. It is important, therefore, to eliminate air and to remove water from the distribution system. All hot pipe lines exposed to contact by residents must be properly insulated or guarded.

Steam heating systems are classified according to the method of returning the condensate to the boiler.

1 Gravity One-pipe Air-vent System — The gravity one-pipe air-vent system is one of the earliest types used. The condensate is returned to the boiler by gravity. This system is generally found in one-building-type heating systems. The steam is supplied by the boiler and carried through a single system or pipe to radiators as shown in Figure 7. Return of the condensate is dependent on hydrostatic head. Therefore, the end of the steam main, where it attaches to the boiler, must be full of water (termed a wet return) for a distance above the boiler line to create a pressure drop balance between the boiler and the steam main.

Radiators are equipped with an inlet valve and with an air valve (see Figure 8). The air valve permits venting of air from the radiator and its displacement by steam. Condensate is drained from the radiator through the same pipe that supplies steam.

2 Two-pipe Steam Vapor System with Return Trap — The two-pipe vapor system with boiler return trap and air eliminator is an improvement of the one-pipe system. The return connection of the radiator has a thermostatic trap that permits flow of condensate and air only from the radiator and prevents steam from leaving the radiator. Since the return main is at atmospheric pressure or less, a boiler return trap is installed to equalize condensate return pressure with boiler pressure.

B **Hot Water Heating Systems** — All hot water heating systems are similar in design and operating principle.

1 One-pipe Gravity System —The one-pipe gravity hot water heating system is the most elementary of the gravity systems and is shown in Figure 9. Water is heated at the lowest point in the system. It rises through a single main because of a difference in density between hot and cold water. The supply rise or radiator branch takes off from the top of the main to supply water to the radiators. After the water gives up heat in the radiator it goes back to the same main through return piping from the radiator. This cooler return water mixes with water in the supply main and causes the water to cool a little. As a result, the next radiator on the system has a lower emission rate and must be larger.

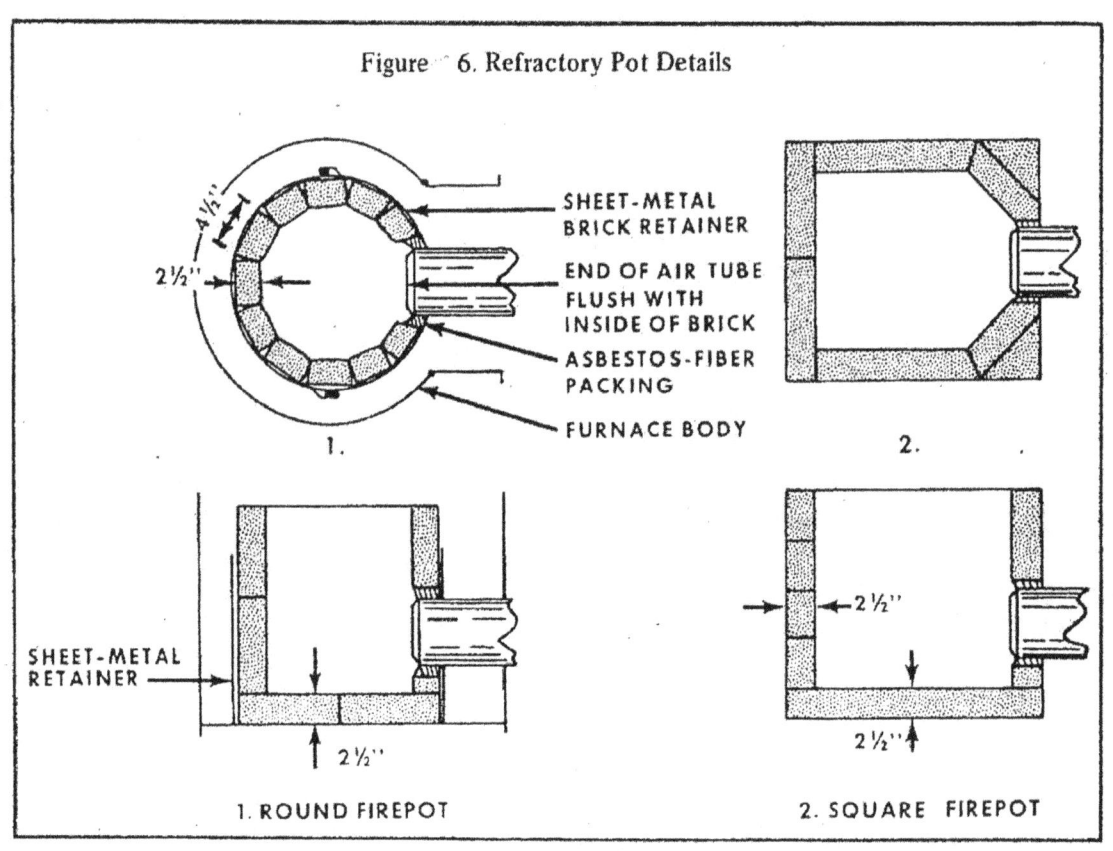

Figure 6. Refractory Pot Details

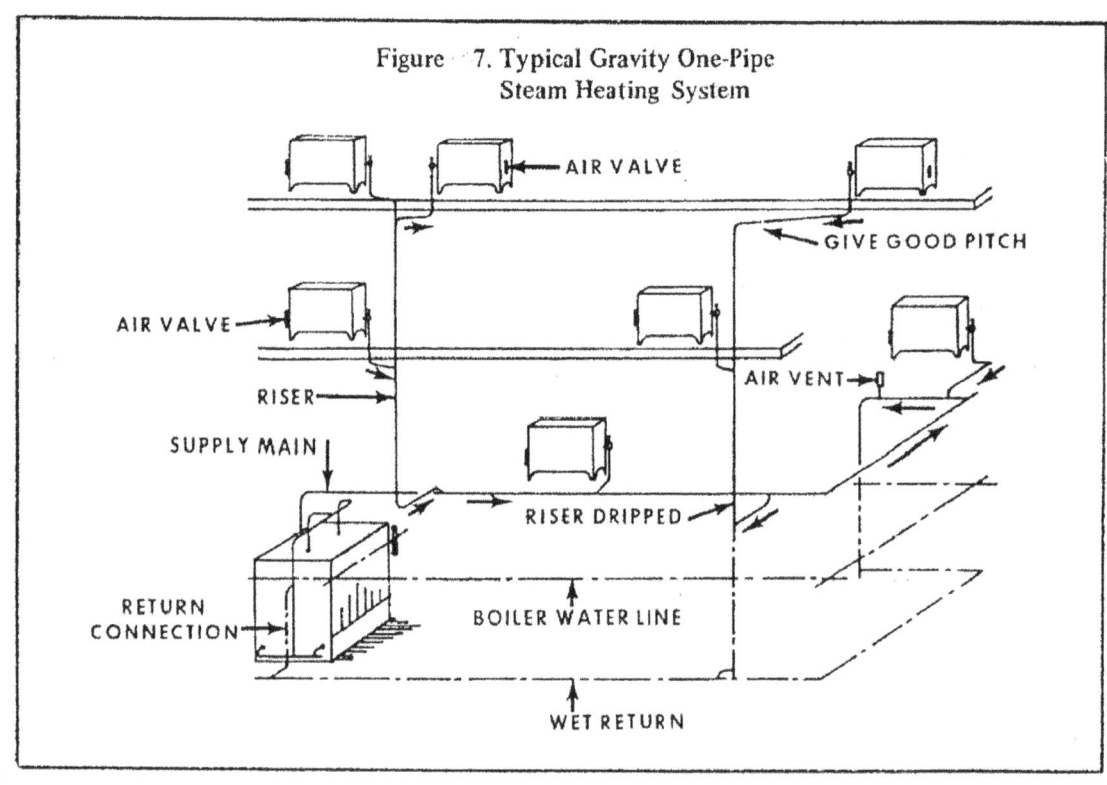

Figure 7. Typical Gravity One-Pipe Steam Heating System

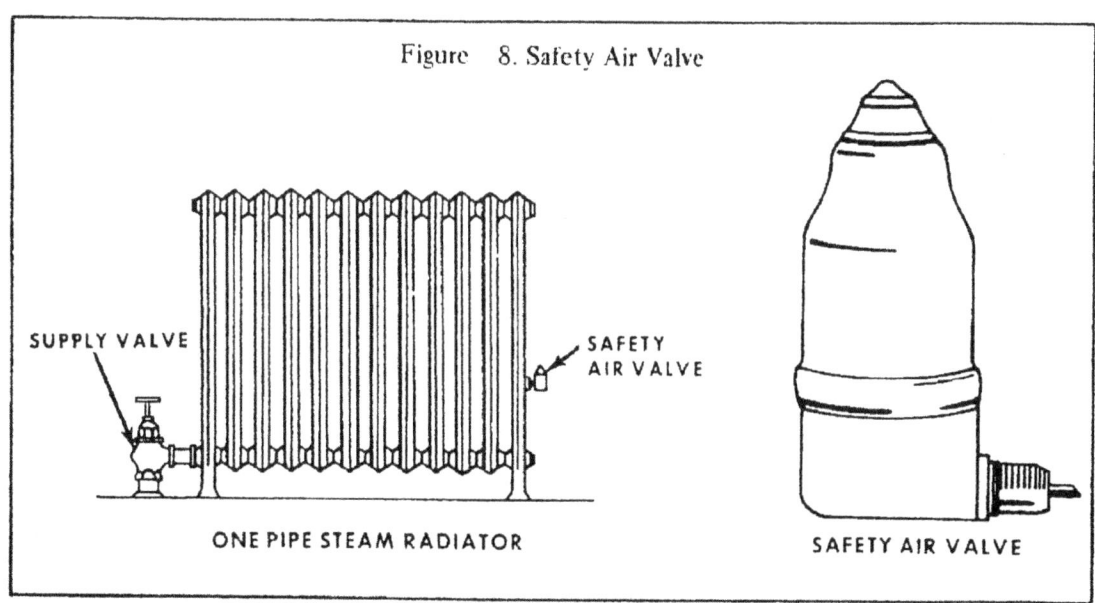

Figure 8. Safety Air Valve

Note in Figure 9 that the high points of the hot water system are vented and the low points are drained. In this case, the radiators are the high points and the heater is the low point.

2 **One-pipe Forced-feed System** — If a pump or circulator is introduced in the main near the heater of the one-pipe system, we have a forced system that can be used for much larger applications than the gravity type. This system can operate at higher water temperatures than the gravity system. The faster moving higher temperature water "Hakes a more responsive system with a smaller temperature drop through each radiator. Higher operating temperatures and lower temperature drops permit the use of smaller radiators for the same heating load.

3 **Two-pipe Gravity Systems** — One-pipe gravity systems may become a two-pipe system if the return radiator branch connects to a second main that returns water to the heater (see Figure 10). Water temperature is practically the same in all the radiators.

4 **Two-pipe Forced-circulation System** — This system is similar to a one-pipe forced-circulation system except that the same piping arrangement is found in the two-pipe gravity flow system.

5 **Expansion Tanks** — When water is heated it tends to expand. Therefore, in a hot water system an expansion tank is necessary. The expansion tank, either of open or closed type, must be of sufficient size to permit a change in water volume within the heating system. If the expansion tank is of the open type it must be placed at least 3 feet above the highest point of the system. It will require a vent and an overflow. The open tank is usually in an attic, where it needs protection from freezing.

The enclosed expansion tank is found in modern installations. An air cushion in the tank compresses and expands according to the change of volume and pressure in the system. Closed tanks are usually at the low point in the system and close to the heater. They can, however, be placed at almost any location within the heating system.

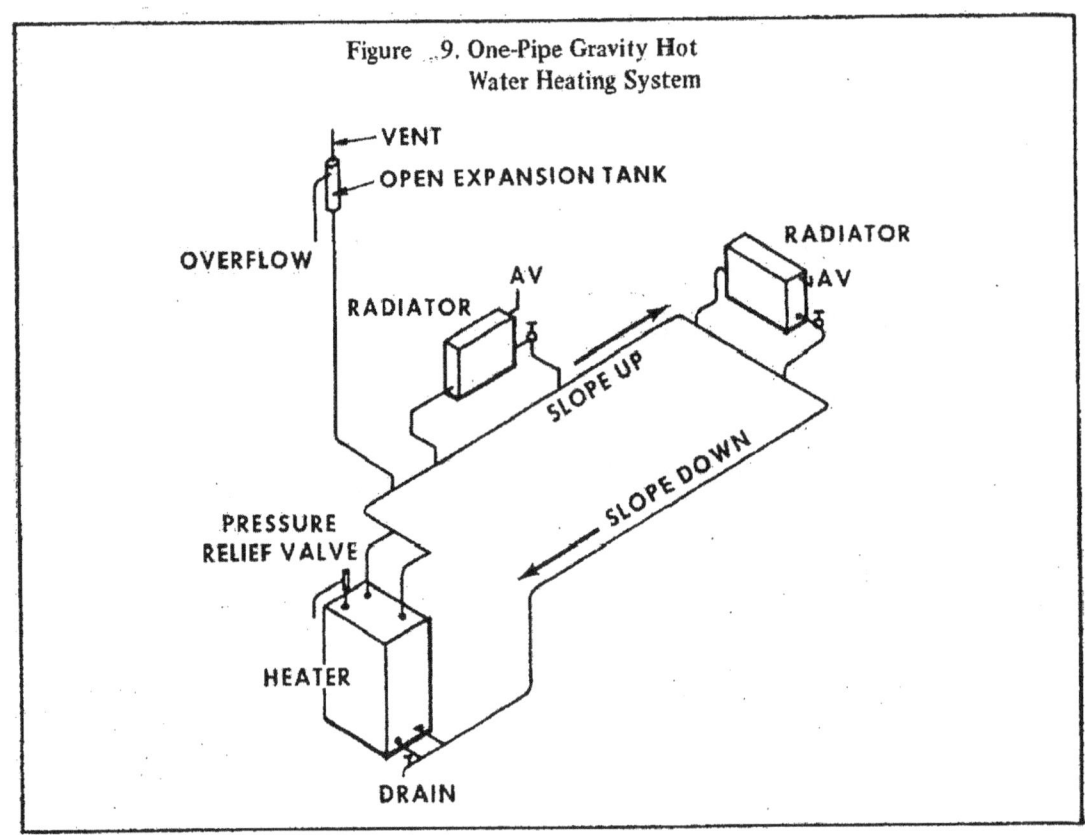

Figure 9. One-Pipe Gravity Hot Water Heating System

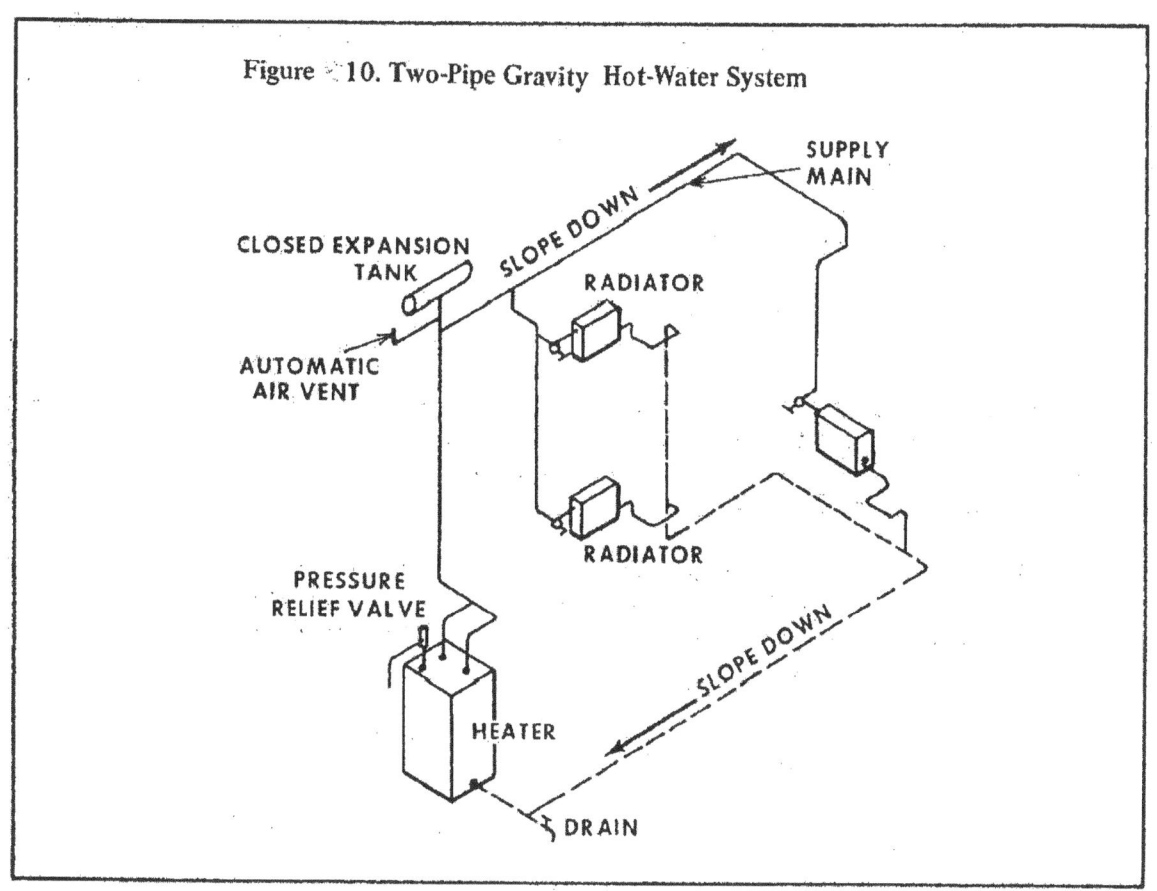
Figure 10. Two-Pipe Gravity Hot-Water System

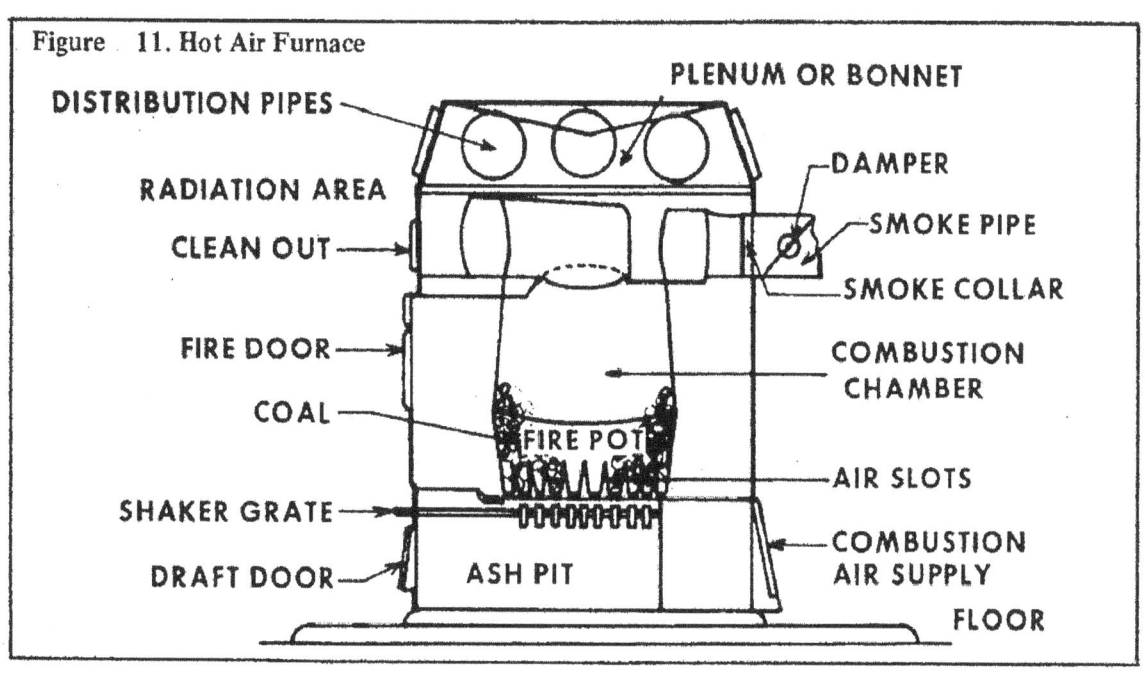
Figure 11. Hot Air Furnace

COAL NOTES

1. Approximately 12 pounds of air is required for complete combustion of 1 pound of hard coal.

2. Approximately 5 pounds of hard coal is consumed per hour for each square foot of grate area.

3. Approximately 12 inches of fire bed will heat most efficiently.

4. Anthracite coal burns more slowly than soft coal, is cleaner to handle-hence more widely used.

5. Large-size coal does not compact-hence the air spaces are too great and allows gases to escape into the flue unburned. Small size coal compacts too much and inhibits airflow through the coal to allow for good combustion. Mixing of coal size is recommended, i.e., stove and chestnut.

6. Fires burn best when the weather is clear and cold, because of reduced atmospheric pressure on the air in the flue—hence greater draft velocity. During periods of heavy atmosphere or rainy weather the temperature of flue gases must exceed normal temperatures to overcome the heavier atmospheric weight.

7. During extreme cold weather, coal should be added to a fire once in approximately 8 hours; moderate weather-12 hours.

C **Hot Air Heating Systems**

1. **Gravity-Warm-Air Heating Systems** — These operate because of the difference in specific gravity of warm air and cold air. Warm air is lighter than cold air and rises if cold air is available to replace it (see Figure 11).

   a **Operation** — Satisfactory operation of a gravity-warm-air heating system depends on three factors. They are: (1) size of warm air and cold ducts, (2) heat loss of the building, (3) heat available from the furnace.

   b **Heat distribution** — The most common source of trouble in these systems is insufficient pipe area usually in the return or cold air duct. The total cross-section area of the cold duct or ducts must be at least equal to the total cross-section area of all warm ducts.

   c **Pipeless furnaces** — The pipeless hot-air furnace is the simplest type of hot-air furnace and is suitable for small homes where all rooms can be grouped about a single large register (see Figure 3). Other pipeless gravity furnaces are often installed at floor level. These are really oversized jacketed space heaters. The most common difficulty experienced with this type of furnace is supplying a return air opening of sufficient size on the floor.

2. **Forced-Warm-Air Heating** Systems — The mechanical warm-air furnace is the most modern type of warm-air equipment (see Figure 12). It is the safest type because it operates at low temperatures. The principle of a forced-warm-air heating system is very similar to that of the gravity system, except that a fan or blower is added to increase air movement. Because of the assistance of the fan or blower, the pitch of the ducts or leaders can be disregarded and it is therefore practical to deliver heated air in the most convenient places.

   a **Operation** — In a forced-air system, operation of the fan or blower must be controlled by air temperature in a bonnet or by a blower control furnacestat. The blower control starts the fan or blower when the temperature reaches a certain point and turns the fan or blower off when the temperature drops to a predetermined point.

   b **Heat distribution** — Dampers in the various warm-air ducts control distribution

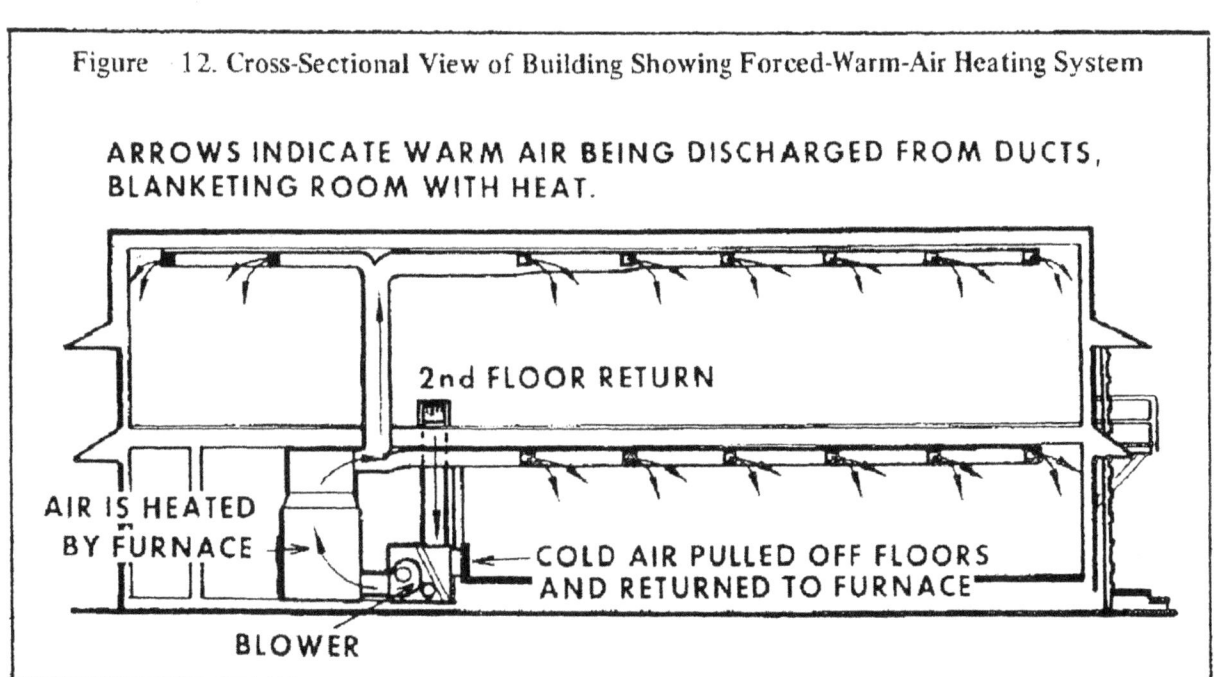

Figure 12. Cross-Sectional View of Building Showing Forced-Warm-Air Heating System

of warm air either at the branch takeoff or at the warm-air outlet.

Humidifiers are often mounted in the supply bonnet in order to regulate the humidity within the residence.

D Space Heaters — Space unit heaters are the least desirable from the viewpoint of fire safety and housing inspection. All space unit heaters must be vented to the flue.

1 Coal-Fired Space Heaters (Cannon stove) — This is illustrated in Figure 13 and is made entirely of cast iron. In operation, coal on the grates receives primary air for combustion through the grates from the ash-door draft intake. Combustible gases driven from the coal by heat burn in the barrel of the stove, where they received additional or secondary air through the feed door. Side and top of the stove absorb the heat of combustion and radiate it to the surrounding space.

2 Oil-Fired Space Heaters — Oil-fired space heaters have atmospheric vaporizing-type burners. The burners require a light grade of fuel oil that vaporizes easily and is comparatively low in temperature. In addition, the oil must be such that it leaves only a small amount of carbon residue and ash within the heater. Oil-fired space heaters are basically of two types:

a Perforated-sleeve burner — The perforated-sleeve burner (see Figure 14) consists essentially of a metal base formed of two or more angular fuel-vaporizing bowl burners (see Figure 15) and is widely used in space heaters and some water heaters.

The burner consists essentially of a bowl, 8 to 13 inches in diameter, with perforations in the side that admit air for combustion. The upper part of the bowl has a flame ring or collar. When several space heaters are installed in a building, an oil supply from an

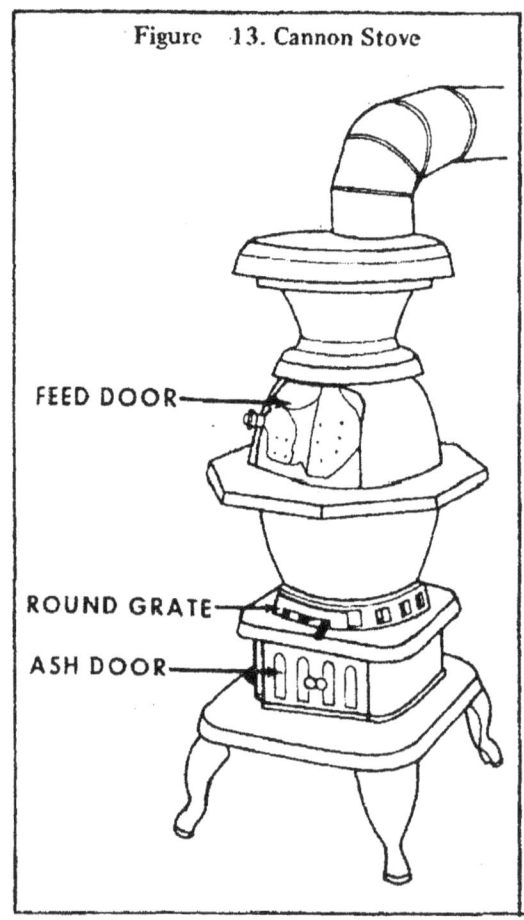

Figure 13. Cannon Stove

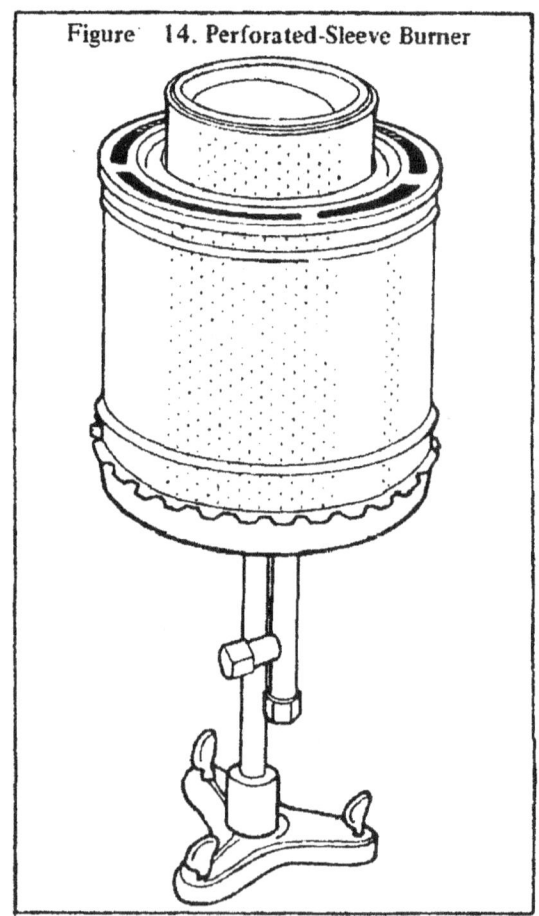

Figure 14. Perforated-Sleeve Burner

outside tank to all heaters is often desirable. Figure 16 shows the condition of a burner flame with different rates of fuel flow and indicates the ideal flame height.

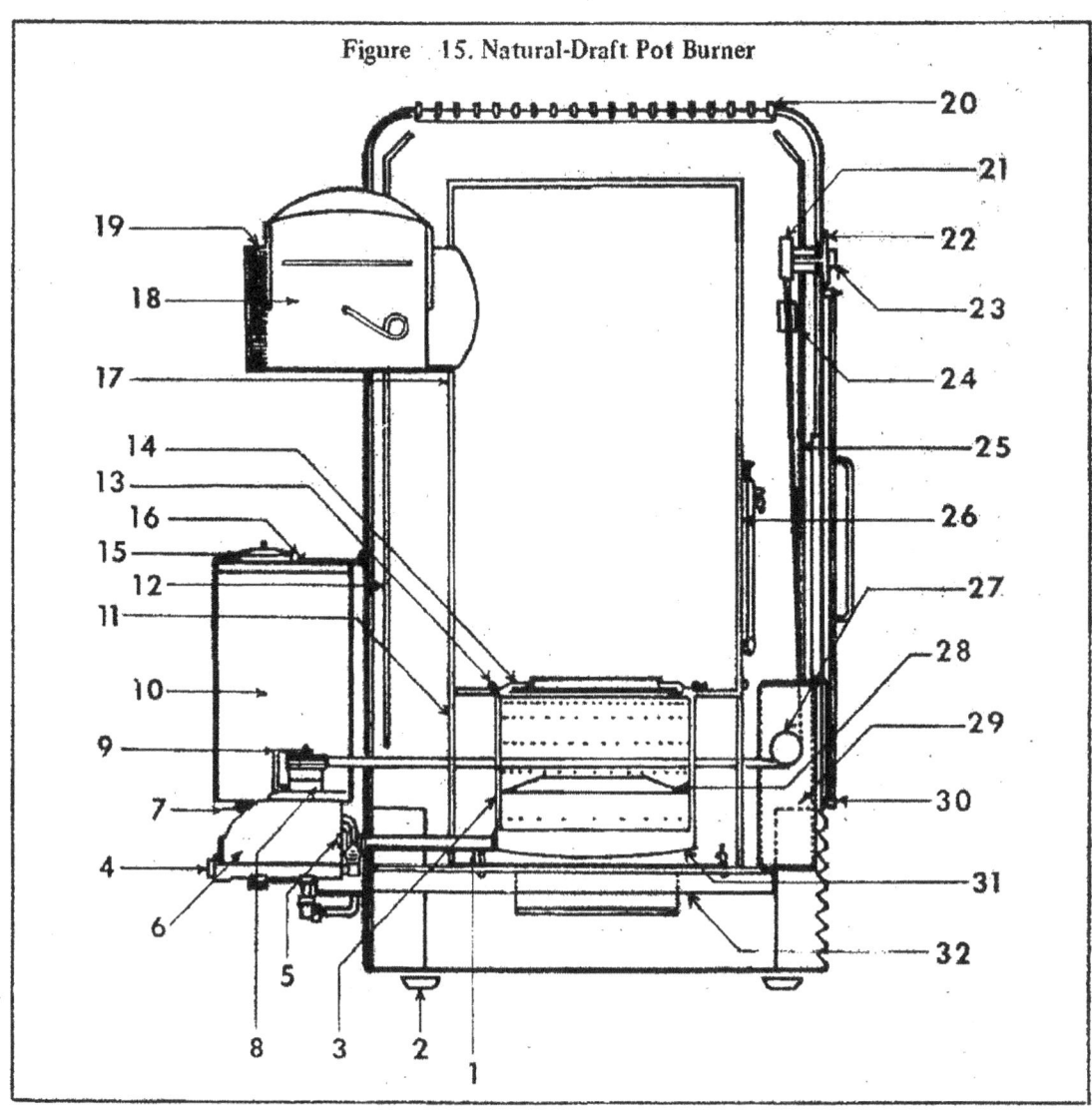

Figure 15. Natural-Draft Pot Burner

1 Burner-pot pipe.
2 Leg Leveler.
3 Pilot-ring clip.
4 Strainer unit.
5 Burner-pot drain plug.
6 Constant-level valve.
7 Tank valve.
8 Control drum (to fit 6).
9 Control pulley bracket
10 Fuel tank.
11 Lower heat unit.
12 Heat shield (rear).
13 Burner-ring clamp.
14 Burner-top ring.
15 Fuel tank cap.
16 Tank fuel gauge.
17 Heat unit.
18 Cold draft regulator.
19 Flue connections, 6-inch diameter.
20 Top grille.
21 Dial control drum.
22 Escutcheon plate.
23 Dial control knob.
24 Pulley assembly (short).
25 Heat shield (front).
26 Heat-unit door.
27 Pulley assembly (long).
28 Pilot ring.
29 Humidifier.
30 Trim bar.
31 Burner pot.
32 Heat-unit support.

3 Gas-Fired Space Heaters—There are three types of gas-fired space heaters: natural, manufactured, and liquified petroleum gas. Space heaters using natural, manufactured, or liquified petroleum gases have a similar construction. All gas-fired space heaters must be vented to prevent a dangerous buildup of poisonous gases.

Each unit console consists of an enamel steel cabinet with top and bottom circulating grilles or openings, gas burners, heating element, gas pilot, and gas valve (see Figure 17). The heating element or combustion chamber is usually cast iron.

CAUTION: All gas-fired space heaters and their connections must be of the type approved by the American Gas Association (AGA). They must be installed in accordance with the recommendations of that organization or the local code.

a Venting — Use of proper venting materials and correct installation of venting for gas-fired space heaters is necessary to minimize harmful effects of condensation and to ensure that combustion products are carried off. (Approximately 12 gallons of water are produced in the burning of 1,000 cubic feet of natural gas. The inner surface of the vent must therefore be heated above the dewpoint of the combustion products to prevent water. from forming in the flue.) A horizontal vent must be given an upward pitch of at least 1 inch per foot of horizontal distance.

When the smoke pipe extends through floors or walls the metal pipe must be insu-

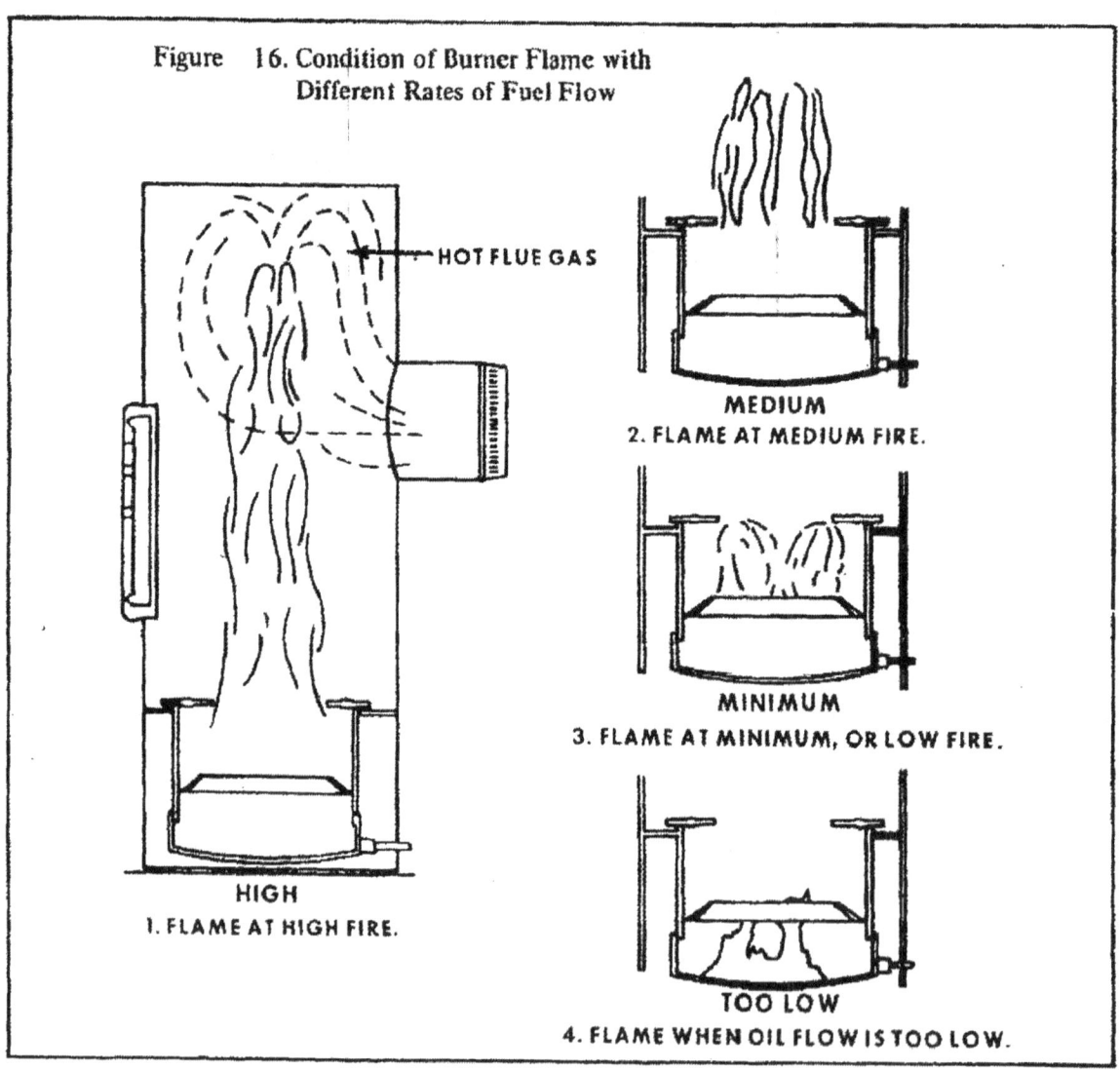

Figure 16. Condition of Burner Flame with Different Rates of Fuel Flow

1. FLAME AT HIGH FIRE.
2. FLAME AT MEDIUM FIRE.
3. FLAME AT MINIMUM, OR LOW FIRE.
4. FLAME WHEN OIL FLOW IS TOO LOW.

lated from the floor or wall system by an air space (see Figure 18). Avoid sharp bends. A 90° vent elbow has a resistance to flow equivalent to a straight section of pipe having a length of 10 times the elbow diameter. Be sure vent is of a rigid construction and resistant to corrosion by flue gas products. Several types of venting material are available such as B-vent and several other ceramic-type materials. A chimney lined with fire-brick type of terra cotta must be relined with an acceptable vent material if it is to be used for venting gas-fired appliances.

Use the same size vent pipe throughout its length. Never make a vent smaller than heater outlet except when two or more vents converge from separate heaters. To determine the size of vents beyond the point of convergence, add one-half the area of each vent to the area of the largest heater's vent.

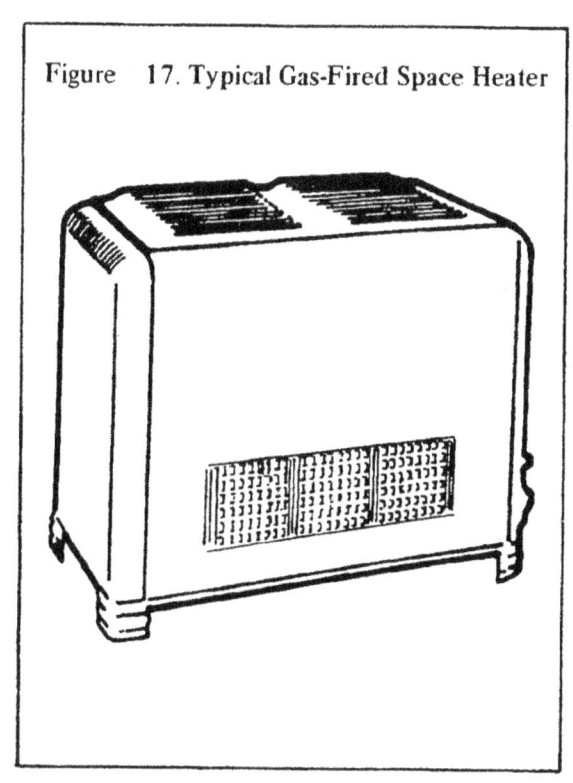

Figure 17. Typical Gas-Fired Space Heater

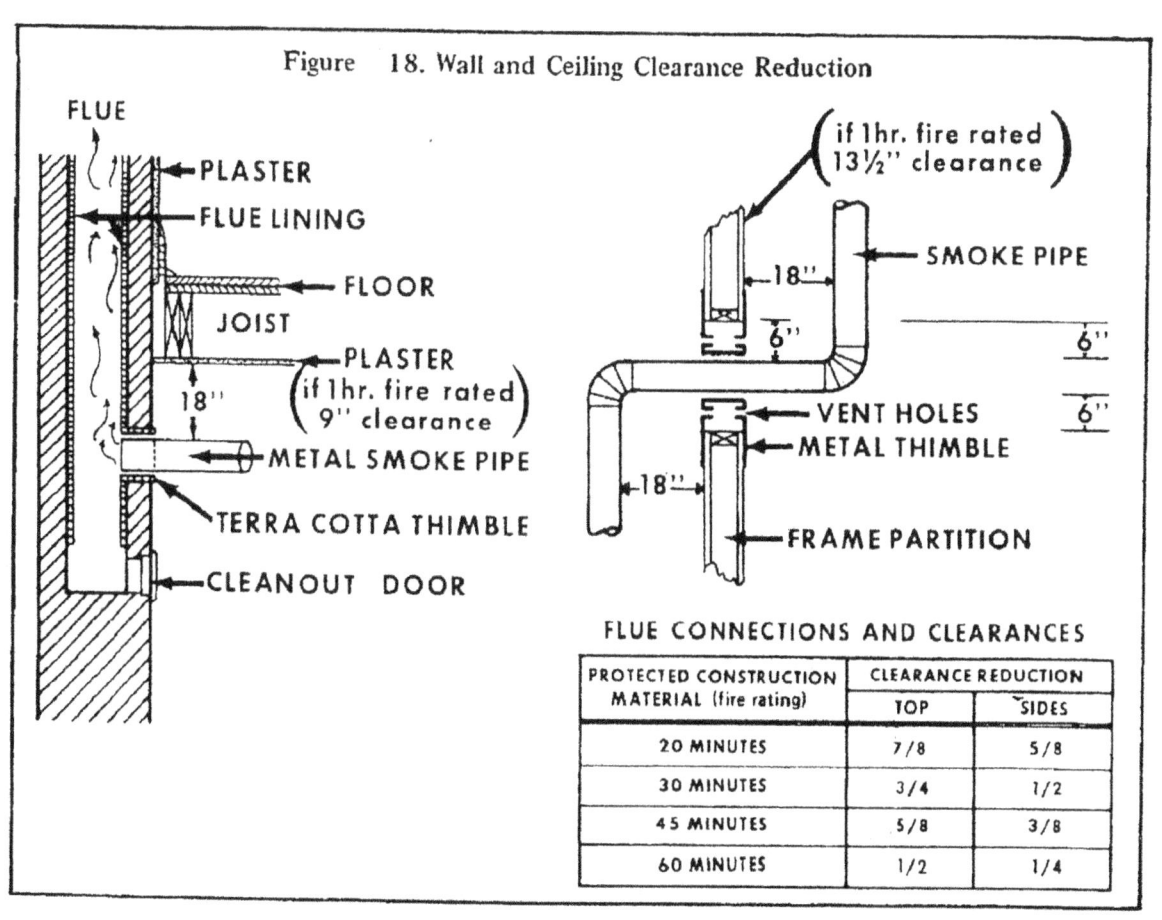

Figure 18. Wall and Ceiling Clearance Reduction

FLUE CONNECTIONS AND CLEARANCES

PROTECTED CONSTRUCTION MATERIAL (fire rating)	CLEARANCE REDUCTION	
	TOP	SIDES
20 MINUTES	7/8	5/8
30 MINUTES	3/4	1/2
45 MINUTES	5/8	3/8
60 MINUTES	1/2	1/4

Install vents with male ends of inner liner down to ensure condensate is kept within pipes on a cold start. The vertical length of each vent or stack should be at least 2 feet greater than the length between horizontal connection and stack.

Run vent at least 3 feet above any projection of the building within 20 feet to place it above a possible pressure zone due to wind currents (see Figure 19). End it with a weather cap designed to prevent entrance of rain and snow.

Gas-fired space heaters as well as gas furnaces and hot water heaters must be equipped with a backdraft diverter (see Figure ,20) designed to protect heaters against downdrafts and excessive updrafts. Use only draft diverters of the type approved by the AGA.

The combustion chamber or firebox must be insulated from the floor, usually with an air-space of 15 to 18 inches, or the firebox is sometimes insulated within the unit and thus allows for lesser clearance for combustibles.

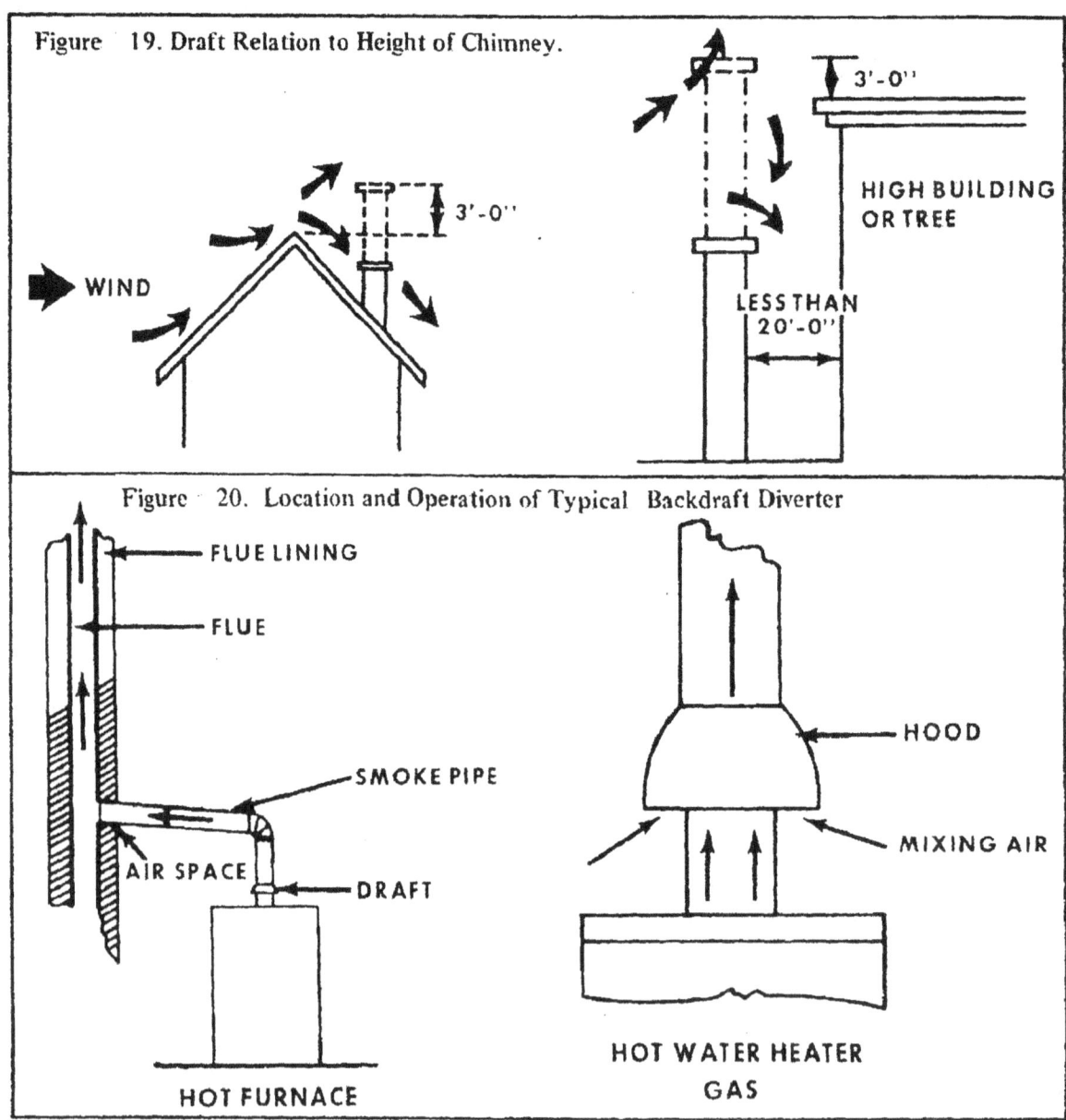

Figure 19. Draft Relation to Height of Chimney.

Figure 20. Location and Operation of Typical Backdraft Diverter

Where coal space heaters are located, a floor protection should be provided. This would be a metal-covered asbestos board or a similar durable insulation material. One reason for the floor protection would be to allow cooling off of hot coals and ashes if they drop out while ashes are being removed from the ash chamber. Walls and ceilings of a non-combustible construction exposed to furnace radiation should be installed, and the following clearances are recommended: Space heaters — A top or ceiling clearance of 36 inches, a wall clearance of 18 inches, and a smoke pipe clearance of 18 inches, (see Figure 18).

VIII. Domestic Hot Water Jack Stoves (Coal Stoves)

Domestic hot water jack stoves (coal stoves) equipped with water jackets to supply hot water for domestic use are to be treated as coal-fired furnaces or boilers previously discussed. Note that flue connections should not exceed two to the same flue unless the draft and size are sufficient to accommodate both exhausting requirements. One flue with one smoke pipe is the rule; however, housing inspectors may find a jack stove and main furnace connected to the same flue. Where these conditions are encountered and no complaint about malfunctioning of this system is found, it can be assumed that the system is operating satisfactorily. Where more than two units, other than gas, are attached to a single flue, the building agency should be notified, since this can be considered an improper installation. Gas, oil, and electric hot water heating units for domestic hot water should be treated the same as previously discussed for central heating units.

IX. Hazardous Installations

A Generalities — The housing inspector should be on the alert for unvented open burning flame heaters, such as manually operated gas logs. Coil-type wall-mounted hot-water heaters that do not have safety relief valves are not permitted. Kerosene (portable) units for cooking or heating should be prohibited. Generally, open-flame portable units are not allowed under fire safety regulations.

In oil heating units, other than integral tank units, the oil filling and vent must be located on the exterior of the building. Filling of oil within buildings is prohibited.

Electric wiring to heating units must be installed as indicated in the electrical section. Cutoff switches should be close to the entry but outside of the boiler room. The inspector should be able to appraise the heating installation and determine its adequacy. Any installation that indicates haphazard location, workmanship, or operation, whether it be building, zoning, plumbing, electrical, or housing, will dictate further inspection.

B Chimneys (see Figure 21 and 22) - Chimneys, as all inspectors know, are an integral part of the building. The chimney is a point of building safety and should be understood by the housing inspector. The chimney, if of masonry, must be tight and sound; flues should be terra cotta lined, and where no linings are installed, the brick should be tight to permit proper draft and elimination of combustion gases.

Chimneys that act as flues for gas-fired equipment must be lined with either B-vent or terra cotta.

To the inspector, on exterior inspection, "banana peel" on the portion of the chimney above the roof will indicate trouble and a need for rebuilding. Exterior deterioration of the chimney will, if let go too long, gradually permit erosion from within the flues and eventually block the flue opening.

Rusted flashing at the roof level will also contribute to the chimney's deterioration. Effervescence on the inside wall of the chimney below the roof and on the outside of the chimney, if exposed, will show salt accumulations — a tell-tale sign of water penetration and flue gas escape and a sign of chimney deterioration. In the spring and fall, during rain seasons, if terra cotta chimneys leak, the joint will be indicated by dark areas permitting actual counting of the number of flues inside the masonry chimney. When this condition occurs, it usually requires 2 or 3 months to dry out. Upon drying out, the mortar joints are discolored (brown), and so after a few years of this type of deterioration the joints can be distinguished wet or dry. The above-listed conditions usually develop during coal operation and become more pronounced usually 2 to 5 years after conversion to oil or gas.

An unlined chimney can be checked for deterioration below the roof line by checking the residue deposited at the base of the chimney, usually accessible through a cleanout (door or plug) or breaching. Red granular or fine powder showing through coal soot or oil soot will generally indicate, if in quantity (a handful), that deterioration is excessive and repairs are needed.

Gas units attached to unlined chimneys will be devoid of soot, but will usually show similar tell-tale brick powder and deterioration as previously mentioned. Manufactured gas has a greater tendency to dehydrate and decompose brick in chimney flues than natural gas. For gas installations in older homes, utility companies usually specify chimney requirements before installation, and so older chimneys may require the installation of terra cotta liners, lead-lined copper liners, or transite pipe. Oil burner operation using a low air ratio and high oil consumption is usually indicated by black carbon deposits around the top of the chimney. Prolonged operation in this burner setting results in long carbon water deposits down the chimney for 4 to 6 feet or more and should indicate to the inspector a possibility of poor burner maintenance. This will accent his need to be more thorough on the ensuing inspection. This type of condition can result from other related causes, such as improper chimney height or exterior obstructions such as trees or buildings that will cause downdrafts or insufficient draft or contribute to a faulty heating operation.

Rust spots and soot-mold usually occur on galvanized smoke pipe deterioration.

C Fireplace — Careful attention should be given to the construction of the fireplace. Improperly built fireplaces are a serious safety and fire hazard (see Figure 22). The most common causes of fireplace fires are thin walls, combustible materials such as studding or trim against sides and back of the fireplace, wood mantels, and unsafe hearths.

Fireplace walls should be not less than 8 inches thick, and if built of stone or hollow masonry units, not less than 12 inches thick. The faces of all walls exposed to fire should be lined with firebrick or other suitable fire-resistive material. When the lining consists of 4 inches of firebrick, such lining thickness may be included in the required minimum thickness of the wall.

The fireplace hearth should be constructed of brick, stone, tile, or similar incombustible material and should be supported on a fireproof slab or on a brick arch. The hearth should extend at least 20 inches beyond the chimney breast and not less than 12 inches beyond each side of the fireplace opening

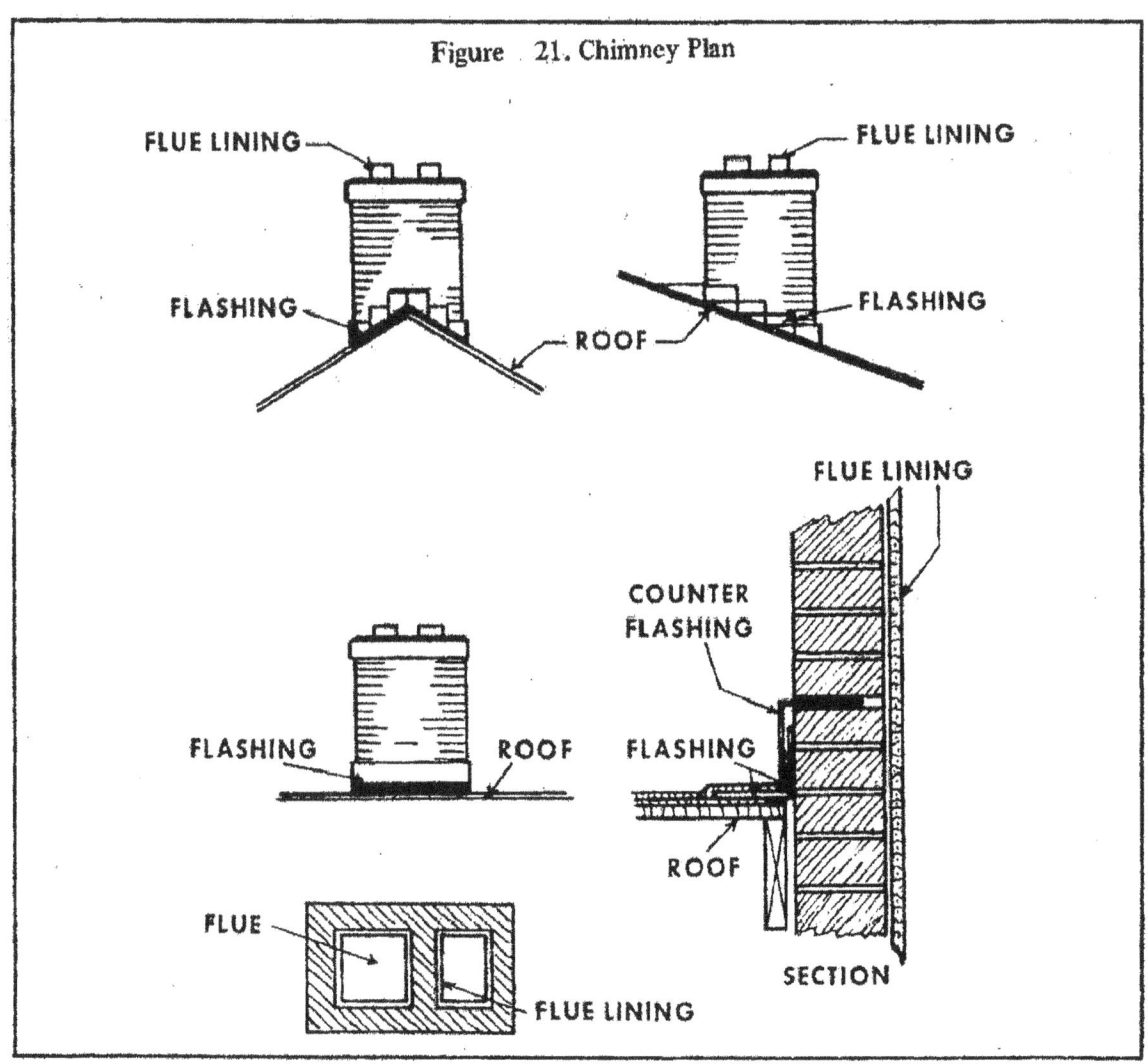

Figure 21. Chimney Plan

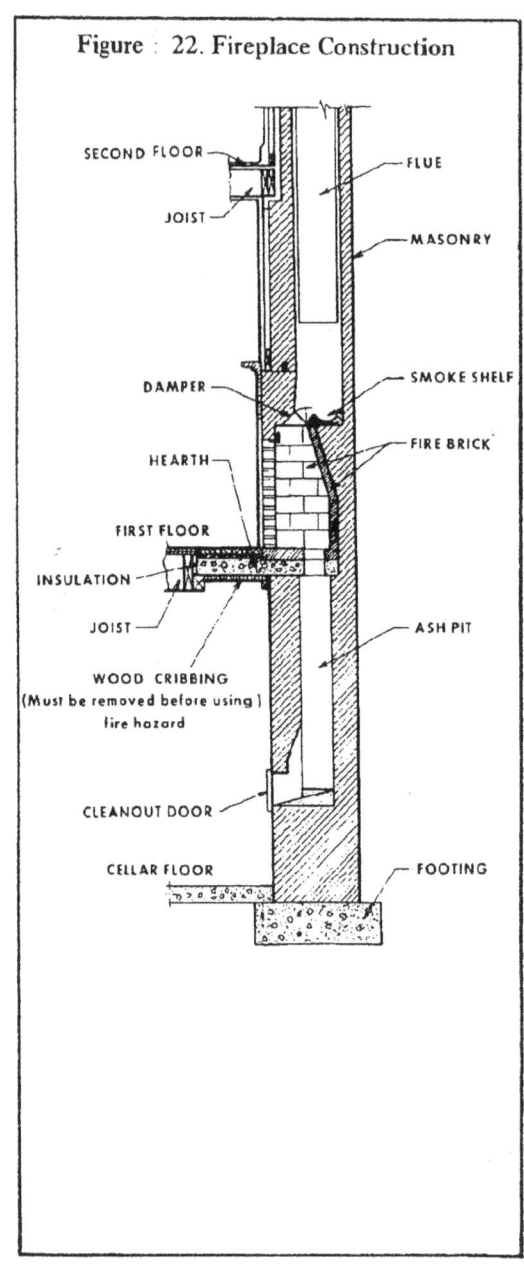

Figure 22. Fireplace Construction

along the chimney breast. The combined thickness of the hearth and its supporting construction should be not less than 6 inches at any point.

It is important that all wooden beams, joists, and studs are set off from the fireplace and chimney so that there is not less than 2 inches of clearance between the wood members and the sidewalls of the fireplace or chimney and not less than 4 inches of clearance between wood members and the back wall of the fireplace.

The housing inspector is a very important person in maintaining sound, safe, and healthful community growth. This should be a challenge to every inspector to provide himself with the necessary tools for better and more efficient housing inspection. He must develop the extra senses so necessary in spotting and correcting faults. He must know when to refer and to whom the referral is to be made; he must be continually seeking knowledge, which may be found by consulting with technicians, tradesmen, and professionals. No finer satisfaction can be realized than to know and feel that the security, safety, and comfort of each and every family within your community has a better and more healthful life because of that extra bit of knowledge you have imparted. "An inspector who stops learning today is uneducated tomorrow."

REFRIGERATION AND AIR CONDITIONING TERMINOLOGY AND TROUBLESHOOTING

TABLE OF CONTENTS

Page

A. TERMINOLOGY

Absolute Pressure ... Bimetallic Element	1
Boiling Point ... Conduction	2
Conductor (Heat or Thermal) ... Equalizer	3
Evaporation ... Humidistat	4
Humidity ... Saturated Liquid	5
Saturated Vapor ... Wet-Bulb Depression	6

B. TROUBLESHOOTING 7

REFRIGERATION AND AIR CONDITIONING

TERMINOLOGY AND TROUBLESHOOTING

A. TERMINOLOGY

Many of the terms used in connection with refrigeration and air conditioning have quite definite and specialized meanings. In order to understand any written material in the field of refrigeration and air conditioning, it is essential to have a thorough knowledge of correct terminology. Some important terms used in connection with refrigeration and air conditioning are defined in the following list.

ABSOLUTE PRESSURE.—Pressure measured from absolute zero rather than from normal atmospheric pressure; the sum of atmospheric pressure plus gage pressure.

ABSOLUTE TEMPERATURE.—Temperature measured from absolute zero (-459.67° F, or -273.15°C).

ABSORBENT.—A material that has the ability to extract certain substances from a liquid or a gas with which it is in contact, causing physical changes, chemical changes, or both during the absorption process.

ACCUMULATOR.—A shell placed in a suction line for separating liquid refrigerant entrained in suction gas; serves as a storage chamber for low side liquid refrigerant; also known as a surge drum or surge header.

ADIABATIC PROCESS.—Any thermodynamic process that is accomplished without the transfer of heat to or from the system while the process is occurring.

ADSORBENT.—A material that has the ability to cause molecules of gases, liquids, and solids to adhere to its internal surfaces without causing any chemical or physical change.

AIR CONDITIONING.—The process of treating air to simultaneously control its temperature, humidity, cleanliness, and distribution to meet the requirements of the conditioned space.

AIR CONDITIONING UNIT.—An assembly of equipment for the control of (at least) the temperature, humidity, and cleanliness of the air within a conditioned space.

AIR DIFFUSER.—A device arranged to promote the mixing of the air leaving the duct with the room air.

AMBIENT AIR TEMPERATURE.—The temperature of the air surrounding an object; in a system using an air-cooled condenser, the temperature of the air entering the condenser.

ANEMOMETER.—An instrument for measuring the velocity of air flow.

ATMOSPHERIC PRESSURE.—Pressure exerted by the weight of the atmosphere; standard atmospheric pressure is 14.696 psia or 29.921 inches of mercury at sea level.

BACK PRESSURE.—Same as suction pressure.

BAFFLE.—A partition to direct the flow of a fluid.

BAROMETER.—An instrument for measuring atmospheric pressure.

BAROMETRIC PRESSURE.—The actual atmospheric pressure existing at any given moment; at certain times, barometric pressure is not identical with standard atmospheric pressure.

BIMETALLIC ELEMENT.—A device formed from two different metals having different

TERMINOLOGY AND TROUBLESHOOTING

coefficients of thermal expansion; used in temperature indicating and controlling instruments.

BOILING POINT.—Temperature at which a liquid boils at a given pressure.

BORE.—Inside diameter of a cylinder.

BRINE.—Any liquid cooled by the refrigerant and used for the transmission of heat without change of state.

BRITISH THERMAL UNIT.—The amount of heat required to produce a temperature rise of 1° F in 1 pound of water. Abbreviated Btu.

CENTIGRADE.—A thermometric system in which the freezing point of water is 0° C and the boiling point of water is 100° C, at standard atmospheric pressure.

CENTRAL FAN SYSTEM.—A mechanical, indirect system of air conditioning in which the air is treated by equipment outside the area served and is conveyed to and from the area by means of a fan and a distributing duct system.

CENTRIFUGAL MACHINE.—A compressor employing centrifugal force for compression.

CHANGE OF AIR.—The introduction of new, cleansed, or recirculated air to conditioned spaces, measured in the number of complete air changes in a specified time.

CHANGE OF STATE.—The change from one phase (solid, liquid, or gas) to another.

CHARGE.—The amount of refrigerant in a system; also the act of putting refrigerant into a system.

CHILL.—To refrigerate meats, water, etc., moderately, without freezing.

COEFFICIENT OF EXPANSION.—The change in length per unit length per degree of change in temperature of a material; or the change in volume per unit volume per degree of change in temperature of a material.

COEFFICIENT OF PERFORMANCE.—The ratio of the refrigeration produced to the work supplied, with refrigeration and work being expressed in the same units.

COIL.—Any cooling or heating element made of pipe or tubing.

COMFORT CHART.—A chart showing effective temperature, with dry-bulb temperature and humidity, by which the effects of various conditions on human comfort may be determined.

COMFORT COOLING.—Refrigeration for comfort, as opposed to refrigeration for manufacture or storage.

COMFORT ZONE.—The range of effective temperatures over which the majority of adults feel comfortable.

COMPRESSION, MULTI-STAGE. — Compression in two or more stages, as when the discharge of one compressor is connected to the suction of another.

COMPRESOR, HERMETIC.—A compressor in which the electric motor and the compressor are enclosed within a sealed housing.

COMPRESSOR, "V" AND "W".—High speed, single-acting, multi-cylinder compressor with straight-line piston movement in the various cylinders; the cylinders are in the "V" position or the "W" position with respect to the shaft axis.

CONDENSATE.—The liquid formed by the condensation of a vapor. In steam heating, water condensed from steam; in air conditioning, water removed from air by condensation on the cooling coil of a refrigeration system.

CONDENSATION.—The process by which a vapor changes to a liquid when heat is removed from the vapor.

CONDENSER.—A vessel or an arrangement of pipe or tubing in which the compressed refrigerant vapor is liquefied by the removal of heat.

CONDENSING UNIT.—A specific refrigerating machine combination for a given refrigerant; the unit consists of one or more power-driven compressors, condensers, liquid receivers (when required), and the necessary accessories.

CONDUCTION.—The method of heat transfer by which heat is transferred from molecule to

REFRIGERATION AND AIR CONDITIONING

molecule within a homogeneous substance or between two substances that are in physical contact with each other.

CONDUCTOR (HEAT OR THERMAL).—A material that readily transmits heat by conduction; the opposite of an insulator.

CONTROL.—Any device for the regulation of a machine in normal operation. May be manual or automatic; if automatic, it is responsive to changes in temperature, pressure, liquid level, time, or other variables.

CONVECTION.—The movement of a mass of fluid (liquid or gas) caused by differences in density in different parts of the fluid; the differences in density are caused by differences in temperature. As the fluid moves, it carries with it its contained heat energy, which is then transferred from one part of the fluid to another and from the fluid to the surroundings.

COOLER, OIL.—A heat exchanger used for cooling oil in a lubrication system.

COOLING TOWER.—A device for lowering the temperature of water by evaporative cooling, as the water is showered through a space in which outside air is circulated.

COOLING WATER.—Water used in a condenser to cool and condense a refrigerant.

COPPER PLATING.—The depositing of a film of copper on the surface of another metal (such as iron or steel) by electrochemical action; in refrigeration, copper plating usually occurs on compressor walls, pistons, discharge valves, shafts, and seals.

COUNTERFLOW.—In a heat exchanger, opposite direction of flow of the cooling liquid and the cooled liquid (or of the heating liquid and the heated liquid).

CRYOGENICS.—The branch of physics that relates to the production and the effects of very low temperatures.

CYCLE.—The complete course of operation of a refrigerant, from starting point back to starting point, in a closed refrigeration system; also, a general term for any repeated process in any system.

DEGREE.—Unit of temperature.

DEGREE OF SUPERHEAT.—The amount by which the temperature of a superheated vapor exceeds the temperature of the saturated vapor at the same pressure.

DEHUMIDIFIER.—An air cooler or washer used for lowering the moisture content of the air passing through it.

DEHUMIDIFY.—To reduce, by any process, the quantity of water vapor within a given space.

DEHYDRATE.—To remove water (in any form) from some other substance.

DENSITY.—Mass per unit volume or weight per unit volume.

DESICCANT.—Any absorbent or adsorbent, liquid or solid, that removes water or water vapor from a material. In a refrigeration circuit, the desiccant should be insoluble in the refrigerant and refrigerant oils.

DEWPOINT.—The temperature at which water vapor begins to condense in any given sample of air; dewpoint depends upon humidity, temperature, and pressure.

DISTRIBUTOR.—A device for guiding the flow of liquid into parallel paths in an evaporator.

DRIER.—A device containing a desiccant placed in a refrigerant circuit for the purpose of collecting and holding within the desiccant all water in the system above the amount that can be tolerated in the circulating refrigerant.

ELECTROLYSIS.—Chemical decomposition caused by action of an electric current in a solution.

ENTHALPY.—A term used to mean TOTAL HEAT or HEAT CONTENT.

EQUALIZER.—Piping arrangement on an enclosed compressor to equalize refrigerant gas pressure in the crankcase and suction; device for dividing the liquid refrigerant between parallel low-side coils; a piping arrangement to divide the lubricating oil between the crankcases of compressors operating in parallel; the method by which refrigerant pressure is

TERMINOLOGY AND TROUBLESHOOTING

transmitted to the diaphragm or bellows of a thermostatic expansion valve.

EVAPORATION.—The change of state from the liquid phase to the vapor phase.

EVAPORATOR.—The unit in a refrigeration system in which the refrigerant is vaporized to produce refrigeration.

EXFILTRATION.—The flow of air outward from a space through walls, leaks, etc.

EXPANSION VALVE SUPERHEAT.—The difference between the temperature of the thermal bulb and the temperature corresponding to the pressure at the coil outlet or at the equalizer connection (where provided).

FAHRENHEIT.—Thermometric scale in which 32° F denotes the freezing point of water and 212° F denotes the boiling temperature of water under standard atmospheric pressure at sea level.

FIN.—An extended surface used on tubes in some heat exchangers to increase the heat transfer area.

FLASH CHAMBER. — A separation tank placed between the expansion valve and the evaporator in a refrigeration system to separate and bypass any flash gas formed in the expansion valve.

FLASH GAS.—The gas resulting from the instantaneous evaporation of refrigerant in a pressure-reducing device, to cool the refrigerant to the evaporating temperature corresponding to the reduced pressure.

FLUID.—The general term that includes liquids and gases (or vapors).

FOAMING.—The formation of a foam or froth on an oil-refrigerant mixture; caused by a reduction in pressure with consequent rapid boiling out of the refrigerant.

FREEZING.—The change of state from the liquid phase to the solid phase.

GAGE PRESSURE.—Absolute pressure minus atmospheric pressure.

GAS.—A substance in the gaseous state; a highly superheated vapor that satisfies the perfect gas laws, within acceptable limits of accuracy. See VAPOR.

GAS, INERT.—A gas that does not readily enter into or cause chemical reactions.

GAS, NONCONDENSABLE.—A gas in a refrigeration system which does not condense at the temperature and partial pressure existing in the condenser, thereby exerting a higher head pressure on the system.

GRILLE.—A lattice or grating for an intake opening or a delivery opening.

HEAD PRESSURE.—The operating pressure measured in the discharge line at the compressor outlet.

HEAT.—A basic form of energy, which is transferred by virtue of a temperature difference.

HEAT OF CONDENSATION.—The latent heat given up by a substance as it changes from a gas to a liquid.

HEAT OF FUSION.—The latent heat absorbed when a substance changes from a solid state to a liquid state.

HEAT OF VAPORIZATION.—The latent heat absorbed by a substance as it changes from a liquid to a vapor.

HEAT PUMP.—Refrigeration equipment; used for year-round air conditioning. In summer used to cool and condition the air in a space; in winter used to warm and condition the air.

HOT-GAS DEFROSTING.—The use of high pressure or condenser gas in the low side or condenser gas in the evaporator to effect the removal of frost.

HUMIDIFY.—To increase the percentage of water vapor within a given space.

HUMIDISTAT.—A control instrument or device, actuated by changes in humidity within the conditioned areas, which automatically regulates the relative humidity of the area.

REFRIGERATION AND AIR CONDITIONING

HUMIDITY.—The water vapor within a given space.

HUMIDITY, SPECIFIC.—The weight of water vapor mixed with 1 pound of dry air, expressed as the number of grains of moisture per pound of dry air.

HYDROLYSIS.—The splitting up of compounds by reaction with water. For example, the reaction of R-12 with water which results in the formation of acid materials.

INDUSTRIAL AIR CONDITIONING.—Air conditioning used for purposes other than comfort.

JACKET WATER.—The water used to cool the cylinder head and cylinder walls of a water-cooled compressor.

LATENT HEAT.—Heat transfer that is NOT reflected in a temperature change but IS reflected in a changing physical state of the substance involved.

LIQUEFACTION.—The change of state from a gas to a liquid. (The term liquefaction is usually used instead of condensation when referring to substances which are in a gaseous state at ordinary pressures and temperatures.)

LIQUID LINE.—The tube or pipe through which liquid refrigerant is carried from the condenser or receiver to the pressure-reducing device.

LIQUID RECEIVER.—A vessel permanently connected to the high side of a system for the storage of liquefied refrigerant.

LOAD.—The amount of heat imposed upon a refrigeration system in any specified period of time, or the required rate of heat removal; usually expressed in Btu per hour.

LOW SIDE.—The parts of the refrigeration system that are at or below the evaporating temperature.

MANOMETER.—A U-tube, or a single tube and reservoir arrangement, used with a suitable fluid to measure pressure differences.

MELTING.—The change of state from a solid to a liquid.

OZONE.—Triatomic oxygen (O_3). Sometimes used in cold storage or air conditioning installations as an odor eliminator. Can be toxic in certain concentrations.

PLENUM CHAMBER.—An air compartment maintained under pressure for receiving air before distribution to the conditioned spaces.

PNEUMATIC.—Operated by air pressure.

PREHEATING.—In air conditioning, to heat the air in advance of other processes.

PRESSURE.—Force per unit area.

PRESSURE DROP.—Loss of pressure, as from one end of a refrigerant line to the other, because of friction.

PRESSURE EQUALIZING.—Allowing the high side and the low side of the refrigeration system to become equal or nearly equal in pressure during idle periods, to prevent excessive starting loads on the compressor.

PRESSURE REGULATOR, SUCTION.—An automatic valve designed to limit the suction pressure to prevent motor overload.

PSYCHROMETER.—An instrument for measuring relative humidities by means of wet-bulb and dry-bulb temperatures.

PSYCHROMETRIC CHART.—A graphical representation of the properties of water vapor and air mixtures.

PURGING.—The act of blowing out gas from a refrigeration system, usually for the purpose of removing air or other noncondensable gases.

REFRIGERATION TON.—The removal of heat at a rate of 288,000 Btu in 24 hours or 12,000 Btu in 1 hour.

RETURN AIR.—The air returned from a space being conditioned.

SATURATED LIQUID.—A liquid which is at saturation pressure and saturation temperature; in other words, a liquid which is at its boiling point for any given pressure.

TERMINOLOGY AND TROUBLESHOOTING

SATURATED VAPOR.—A vapor which is at saturation pressure and saturation temperature. A saturated vapor cannot be superheated as long as it is in contact with the liquid from which it is being generated.

SATURATION PRESSURE and SATURATION TEMPERATURE.—The pressure and temperature at which a liquid and the vapor it is generating can exist in equilibrium contact with each other. The boiling point of any liquid depends upon pressure and temperature; a liquid boils when it is at the saturation temperature for any particular saturation pressure.

SELF-CONTAINED UNIT.—A refrigeration unit that can be removed from the premises without disconnecting any refrigerant-containing part.

SENSIBLE HEAT.—Heat transfer that is reflected in a change of temperature.

SILICA GEL.—A form of silicon dioxide which absorbs moisture readily; used as a drying agent.

SPECIFIC GRAVITY.—The density of a substance compared to the density of a standard material such as water.

SPECIFIC VOLUME.—The space occupied by unit amount of a substance at a specified pressure and temperature; often measured in cubic feet per pound.

SUBCOOLED LIQUID.—A liquid that is at a temperature below its boiling point for any given pressure.

SUBCOOLING.—The process of cooling a liquid to a temperature below its saturation temperature for any given saturation pressure.

SUPERHEATING.—The process of adding heat to a vapor in order to raise its temperature above saturation temperature. It is impossible to superheat a saturated vapor as long as it is in contact with the liquid from which it is being generated; hence the vapor must be led away from the liquid before it can be superheated.

TEMPERATURE.—A measure of the concentration of heat (thermal energy) in a body or substance.

THERMODYNAMICS.—The branch of physics that deals with heat and its transformations to and from other forms of energy.

THERMOSTAT.—A temperature-sensing automatic control device.

TOXIC.—Having temporary or permanent poisonous effects.

TUBE, CAPILLARY.—In refrigeration, a tube of small internal diameter used as a liquid refrigerant flow control or expansion device between the high side and the low side of the refrigeration system.

UNLOADER.—A device in or on the compressor for equalizing high-side and low-side pressures for a brief time during starting and for controlling compressor capacity by rendering one or more cylinders ineffective.

VACUUM.—Pressure that is less than atmospheric pressure.

VALVE, KING.—A stop valve between the receiver and the expansion valve, normally close to the receiver.

VAPOR.—A gaseous substance, particularly one that is at or near saturation temperature and pressure.

VENTILATION.—The process of supplying or removing air by natural or mechanical means, to or from a space; such air may or may not have been conditioned.

VITAL HEAT.—The heat generated by fruits and vegetables in storage; caused by ripening.

VOLATILE LIQUID.—A liquid that evaporates (vaporizes) readily at atmospheric pressure and room temperature.

WATER (OR BRINE) COOLER.—A factory-made assembly or elements in which the water or brine and the refrigerant are in heat transfer relationship causing the refrigerant to evaporate and absorb heat from the water or brine.

WATER VAPOR.—In air conditioning, the water in the atmosphere.

WET-BULB DEPRESSION.—The difference between the dry-bulb temperature and the wet-bulb temperature.

REFRIGERATION AND AIR CONDITIONING

B. TROUBLESHOOTING

The two trouble charts that follow may be used as a guide for locating and correcting malfunctions in refrigeration systems. The first chart deals with troubles that may be encountered in vapor compression systems. The second chart deals with troubles that may be encountered in absorption-type (lithium bromide) systems. If the points and procedures outlined in these charts are closely adhered to, a great deal of time can be saved in troubleshooting.

To use these charts, the first thing to do is to isolate the trouble. Then check all possible causes. And finally, make the indicated corrections. In general, the correction of a malfunction is a process of elimination. The easiest corrections should be made first; then, if necessary, the more difficult corrections should be made.

TERMINOLOGY AND TROUBLESHOOTING

Trouble	Possible Cause	Corrective Measure
High condensing pressure.	Air on non-condensable gas in system.	Purge air from condenser.
	Inlet water warm.	Increase quantity of condensing water.
	Insufficient water flowing through condenser.	Increase quantity of water.
	Condenser tubes clogged or scaled.	Clean condenser water tubes.
	Too much liquid in receiver, condenser tubes submerged in liquid refrigerant.	Draw off liquid into service cylinder.
Low condensing pressure.	Too much water flowing through condenser.	Reduce quantity of water.
	Water too cold.	Reduce quantity of water.
	Liquid refrigerant flooding back from evaporator.	Change expansion valve adjustment, examine fastening of thermal bulb.
	Leaky discharge valve.	Remove head, examine valves. Replace any found defective.
High suction pressure.	Overfeeding of expansion valve.	Regulate expansion valve, check bulb attachment.
	Leaky suction valve.	Remove head, examine valve and replace if worn.
Low suction pressure.	Restricted liquid line and expansion valve or suction screens.	Pump down, remove, examine and clean screens.
	Insufficient refrigerant in system.	Check for refrigerant storage.
	Too much oil circulating in system.	Check for too much oil in circulation. Remove oil.
	Improper adjustment of expansion valves.	Adjust valve to give more flow.
	Expansion valve power element dead or weak.	Replace expansion valve power element.

Trouble Chart for Vapor Compression Refrigeration Systems.

REFRIGERATION AND AIR CONDITIONING

Trouble	Possible Cause	Corrective Measure
Compressor short cycles on low pressure control.	Low refrigerant charge.	Locate and repair leaks. Charge refrigerant.
	Thermal expansion valve not feeding properly.	Adjust, repair or replace thermal expansion valve.
	(a) Dirty strainers.	(a) Clean strainers.
	(b) Moisture frozen in orifice or orifice plugged with dirt.	(b) Remove moisture or dirt (Use system dehydrator).
	(c) Power element dead or weak.	(c) Replace power element.
	Water flow through evaporators restricted or stopped. Evaporator coils plugged, dirty, or clogged with frost.	Remove restriction. Check water flow. Clean coils or tubes.
	Defective low pressure control switch.	Repair or replace low pressure control switch.
Compressor runs continuously.	Shortage of refrigerant.	Repair leak and recharge system.
	Leaking discharge valves.	Replace discharge valves.
Compressor short cycles on high pressure control switch.	Insufficient water flowing through condenser, clogged condenser.	Determine if water has been turned off. Check for scaled or fouled condenser.
	Defective high pressure control switch.	Repair or replace high pressure control switch.
Compressor will not run.	Seized compressor.	Repair or replace compressor.
	Cut-in point of low pressure control switch too high.	Set L.P. control switch to cut-in at correct pressure.
	High pressure control switch does not cut-in.	Check discharge pressure and reset H.P. control switch.
	1. Defective switch.	1. Repair or replace switch.
	2. Electric power cut off.	2. Check power supply.
	3. Service or disconnect switch open.	3. Close switches.

Trouble Chart for Vapor Compression Refrigeration Systems—Continued.

TERMINOLOGY AND TROUBLESHOOTING

Trouble	Possible Cause	Corrective Measure
Compressor will not run. (Cont'd)	4. Fuses blown.	4. Test fuses and renew if necessary.
	5. Over-load relays tripped.	5. Re-set relays and find cause of overload.
	6. Low voltage.	6. Check voltage (should be within 10 percent of nameplate rating).
	7. Electrical motor in trouble.	7. Repair or replace motor.
	8. Trouble in starting switch or control circuit.	8. Close switch manually to test power supply. If OK check control circuit including temperature and pressure controls.
	9. Compressor motor stopped by oil pressure differential switch.	9. Check oil level in crankcase. Check oil pump pressure.
Sudden loss of oil from crankcase.	Liquid refrigerant slugging back to compressor crank case.	Adjust or replace expansion valve.
Capacity reduction system fails to unload cylinders.	Hand operating stem of capacity control valve not turned to automatic position.	Set hand operating stem to automatic position.
Compressor continues to operate at full or partial load.	Pressure regulating valve not opening.	Adjust or repair pressure regulating valve.
Capacity reduction system fails to load cylinders.	Broken or leaking oil tube between pump and power element.	Repair leak.
Compressor continues to operate unloaded.	Pressure regulating valve not closing.	Adjust or repair pressure regulating valve.

Trouble Chart for Vapor Compression Refrigeration Systems—Continued.

REFRIGERATION AND AIR CONDITIONING

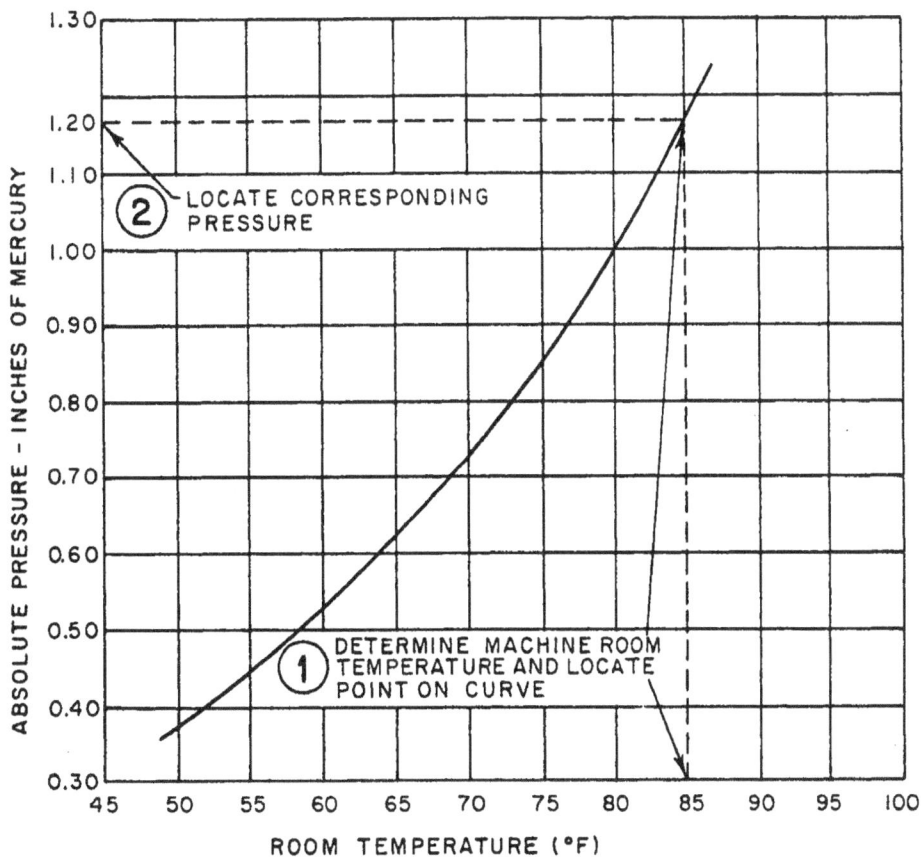

Figure 1.—Pressure temperature curve for lithium-bromide machine.

TROUBLE CHART FOR ABSORPTION TYPE (LITHIUM-BROMIDE) REFRIGERATION SYSTEM

TROUBLE: SOLUTION SOLIDIFIED AT START-UP

	CAUSE	CHECK	CORRECTION
1.	Dilution cycle too short.	- dilution cycle time delay relay.	- Reset time delay relay to 10 minutes.
2.	Steam valve did not close during dilution cycle.	- operation of steam valve and steam EP relay.	- Repair faulty operation. Steam EP relay should close when stop button is pushed and control air pressure at steam valve should go to 0 PSIG.
3.	Cooling load lost during dilution cycle.	- Shut down procedure.	Make certain that the cooling load remains on during the dilution cycle.

TERMINOLOGY AND TROUBLESHOOTING

TROUBLE CHART FOR ABSORPTION TYPE (LITHIUM-BROMIDE) REFRIGERATION SYSTEM—Continued.

TROUBLE: SOLUTION SOLIDIFIED AT START-UP—Continued

	CAUSE	CHECK	CORRECTION
4.	Condenser sea water too cold.	- 3 way mixing valve and sea water thermostat.	-Maintain a constant inlet sea water temperature of 85°F.
5.	Air in machine.	- absolute pressure indicator before starting.	-Turn "Not Purged-Purged" switch to "Not Purged" until machine vacuum corresponds to that given in Fig. 12-1. Find reason for air entering machine.
6.	Machine shut down on safety.	-All safety switches and settings. The following safeties will do this: 1. Low temp. cutout. 2. High temp. cutout. 3. Chilled water pump overload. 4. Absorber - generator pump overload. 5. Refrigerant pump overload. 6. Chilled water failure switch.	-Correct reason for safety cutout or reason for pump overload. -Correct reason for loss of chilled water flow.

TROUBLE: OVER CONCENTRATION OF SOLUTION IN ABSORBER

	CAUSE	CHECK	CORRECTION
1.	High solution temperature in absorber	- solution temperature at generator pump and condensing water temperature leaving absorber. If difference is greater than 10°F, poor heat transfer is indicated.	Add octyl alcohol. If this does not correct the trouble, clean the absorber tubes and check condensing water flow through the absorber.
2.	Plugged spray nozzles in absorber	- discharge pressure of the absorber pump. This should be approximately 11" Hg. Vac.	Inspect and clean spray header and nozzles.

REFRIGERATION AND AIR CONDITIONING

TROUBLE CHART FOR ABSORPTION TYPE (LITHIUM-BROMIDE) REFRIGERATION SYSTEM—Continued.

TROUBLE: OVER CONCENTRATION OF SOLUTION IN ABSORBER—Continued

CAUSE	CHECK	CORRECTION
3. Low condensing sea water flow	- condensing water rise across absorber. At full load this should be 10°F or lower.	Clean inlet sea water strainer. Reset condenser bypass valve.
4. Air in machine	- refrigerant vapor pressure to absorber vapor pressure. Measure temperature at discharge of refrigerant pump and read corresponding vapor pressure on equilibrium diagram. Should be 2° or 3°F.	Reset purge pressure stat to allow more purge operation.
5. Insufficient purging	- purge cycle. With purge pump in operation the purge pump cycle should be about 1 - 1/2 hours. - specific gravity and temperature of purge solution.	Adjust drip tube. Purge valve not opening. This should be about 70° or less with a specific gravity of 1.57 or more to give a purge vapor pressure of less than .18" Hg.
	- pump impeller and jet evacuator for wear	If worn - replace
	- purge system for leaks	Turn off purge pump at the panel board. Blank off the carbon filter tube. Raise pressure in purge system to 25 PSIG and leak test. Correct any leaks

TROUBLE: POOR EVAPORATOR PERFORMANCE

CAUSE	CHECK	CORRECTION
1. Fouled heat transfer surface on chilled water coil	- at full load, check spread between evaporator temperature (at discharge of refrigerant pump) and	Clean tubes - chilled water side. Check division plate gasket in water box, if

TERMINOLOGY AND TROUBLESHOOTING

TROUBLE CHART FOR ABSORPTION TYPE (LITHIUM-BROMIDE) REFRIGERATION SYSTEM—Continued.

TROUBLE: Poor Evaporator Performance—Continued.

CAUSE	CHECK	CORRECTION
	leaving chilled water temperature. Spread should not be greater than 3°F.	out of position, reposition or replace.
2. Incorrect refrigerant pump discharge pressure	- pump pressure; should be approximately 4 PSIG.	Inspect evaporator spray nozzles. Clean if necessary.
	- Refrigerant charge.	Add refrigerant at full load until overflow temperature begins to drop.
	- refrigerant pump impeller.	If worn, replace.
	- pump rotation, should be counter-clockwise as viewed from the pump end.	If incorrect reverse motor rotation.

TROUBLE: WEAK SOLUTION IN ABSORBER, UNABLE TO CONCENTRATE WITH STEAM VALVE WIDE OPEN AT FULL LOAD. —Continued.

1. Vapor condensate above 110°F	- condensing water approach, leaving condenser water temperature to vapor condensate temperature should not be greater than 8°F.	Clean condenser tubes.
	- condensing sea water flow	Clean inlet sea water strainer - adjust condenser bypass valve.
	- refrigerant overflow temperature	If below 45°F, remove refrigerant until temperature begins to rise.
	- calibration of vapor condensate thermometer	recalibrate
2. Strong solution Temperature below 205°F.	- steam pressure	Raise steam pressure to 18 PSIG at generator inlet.
	- steam strainer	Clean strainer
	- steam traps	Open bypass valve, if any change is noted in solution temperature, repair traps.

REFRIGERATION AND AIR CONDITIONING

TROUBLE CHART FOR ABSORPTION TYPE (LITHIUM-BROMIDE) REFRIGERATION SYSTEM—Continued.

TROUBLE: SOLIDIFICATION DURING OPERATION—Continued

CAUSE	CHECK	CORRECTION
3. Low solution flow to generator	- calibration of strong solution thermometer	Recalibrate
	- generator pump discharge pressure. Should be 4 PSIG, approximately.	Inspect valves for restrictions. Inspect generator spray nozzles. Clean or replace.

TROUBLE: SOLIDIFICATION DURING OPERATION

CAUSE	CHECK	CORRECTION
1. See over concentration of solution in absorber.		
2. See poor evaporator performance.		Desolidify machine
3. Sudden drop in entering condensing sea water temperature.	- 3-way pneumatic mixing valve (4) and condensing water temperature control.	Correct reason for malfunction of valve or control.
4. Sudden rise in steam pressure above 18 PSIG.	- control air pressure to steam control pilot and steam regulating valve bypass (12).	Reduce control air pressure to 15 PSIG and make certain valve is closed.

TROUBLE: LOST SOLUTION LEVEL IN ABSORBER

CAUSE	CHECK	CORRECTION
1. Heat exchanger strong solution valve restricted	- valve closed or collapsed diaphragm	Open valve. Replace diaphragm.

TROUBLE: PURGE WILL NOT OPERATE

CAUSE	CHECK	CORRECTION
1. Off on safety	- solution level in purge tank	Drain solution from tank. Clean probes.
2. Malfunction of purge pump.	- purge pump starter - purge level control - purge pressurestat - purge pump motor	Repair or replace if necessary.

TROUBLE: LOSS OF VACUUM DURING SHUT DOWN PERIOD

CAUSE	CHECK	CORRECTION
1. Valve open.	- all of these valves	Close valves and pull vacuum on machine.

TERMINOLOGY AND TROUBLESHOOTING

TROUBLE CHART FOR ABSORPTION TYPE (LITHIUM-BROMIDE) REFRIGERATION SYSTEM—Continued.

TROUBLE: LOSS OF VACUUM DURING SHUT-DOWN PERIOD. —Continued.

	CAUSE	CHECK	CORRECTION
2.	Pneumatic purge valve stuck open.	- purge valve operation air pressure to valve diaphragm	Repair if necessary. Open air bleed or correct reason for purge EP relay not closing and bleeding air.
3.	Seal leak	- water level in seal water tank, should be above suction and connection of seal water pump.	Replace leaking seal
4.	Check valve in seal water make up line did not seat	- ball check and check valve seat.	Replace ball check or repair valve seat.
5.	Leak in machine proper	- leak test machine.	Repair all leaks

TROUBLE: LOSS OF VACUUM DURING OPERATION

	CAUSE	CHECK	CORRECTION
1.	Seal leak	- all pump seals	Replace faulty seal.
2.	Malfunction of purge pump	- purge pump starter - purge pump motor	Repair if necessary Replace if burned out.

TROUBLE: REFRIGERANT OVERFLOW TEMPERATURE ALWAYS COLD MUST REMOVE REFRIGERANT PERIODICALLY

	CAUSE	CHECK	CORRECTION
1.	Tube leak.	- leak test across all tube bundles.	-Repair any leaks.
2.	Purge cooling coil.	- level in purge tank for an extended period while purge pump is off.	-Repair leaky coil if level in tank rises during test.

TROUBLE: COPPER PLATING

	CAUSE	CHECK	CORRECTION
1.	Air leakage into machine.	- leak test.	-Repair any leaks.
2.	Did not break vacuum with nitrogen and provide continuous bleed during repair work.	- procedure for breaking vacuum with nitrogen.	

REFRIGERATION AND AIR CONDITIONING

TROUBLE CHART FOR ABSORPTION TYPE (LITHIUM-BROMIDE) REFRIGERATION SYSTEM—Continued.

TROUBLE: MACHINE SHUT DOWN ON SAFETY

CAUSE	CHECK	CORRECTION
1. Power failure and control failure.	- fuses and power supply.	-Replace blown fuses and restore power.
2. Shutdown on low temperature cutout switch.	- switch setting.	-Set at 36°F.
	- chilled water temperature and steam valve.	-Recalibrate control and adjust steam valve.
3. Shutdown on chilled water failure switch.	- switch setting	-Set at 360 GPM minimum.
	- chilled water pump operation.	-Start pump.
	- chilled water flow.	-Open chilled water line valves.
4. Sea water pump, chilled water pump, refrigerant pump, or absorber-generator pump motor trips out on overload.	- heater elements.	-Install correct size.
	- amperage draw of motor.	-Find reason for overload if present.
	- power supply to all phases.	-Should be 440-3-60AC.
	- ambient temperature around starter too high.	-Provide air circulation or move starter.
	- pump head against pump curves.	-Correct reason for abnormal pump head.
	- binding due to impeller or bearing wear.	-Change impeller or bearings.
	- solidification in absorber-generator pump.	-Desolidify.